IMAGES
of America

CLARK'S TRADING POST AND THE WHITE MOUNTAIN CENTRAL RAILROAD

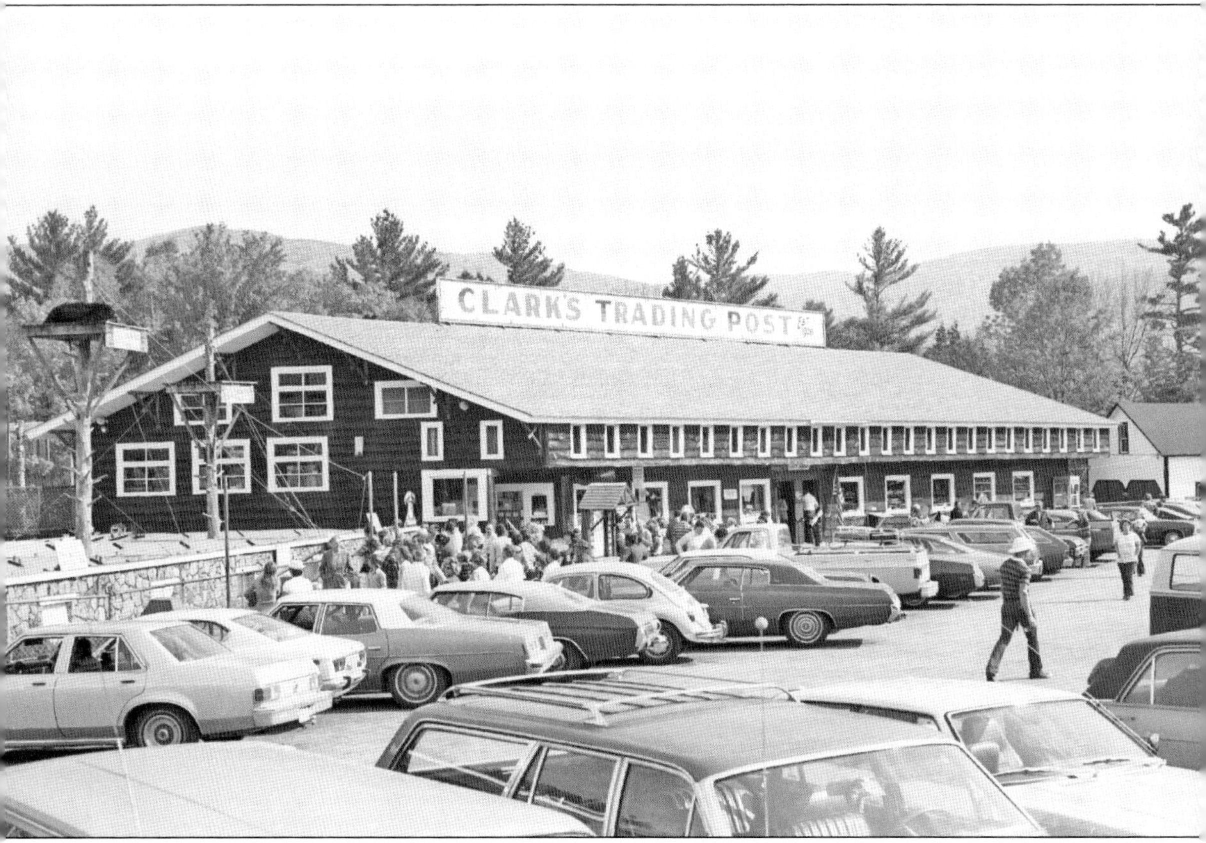

This was a busy day at Clark's Trading Post around 1976, shortly after completion of the south end of the building. While the interior has received updates periodically, the exterior has not changed substantially since the last nail was driven home in the south end. There is a bear on one of the platforms on the north end, and the white building visible on the right houses unused locomotives. (Courtesy of the Clark family.)

On the Cover: Pictured out for a ride in the 1909 Ford Model T in 1955 are (front seat) Ebony and Edward Murray Clark; (back seat) W. Murray Clark and Midnight. The Lima Shay locomotive can be seen on the left, and the dog pens are just visible on the right. Murray set up his camera on a tripod and Joyce Clark snapped this classic picture, which has become synonymous with the Trading Post. (Courtesy of the Clark family.)

IMAGES
of America

CLARK'S TRADING POST AND THE WHITE MOUNTAIN CENTRAL RAILROAD

Linda Eisenhart

ARCADIA
PUBLISHING

ISBN 978-1-4671-2910-7

Published by Arcadia Publishing
Charleston, South Carolina

Printed in the United States of America

Library of Congress Control Number: 2017962861

For all general information, please contact Arcadia Publishing:
Telephone 843-853-2070
Fax 843-853-0044
E-mail sales@arcadiapublishing.com
For customer service and orders:
Toll-Free 1-888-313-2665

Visit us on the Internet at www.arcadiapublishing.com

Dedicated to those upon whose shoulders we stand:
Edward Pullman and Florence Murray Clark;
Edward Murray and Joyce Avery Clark;
W. Murray and Barbara Avery Clark.

Contents

Acknowledgments

Without the enthusiastic support of the entire Clark family, this book would never have seen the light of day. However, a few people deserve special recognition. I owe a large debt of gratitude to Ruth Bossie. Her research and writings on the Clark family laid the tracks that made this book much easier to write. Carol Govoni, thank you for having more faith in me than I did. From conception to conclusion, your deft hand on the tiller helped steer us to port. Maureen Clark, you managed to train bears, put on shows, and still find exactly the right pictures for me; your help was invaluable. Thank you so much! Andrew Clark, I owe you a great deal for your technical wizardry and willingness to go through endless scans with me. To David Clark, huge thanks for answering questions and sharing photographs of the White Mountain Central Railroad. It would have been a very skimpy chapter on the railroad without your generosity. Barbara Clark, Fred and Anne Englert, Katie Mack, Murray Avery Clark, Callum and Nola Grant, Elise Clark, Bob Henderson, and Leon Noel—thank you all for talking with me. Your memories really wrote the book. All photographs appear courtesy of the Clark family. Photographers have been listed where known.

Introduction

After World War II, with an increase in automobile travel, the phenomenon of roadside Americana blossomed. Small, usually family-owned zoos, amusement parks, and private natural attractions arose, designed to persuade travelers to stop and spend a little time and a little money. By the end of the 20th century, however, most had been sold to large conglomerates or were closed due to interstate highways bypassing small towns.

It is surprising, therefore, to find a small, family-owned roadside attraction in the far reaches of New Hampshire that is not only alive but flourishing after nearly 100 years. Most certainly the bears play a large part. To see them loved, respected, and treated as part of the family is endearing. The Clarks themselves, approachable on even the busiest day, working hard to maintain the standards set down by their parents and grandparents, are also part of it. But there is a certain nostalgic magic at work too, which makes the whole greater than the sum of its parts.

The story begins in 1917 when Edward Pullman Clark was sent to Labrador by the fur trading company he worked for. He did not expect to fall in love with the proud, rugged Eskimo sled dogs he encountered there, but fall in love he did. It became his dream to raise, show, and sell Eskimo sled dogs and supplement his living when times were tough as a fur trader. That dream was to change not only the trajectory of his life but that of generations of the Clark family.

Upon returning to Manhattan, he married Florence Loretta Murray and they bought a farm in tiny West Milan, New Hampshire, to pursue the dream. It was a decision, he later admitted, that reflected "more courage than good judgment." Five hard, lean years later, they were no better off financially and now had a great many dogs and two young sons, Ed and Murray, to provide for. In an attempt to find a location with more tourist traffic, they relocated to Lincoln, New Hampshire, and in 1928, Ed Clark's Eskimo Sled Dog Ranch opened for business. Timing for the young business was poor, as the country was slipping into the Great Depression, but with ceaseless hard work, determination, and perseverance—traits that became a family tradition—they held on, hoping for better times. They participated in winter carnivals, races, and promotional events whenever they could. Florence became especially popular with racing fans and the public, and in 1932 drove a team of sled dogs to the top of the 6,288-foot Mount Washington. It took her more than one try, but on April 5, she managed what no woman before her had accomplished: driving her team to the summit platform. The publicity was invaluable for the business.

The boys grew up accustomed to hard, physical labor, and by the time Ed was nine and Murray was six, they were dealing with the public, giving tours and answering questions about the dogs as well as cleaning pens and caring for the dogs on a daily basis. As they grew older, the boys transitioned from simply showing the dogs to leading sled dog tours.

In the mid-1930s, two trappers brought three orphaned bears to the Clark family. The cubs immediately became "road stoppers"—something to entice tourists to visit the dog ranch—and the future of the Clarks became inextricably joined with North American black bears. With the coming of World War II, young Ed was dispatched to Iceland at the age of 18 with teams of sled dogs. They had been acquired from the Clarks by the US government for cold weather operations, and Ed was to train British troops in the handling of the dogs. Murray, at just 16, went to Glen Feshie, Scotland, on a similar mission.

After the war, Ed and Murray began to take increasing responsibility for the running of the Trading Post. In 1948, with public interest in sled dogs diminishing, the brothers, now young men, began training bears for show work, and formal bear shows began in 1949. In the early 1950s, Ed's fascination with steam led the brothers to begin rescuing steam locomotives destined for demolition, creating, as Ed Clark put it, "green pastures for iron horses." In 1958, this led to the founding of the White Mountain Central Railroad as part of the entertainment at the Trading Post. The years 1963 to 1965 saw the addition of a covered bridge spanning the Pemigewasset River, which allowed for an extension of the scenic railroad.

The Clark brothers married the Avery sisters, and between them raised nine children. While several of the children moved away at some point to spread their wings, most eventually returned to work at the family business, bringing with them new expertise and new ideas In 1972, Ed, a "Renaissance Man" of wide and varied interests, left the Trading Post to follow his heart in other directions. This left Murray to shoulder the full burden of managing the business, training the bears, and doing the bear shows. It became crucial for the third generation to begin taking on more of the workload.

The 1970s were a decade of expansion, with something new added almost every year: Wolfman arrived in 1973. The Americana Museum, the Pemigewasset Hook and Ladder Fire Station, the Photo Parlor, Maple Cabin, and the Peppermint Saloon opened on Main Street, and Avery's Garage was completed in 1980. Almost everything was built by family members and a few full-time employees. Very little was contracted out, and everything was done to enhance an "old-time" feeling. The brothers and their families were collectors of all things Americana that were fading from public life. Their desire to rescue and reuse these items has given the Trading Post the look and feel it has today. Little new was used if something the family had gathered was available. Given the brothers' passion for collecting, "something" was almost always available, stored and just waiting to be repurposed.

In the years that followed, new attractions were added at a slower pace but always hewing closely to the ideals and principles laid down by Ed and Murray. The Blaster Boats, Merlin's Mystical Mansion, the Pullman Block, the Climbing Tower, Segways, River City Mining, the Anaconda Escape, and the transformation of Tuttle's Rustic House into Tuttle's Laser Shooting Gallery were all added to keep the Trading Post fun, educational, and family oriented, while retaining the flavor of the past.

Florence and Edward's dream of a family business has survived and evolved in ways they could never have imagined, but they would most certainly approve. Clark's Trading Post and the White Mountain Central Railroad have touched the hearts of millions of visitors and guests to the White Mountains.

One

Affairs of the Heart

When Edward Pullman Clark graduated from business college in 1909, his uncle offered him a position in a fur trading company. Working diligently, he was eventually promoted to buyer. In 1917, he was dispatched to Labrador to check on an agent who was not fulfilling his responsibilities; after reporting back to the home office on the situation, Edward soon found himself the new agent in charge. During the cold, grueling winter months, he discovered that the harsh living conditions suited him, and he fell in love with the beautiful, rugged, intelligent Eskimo sled dogs.

While Edward was in Labrador, Florence Murray was in Manhattan, working as a clerk at an insurance company. Young, strong-willed, and growing restless in a job that seemed impossibly routine, she was ready for a change.

By 1922, Edward had returned to Manhattan. In his mid-30s, he was ready to settle down, but after his Labrador adventure he found it difficult to return to business life in New York. He and Florence grew up in the same neighborhood in Mamaroneck, New York, but it was not until they were adults that they connected over a common interest in dogs. He found her a beautiful, impulsive young woman and was drawn to her intelligence and carefree approach to life. She saw a man with the charisma that cloaks men who have traveled far.

They were married on Friday, October 20, 1922, and that weekend packed their belongings, said goodbye to family, and drove off to begin their new life. Edward was determined to start a business raising and showing Eskimo sled dogs, supplementing his income as a fur trader. He had quit his job and arranged for a team of dogs to be shipped from Labrador to Boston. They were due to arrive in late October. He needed to relocate and there was no time to lose.

A 15-acre farm in West Milan, New Hampshire, became their new home, and within two weeks of their wedding, 10 Eskimo sled dogs arrived. Edward's dream had begun and Florence was excited about a new challenge.

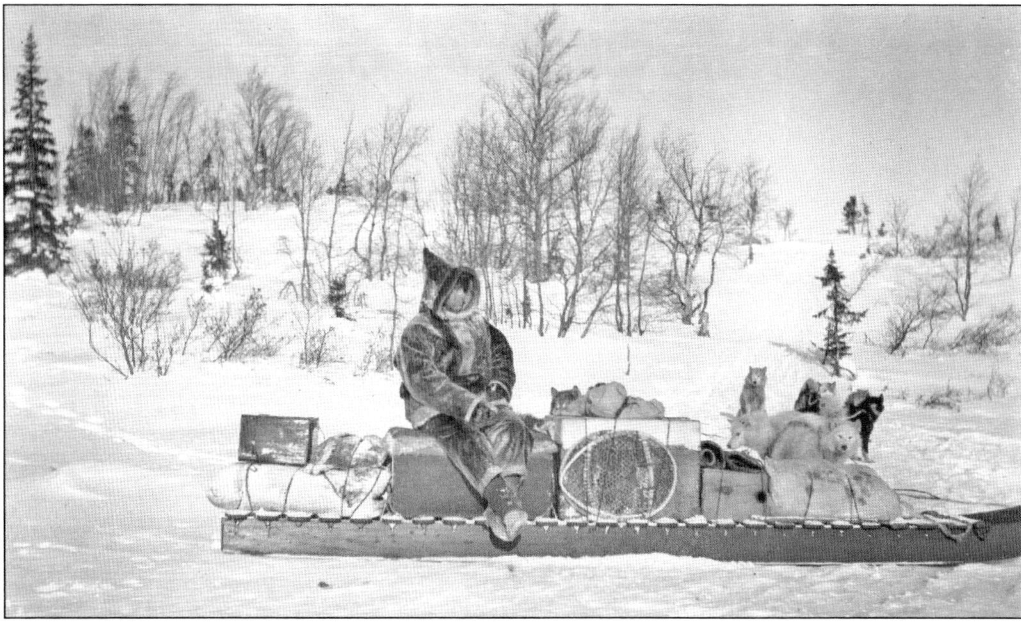

Edward Pullman Clark is seen on a *komatik* sled near Rigoulette, Labrador, in 1918. Paved roads did not exist there at that time. In summer, most travel was accomplished by boat. In winter, however, travel was possible only by dog sled or by walking. Edward, used to a busy social life in New York, faced long, cold, lonely months with only widely scattered fur traders for company. He found solace in the company of his Eskimo sled dogs, who captivated him with their strength, loyalty, and intelligence. Thus began a dream for the future.

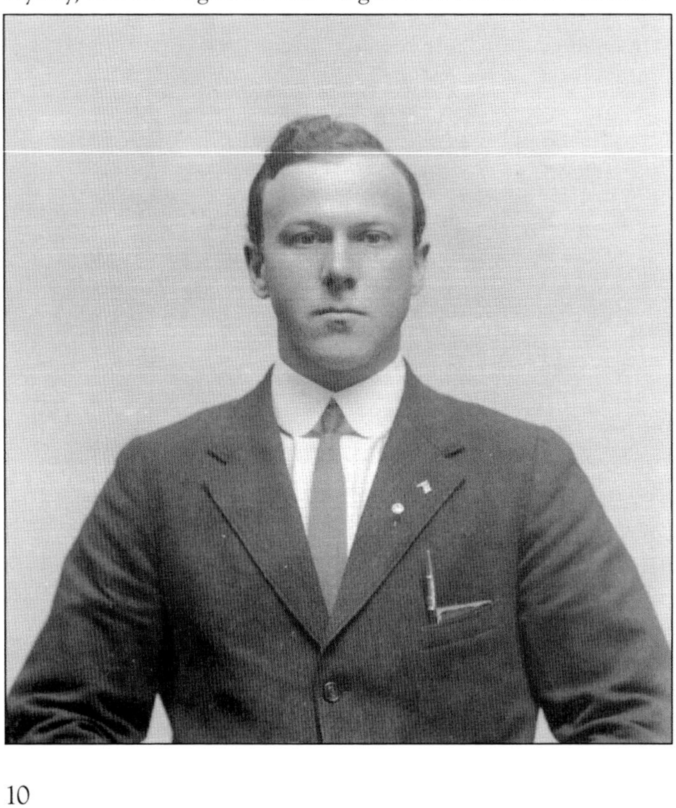

Upon graduation from Merrill Business College in Stamford, Connecticut, Clark was hired by the Charles S. Porter Company, a raw fur wholesaler in New York City. Fashion furs were in high demand, and business was booming. This 1917 passport photograph shows 29-year-old Clark ready to embark for Labrador to inspect the company's northern outposts.

At 18, Florence Murray took a position with the Metropolitan Life Insurance company in New York. On November 11, 1918, the city was wild with excitement at the end of World War I. Florence gathered with fellow workers in the company's 700-foot-high clock tower to watch. The face of the Met Life clock had an opening just large enough for Florence to squeeze through, and with the help of friends, she perched on one of the clock's hands for a "top of the world" view of the celebrations below.

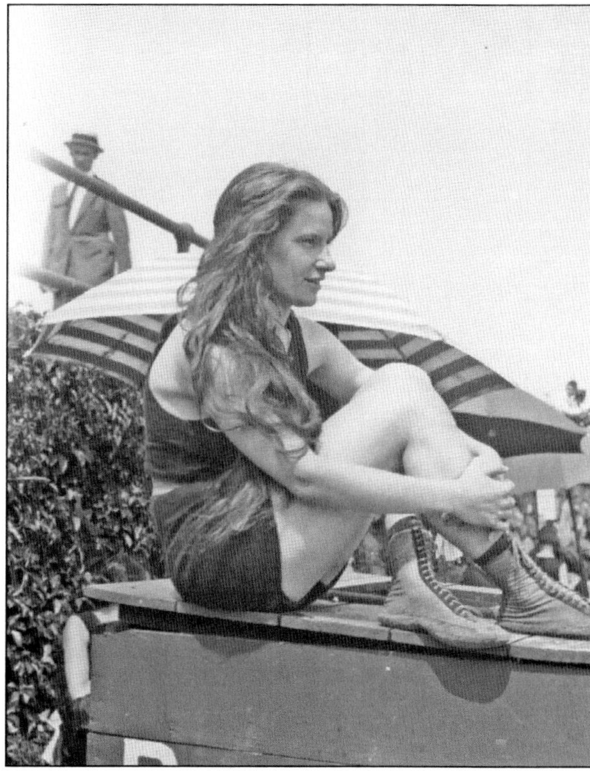

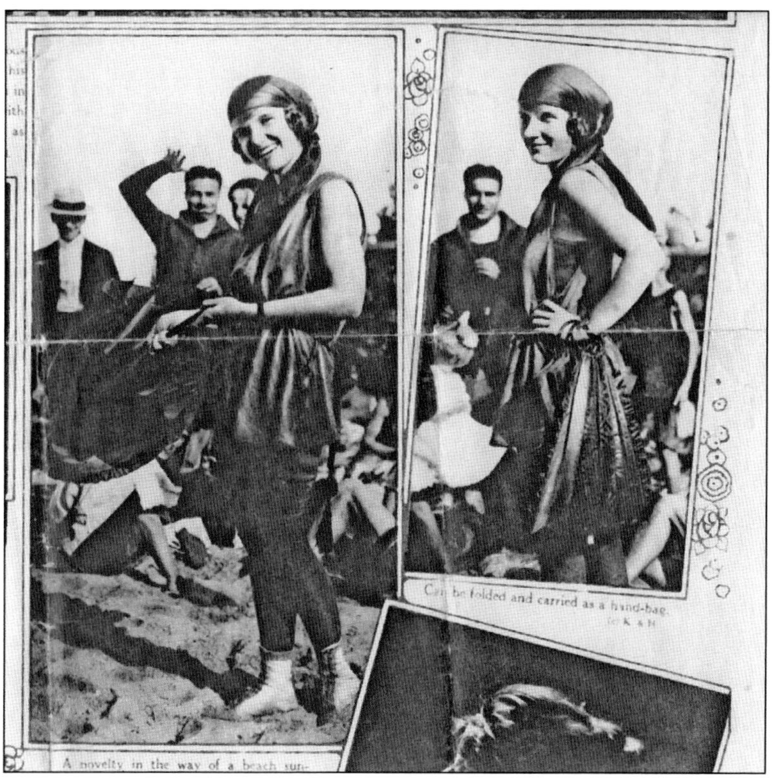

Florence was a carefree girl with no interest in Victorian values. She was featured in the rotogravure section of the *New York World* newspaper on Sunday, August 22, 1920. The caption read: "A novelty in the way of a beach sunshade which can be folded and carried as a handbag." She was 20 years old at the time. (Both photographs by the *New York World*.)

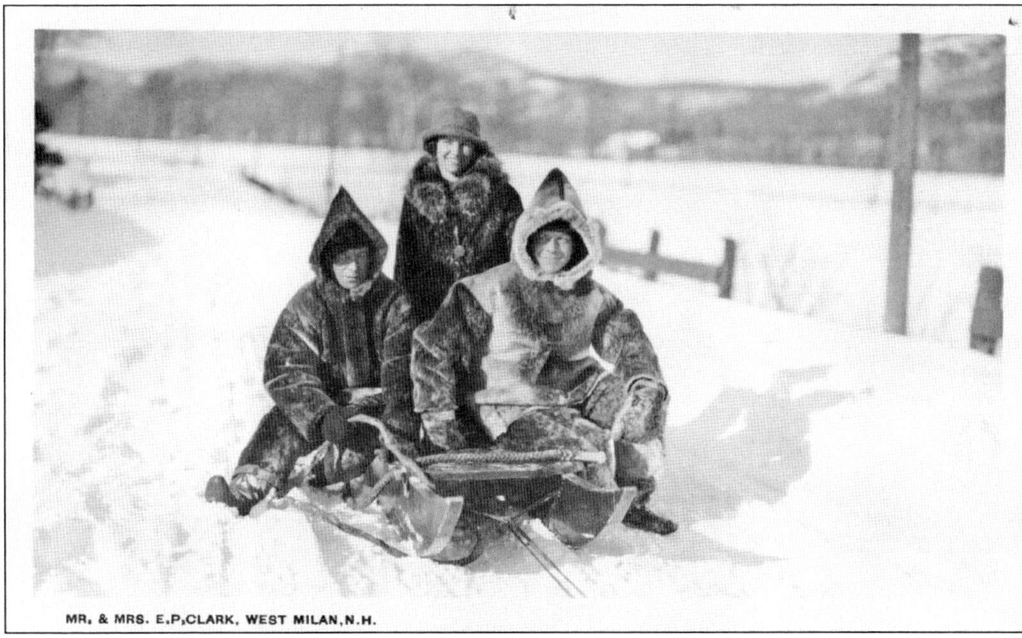

From left to right, Ralph Howland and Florence and Edward Clark are posing for a publicity photograph at the 1923 Gorham Winter Carnival. Eskimo sled dogs were not a well-known breed, and promotion was important if Florence and Edward were to secure their livelihood. This meant participating in every carnival they could. (Photograph by Guy Shorey, Shorey Studio, Gorham, New Hampshire.)

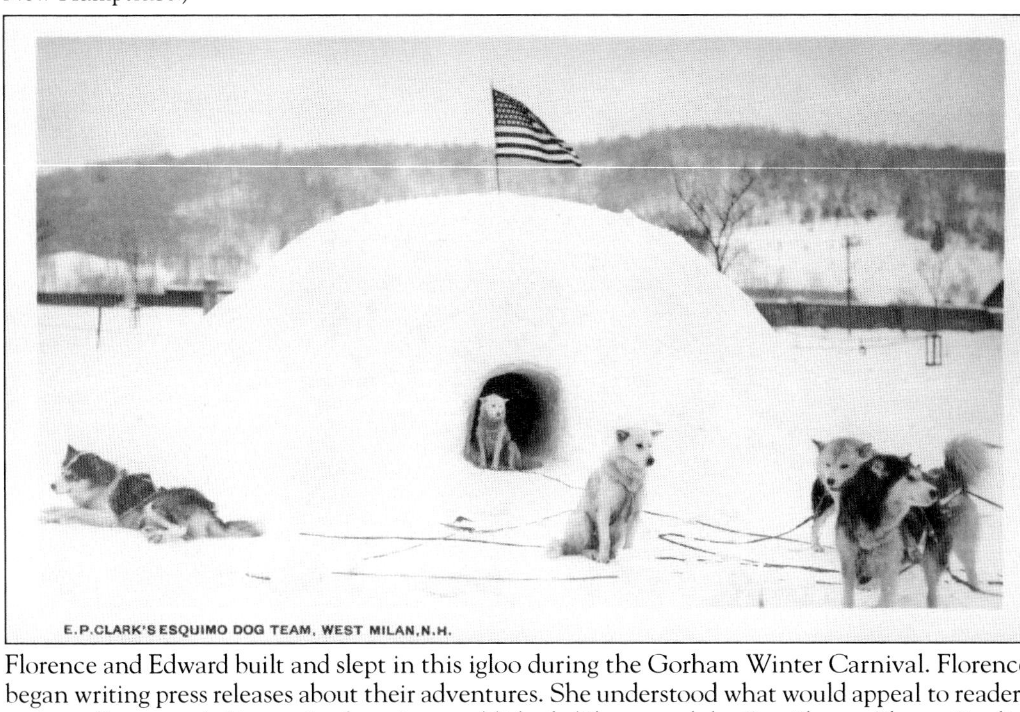

Florence and Edward built and slept in this igloo during the Gorham Winter Carnival. Florence began writing press releases about their adventures. She understood what would appeal to readers and usually succeeded in getting her pieces published. (Photograph by Guy Shorey, Shorey Studio, Gorham, New Hampshire.)

Edward Murray Clark was born February 9, 1924. He was soon making headlines throughout New England, as his parents' decision to include the baby in their adventures created wonderful human interest stories. By the age of one, he had traveled over 500 miles by dog team.

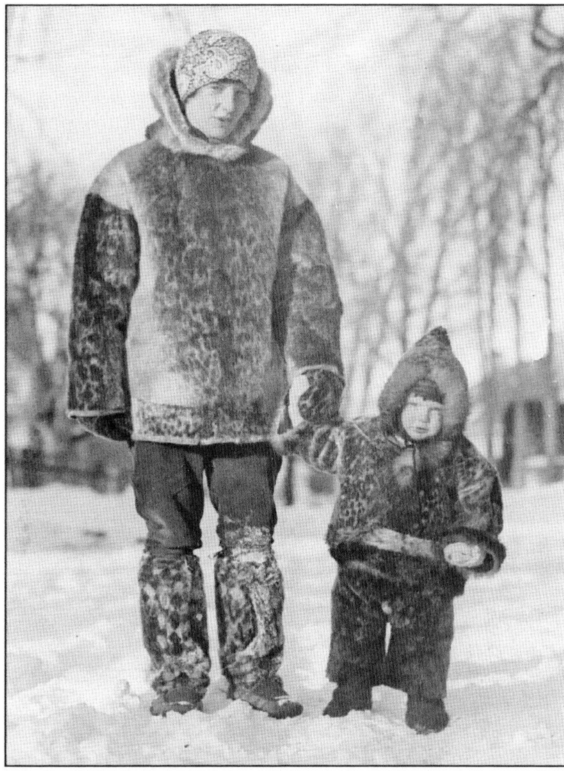

Florence and her son Ed are seen posing with the sled dog Sitty around 1925. Ed once remarked, "The reason we sit here today was more because of her perseverance than it was my father's. She knew the importance of survival. She took her sled dog training very seriously. And she had a rapport with people. Women in the early part of the century were still having a hard time. They were not respected much for putting new footprints in the snow. The woman was to be a mother and help take care of the farm but not have any ideas of her own. My mother always had ideas of her own. And they prevailed."

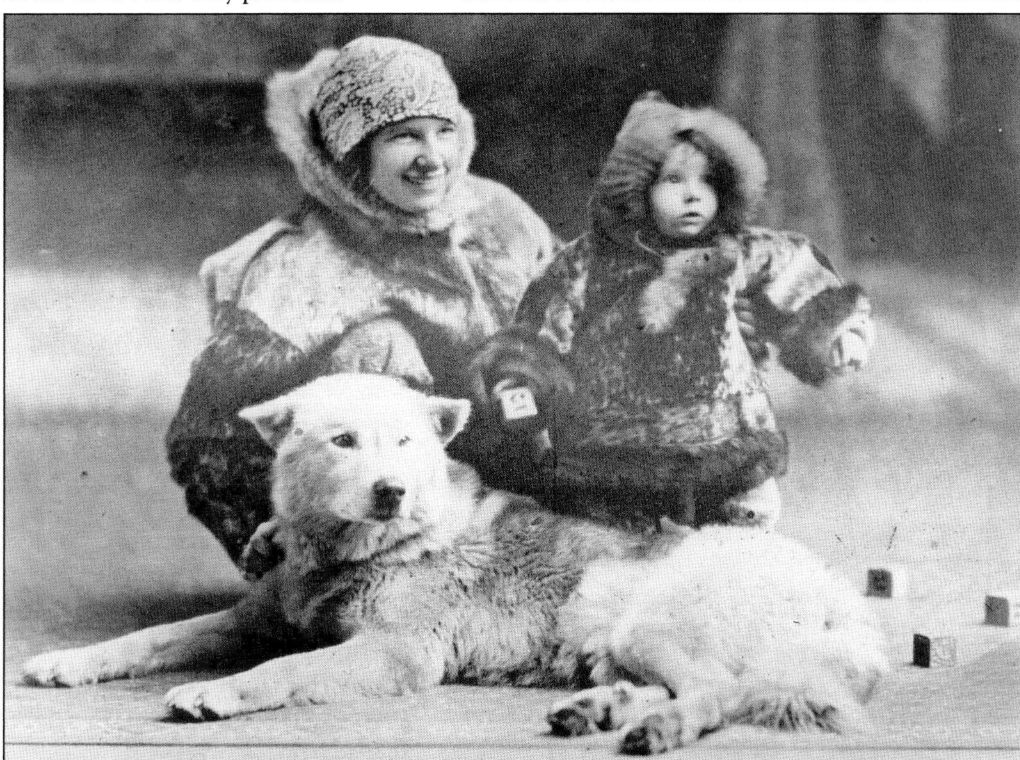

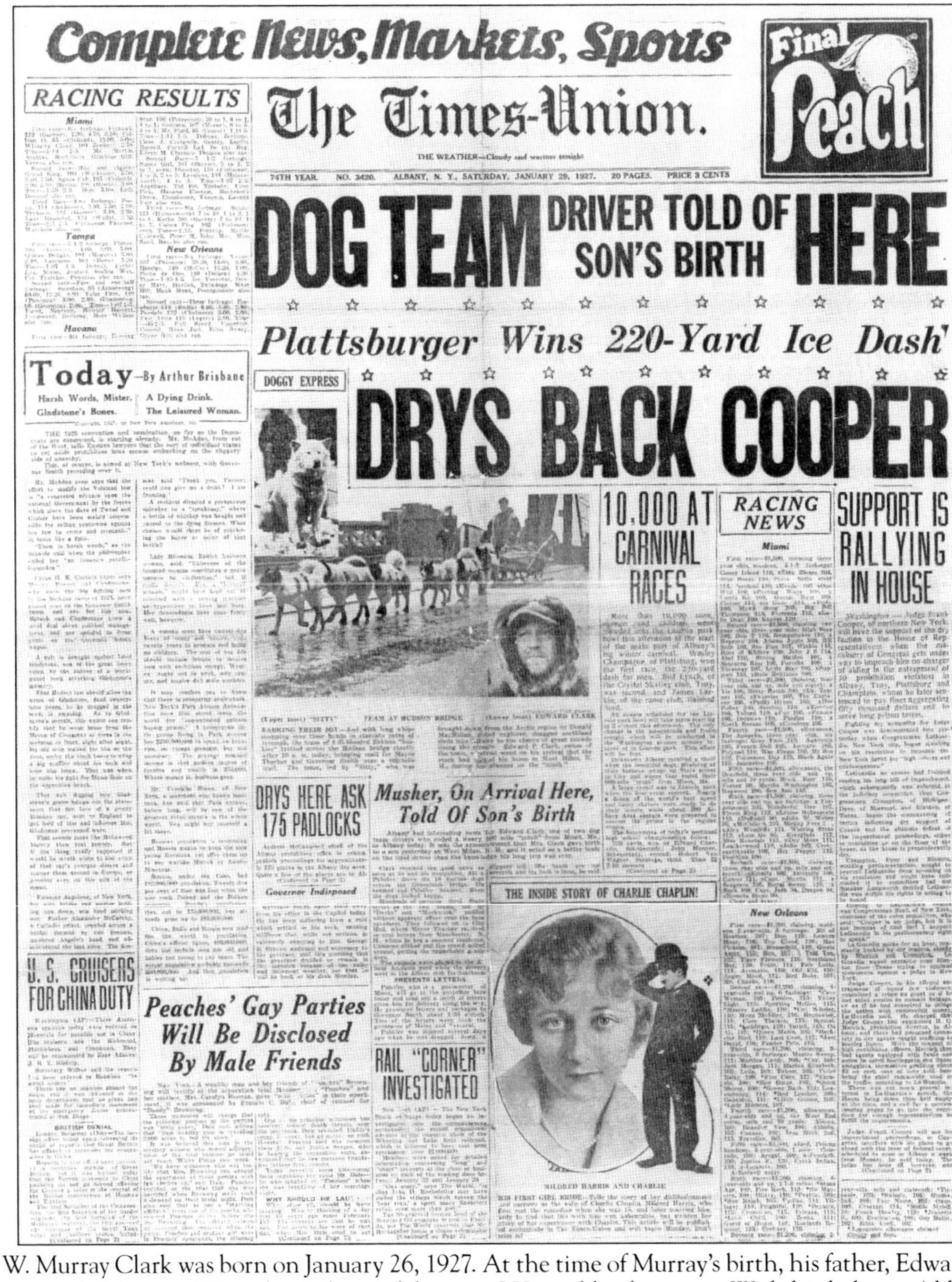

Complete News, Markets, Sports

The Times-Union.

Final Peach

THE WEATHER—Cloudy and warmer tonight

74TH YEAR. NO. 3420. ALBANY, N. Y., SATURDAY, JANUARY 29, 1927. 20 PAGES. PRICE 3 CENTS

RACING RESULTS

Miami

Tampa

New Orleans

Havana

Today—By Arthur Brisbane

Harsh Words, Mister. Gladstone's Bones. A Dying Drink. The Leisured Woman.

DOG TEAM DRIVER TOLD OF SON'S BIRTH HERE

Plattsburger Wins 220-Yard Ice Dash

DOGGY EXPRESS

DRYS BACK COOPER

10,000 AT CARNIVAL RACES

RACING NEWS

Miami

SUPPORT IS RALLYING IN HOUSE

DRYS HERE ASK 175 PADLOCKS

Governor Indisposed

Musher, On Arrival Here, Told Of Son's Birth

THE INSIDE STORY OF CHARLIE CHAPLIN!

New Orleans

U. S. CRUISERS FOR CHINA DUTY

BRITISH DENIAL

Peaches' Gay Parties Will Be Disclosed By Male Friends

RAIL "CORNER" INVESTIGATED

MILDRED HARRIS AND CHARLIE

W. Murray Clark was born on January 26, 1927. At the time of Murray's birth, his father, Edward, was on his famous 600-mile mail run, delivering US mail by dog team. With his helpers, Alden and George Pulsifer, he traveled from Maine through five states, ending in Albany, New York. The headline of the *Times-Union*, an Albany paper, read, "Dog Team Driver Told of Son's Birth Here." In West Milan, Florence had some excitement of her own. The night before Murray's birth, one of the dogs got loose and killed a number of chickens before Florence was able to catch him. She spent the night plucking chickens so they would not go to waste, and gave birth to Murray the following afternoon.

Two

Ed Clark's Eskimo Sled Dog Ranch

It is unlikely that either Edward or Florence had any idea what they were getting into when they decided to follow his dream of raising and showing Eskimo sled dogs. It was to be a hard, cold, primitive existence, which would take great determination and perseverance.

The time in West Milan proved difficult and financially unrewarding. After five years, they were no further toward realizing their dream when a friend from Boston offered Edward some advice: "First, find a well-traveled road." He was suggesting that the young family, which now included two small sons and a great many dogs, should relocate to an area with more traffic, where their dream of creating a successful tourist attraction focusing on the dogs and sled dog racing might be possible.

They settled on property in Lincoln, New Hampshire, just south of Franconia Notch State Park. The Old Man of the Mountain, the Flume, the Indian Head, and Lost River were all nearby, and US Route 3 ran through the property. They had found their well-traveled road, and in July 1928, after some frenzied activity putting up dog pens and constructing a small building to serve as a main entrance for the business—and give the family somewhere to live—Ed Clark's Eskimo Sled Dog Ranch became a reality. For a small fee, visitors could learn the history of the Eskimo sled dogs, enjoy a guided tour, and view an exhibit of furs, clothing, and curios from the far north. By 1937, refreshments, souvenirs, and gifts were also available. Economic patterns were changing: the automobile had made the region more accessible to middle class travelers, and federal, state, and local money was being directed toward new highway construction. A small building boom resulted in tourist cabins, gas stations, and restaurants cropping up. It seemed Florence and Edward might be on the cusp of realizing their dream. Of course, all their water still had to be hauled from the Pemigewasset River by hand, but things looked better than they had in West Milan.

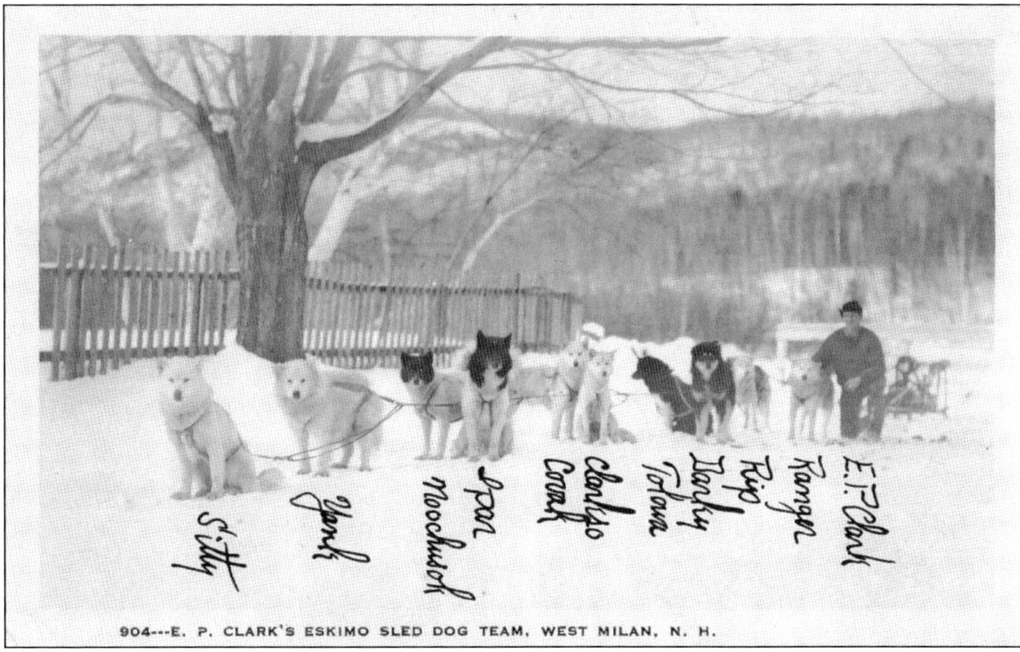

Edward is seen here with several of his original Eskimo sled dogs. He wrote, "The Eskimo dogs are ideally suited for the harsh cold. With their double fur coat they can sleep outside in winter, even when the temperature plunges to 70-degrees below zero. Their bushy, curled tails wrap around their faces when they sleep in the snow, acting as a muffler to keep them warm." (Photograph by Guy Shorey, Shorey Studio, Gorham, New Hampshire.)

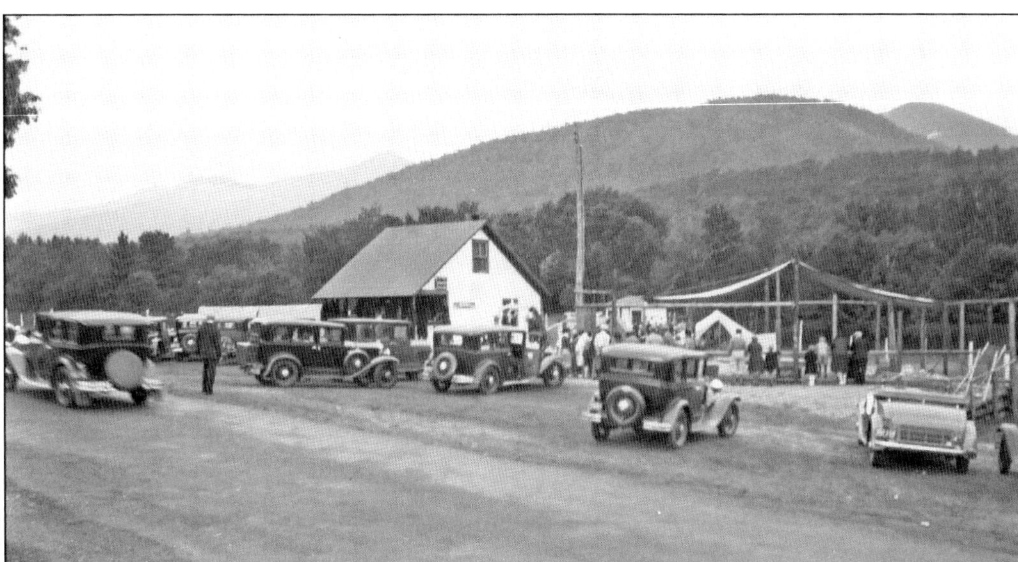

This photograph, taken on Labor Day 1931, is from the early days of Ed Clark's Eskimo Sled Dog Ranch. The cook house for preparing the dogs' food can be seen in the background, and a 1928 or 1929 Ford Model A appears in the foreground. Based on the number of cars in the yard, this was a very busy day.

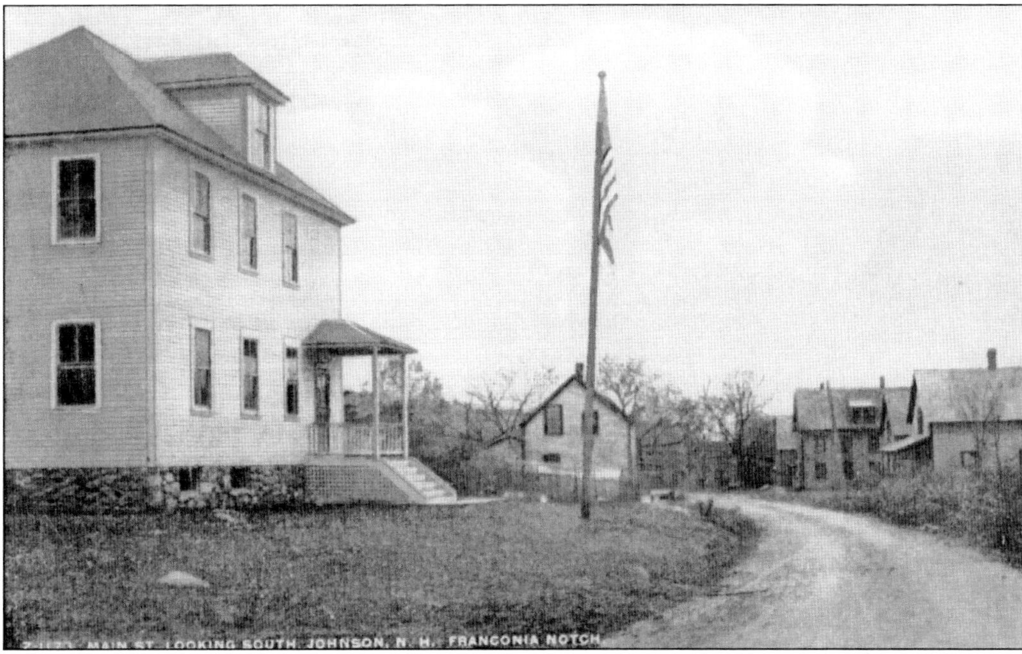

The Johnson schoolhouse was moved from the settlement of Johnson to the site of the former Tuttle Tavern. The Clarks first leased, and then purchased, what had originally been land owned by the Tuttle family. The schoolhouse, across the street from today's Trading Post, is where Ed and Murray Clark were raised. When Florence operated her guesthouse to supplement the family's income, the boys were relegated to the attic.

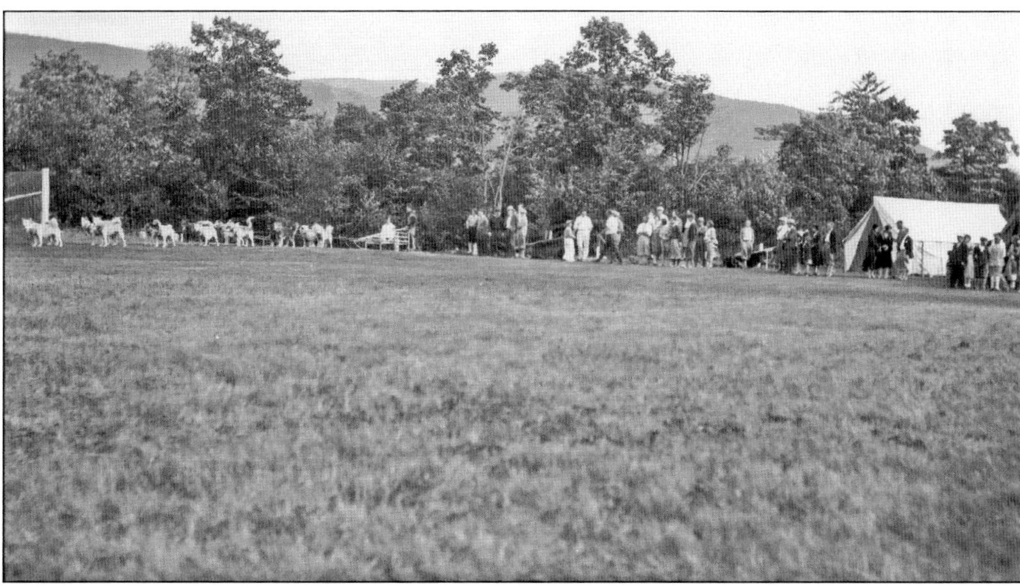

This picture was taken during Labor Day weekend in 1931. According to notes from Edward Clark, the photograph shows people watching the dog teams at Ed Clark's Eskimo Sled Dog Ranch. "We had 946 paid visitors this day and 329 the next day," he wrote.

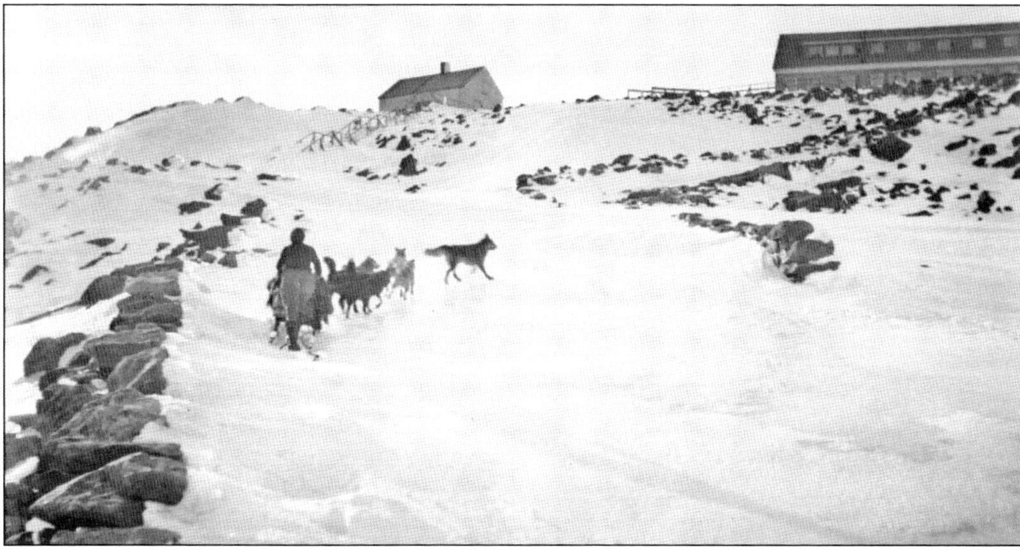

On April 5, 1932, Florence drove her team, with her beloved Clarkso in the lead, to the summit of Mount Washington. She was well aware of the promotional value of being the first woman to make a successful climb to the summit, but she also needed to prove to herself she could do it. Her plan was to make camp, spend the night, and descend the following day. A halo around the sun, however, forecast a coming storm. Exhausted from a day of urging her dogs up the steep, snowy slopes, Florence tumbled into the sled and relied on Clarkso to manage the descent. After a daylong trek to the top, the descent was accomplished in five hours. The sled she used is on display in the Clark Museum at Clark's Trading Post. (Both photographs by Bob Monahan.)

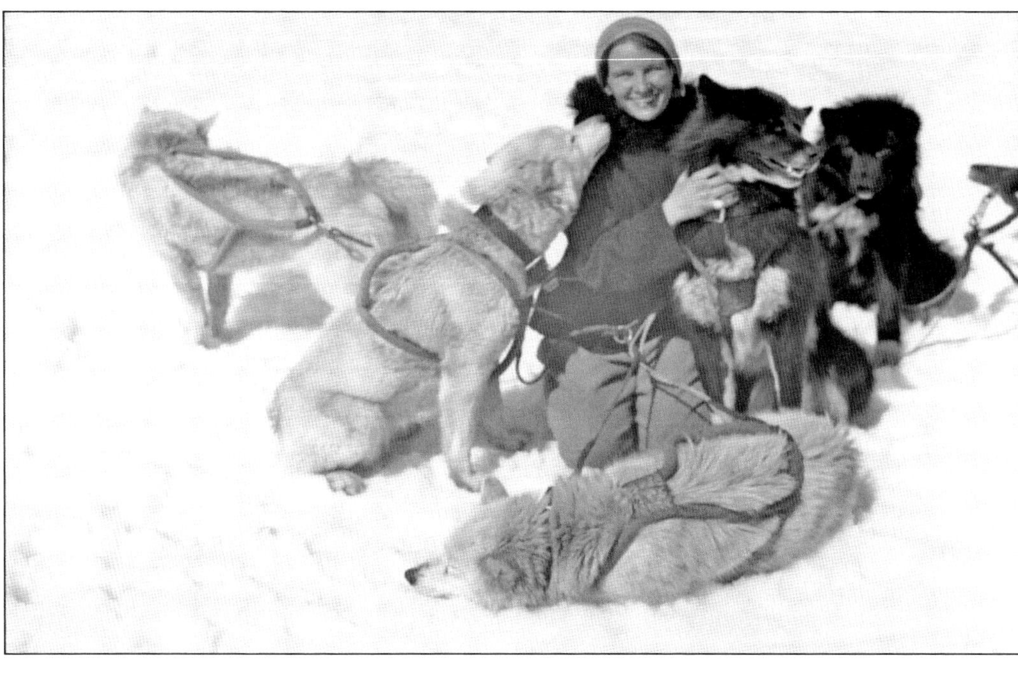

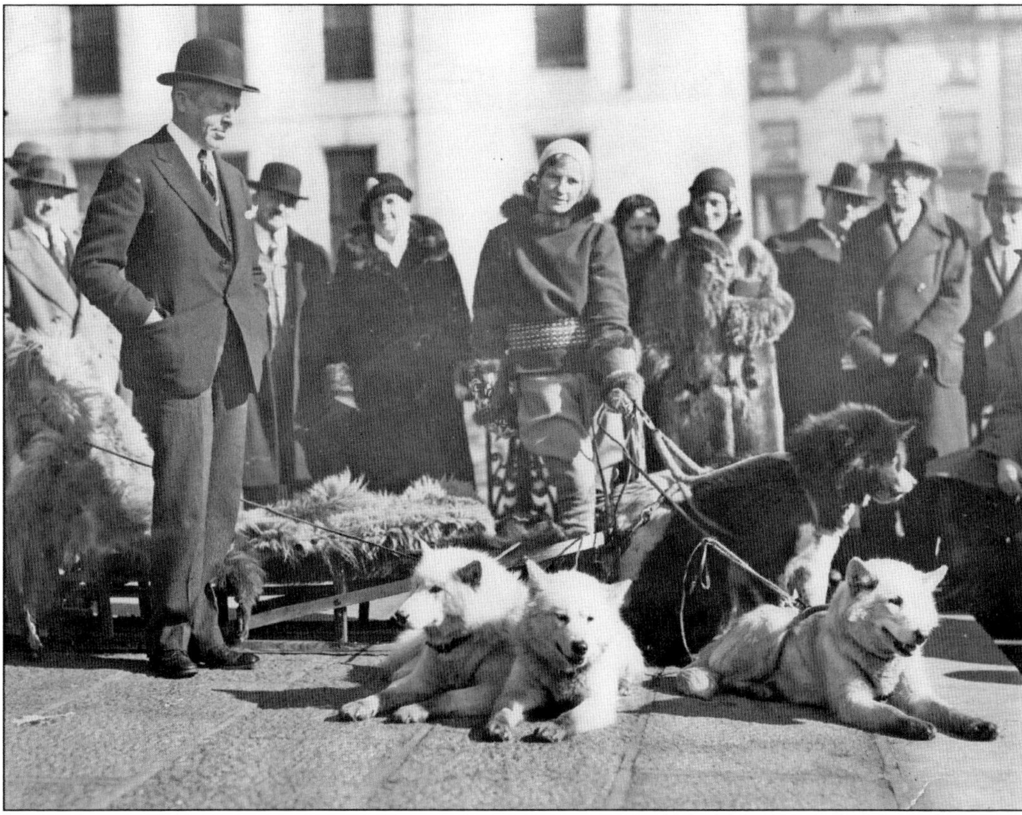

In 1932, Florence had just driven her team to the Massachusetts State House on Beacon Street in Boston when this photograph was taken. Gov. Joseph Buell Ely (left) is shown admiring the dogs. Florence delivered an invitation to Governor Ely from New Hampshire governor John Gilbert Winant to attend the New England Sled Dog Races in Laconia, New Hampshire.

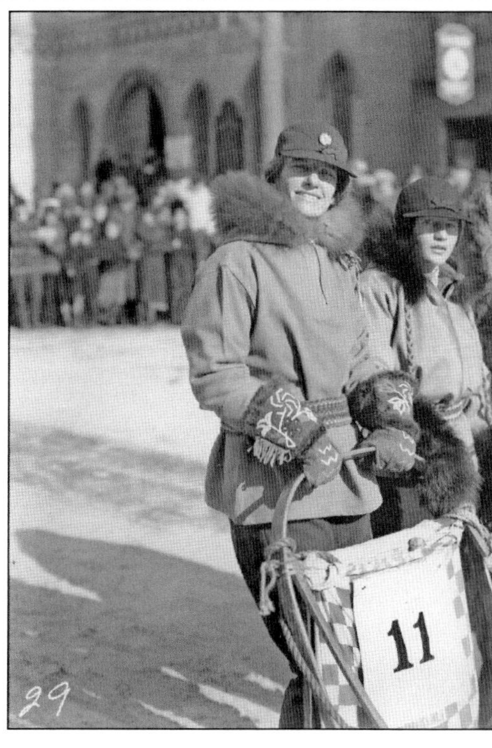

In 1936, Florence ran her last race: the Laconia World's Championship Sled Dog Derby, a grueling contest consisting of 30 miles a day for three consecutive days. She was already showing signs of the tuberculosis that would claim her life, but her smile made it clear that there was nowhere she would rather be. Florence (left) and her nephew Bill MacDonald are pictured at the finish line on the first day of the race. (Photograph by the *Manchester Union*.)

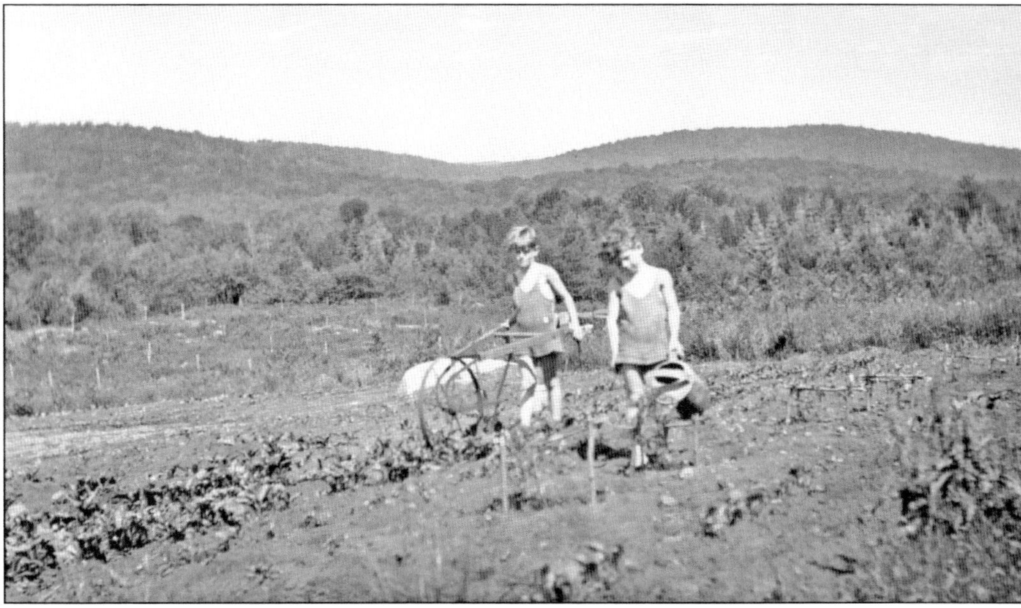

After the stock market crash in 1929, Florence and Edward struggled to put food on the table for two growing boys and upwards of 50 dogs. The Civilian Conservation Corps, working out of North Woodstock, New Hampshire, and workers at the local paper mill, generated quantities of leftovers and Edward arranged to receive the swill to feed the dogs. Food from the garden was essential, and caring for it was the responsibility of young Ed (left) and Murray.

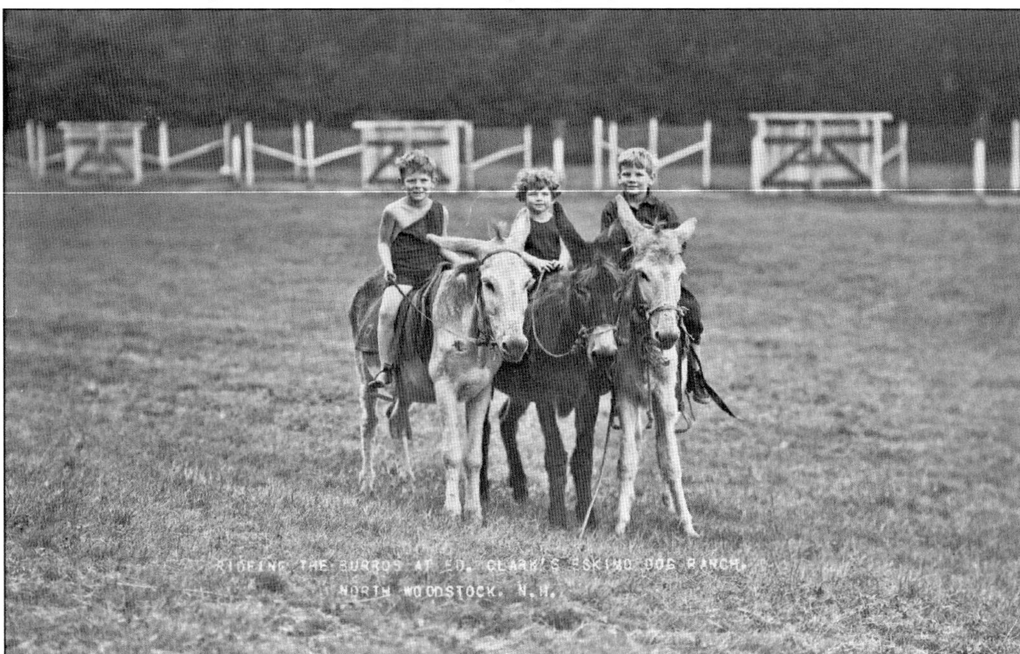

From left to right, Ed Clark, Murray Clark, and their cousin Bill Trowbridge are riding burros. The burros were owned by the Appalachian Mountain Club and were used to haul materials to build the Greenleaf Hut on Mount Lafayette. They were sold to Edward Clark and used around 1931 to give rides at the ranch.

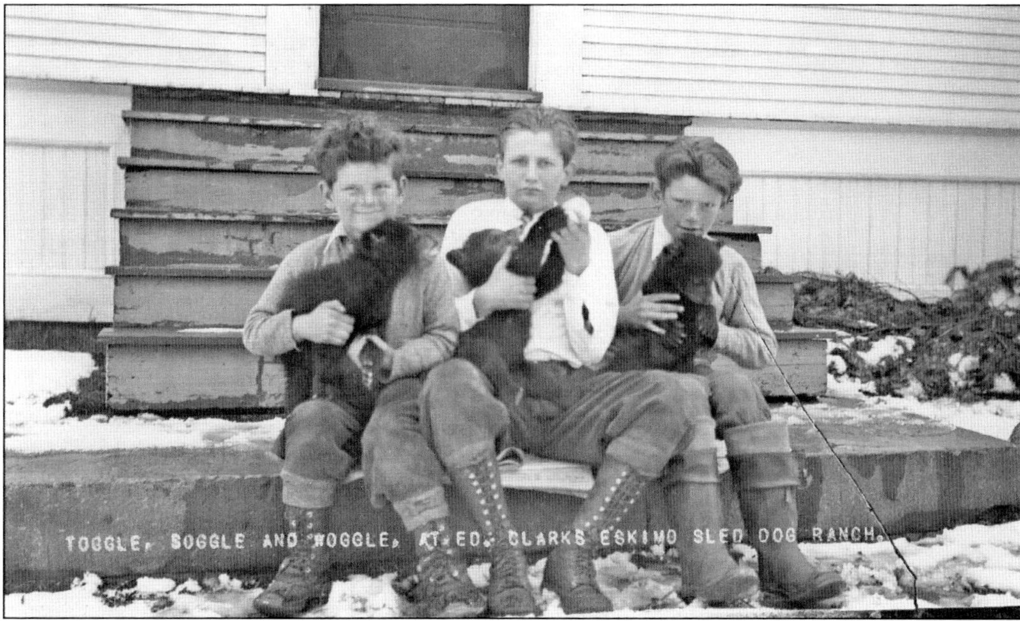

In 1935, Edward Clark acquired three orphaned bear cubs, and Florence promptly named them Soggle, Toggle, and Woggle. From left to right are Murray Clark, Bill MacDonald, and Ed Clark. The stone they are seated on is presently the stepping stone to the south entrance of Kilburn's Photo Parlor. (Photograph by Aria Roberts.)

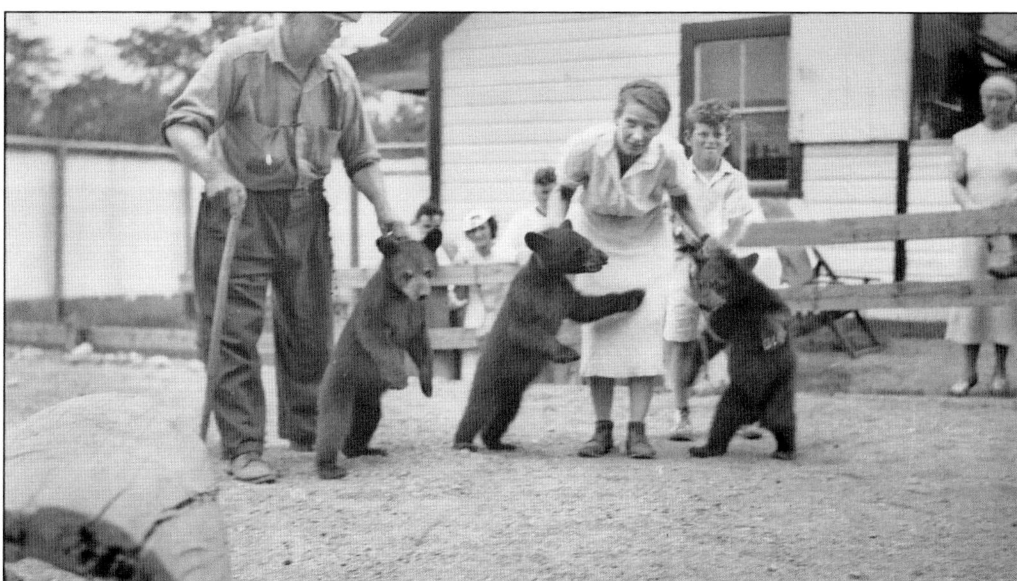

From left to right, Seth Richard Baker, Florence, and Murray Clark are pictured with the three bear cubs; the woman on the right is unidentified. The bears slept in a wooden box in the kitchen and required feeding every four hours. The curious cubs caused mayhem, and Murray later recalled, "You haven't really lived until you've tried to raise bear cubs in your home." (Photograph by Aria Roberts.)

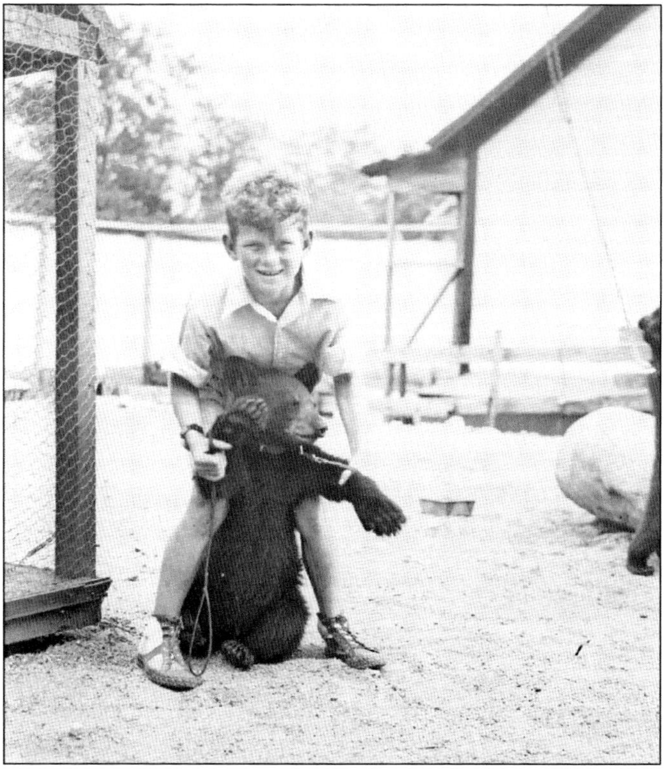

Murray is holding one of the cubs. The bears were used to entice travelers to visit. Behind Murray is the canvas wall used to create mystery and coax people to pay 10¢ admission to come in to view the dogs. The stand through which guests would enter and meet a guide for a tour is seen on the right.

By 1937, furs (which can be seen hanging), maple products, postcards, and New Hampshire souvenirs were being sold at "The Stand." The bears can be seen on the left.

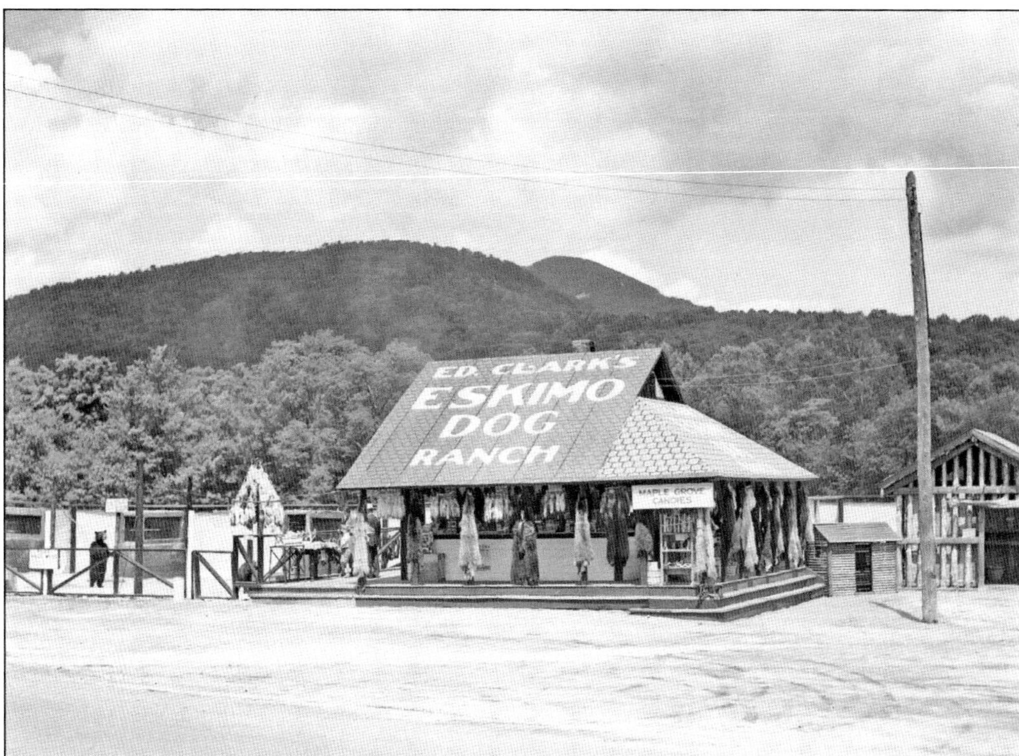

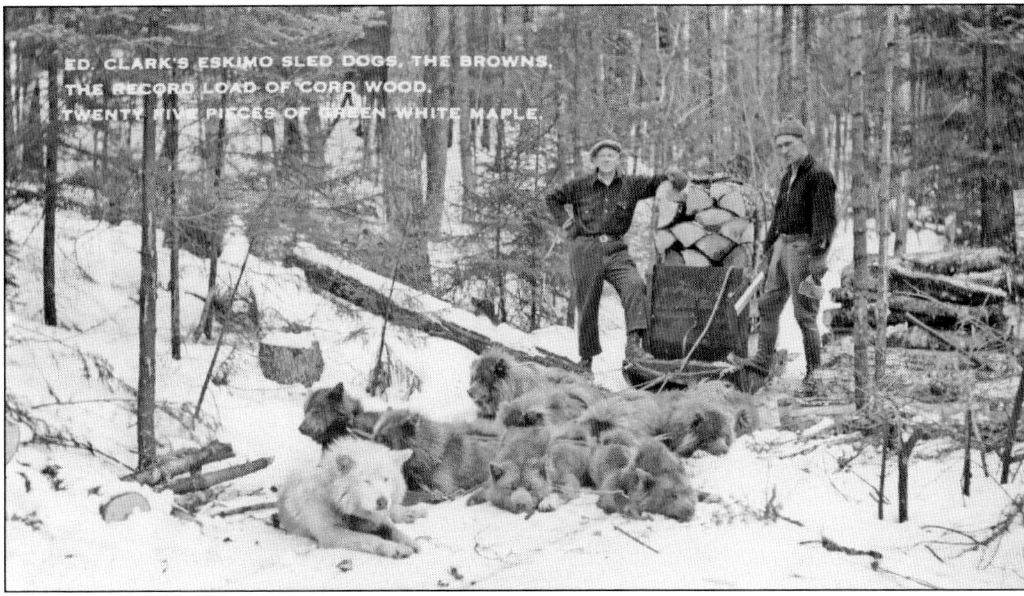

Edward Clark (at left above), Arthur Pinette, and the Brown Team are shown with a record 1,339-pound load of wood. By 1935, with increasing arthritis, Edward began focusing more on his dogs' incredible strength, training them for hauling competitions rather than racing. Florence wrote, "Every dog lays right into his harness and digs, broad shoulders straining and powerful hind legs pumping like pistons of an engine. Heads bent forward and tails—those lovely, expressive tails—arched lightly over their backs. If the load gets stuck, the leader and two or three of the dogs in the team will back up and rush forward and yell a signal to the rest of the team to heave. Sometimes if it just won't start, they will turn on the dog next to them and accuse him of not trying, or else, in their enthusiasm, bite the tail of the dog in front. . . . They arrive at their destination, tails waving, tongues lolling out of the side of their mouth, and heads thrown back laughing."

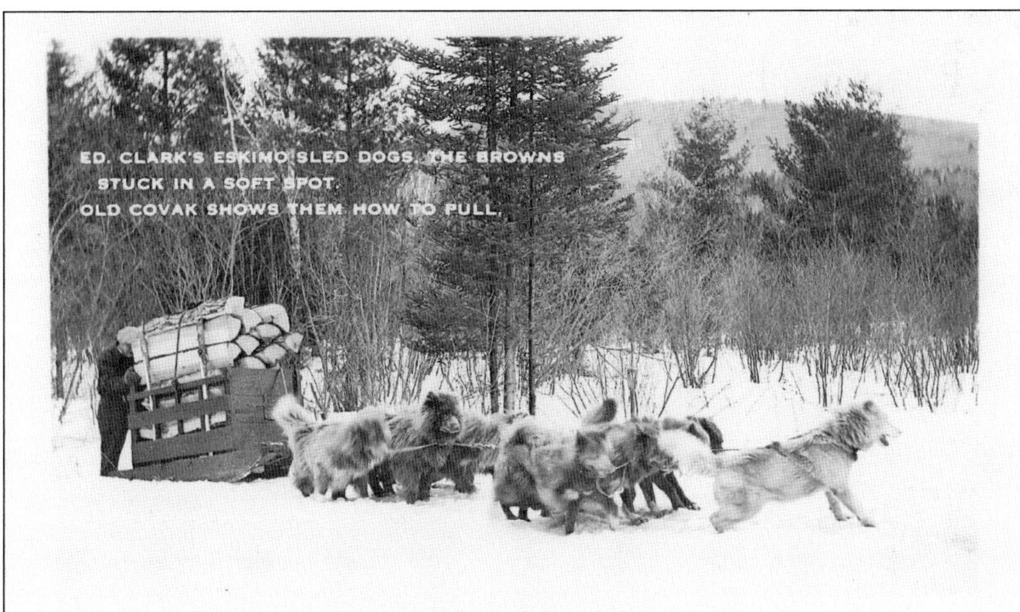

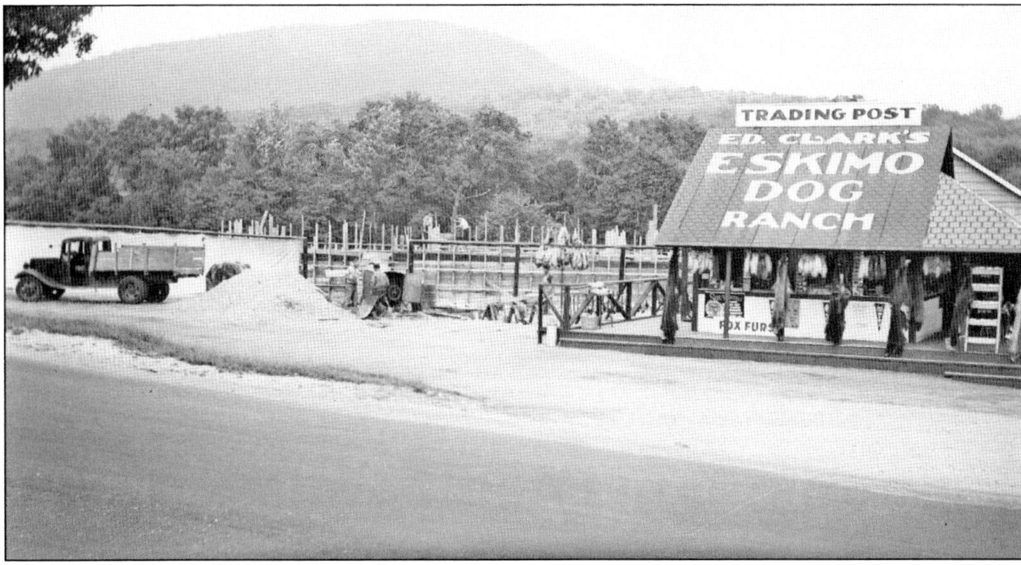

In 1937, the New Hampshire legislature passed laws requiring all wild animals held for public exhibition to be confined in escape-proof enclosures 100 feet back from the center of the roadway. In this 1938 photograph, construction of the bear enclosures is well underway. The pens were designed so that should the laws change, the structure could form the foundation for a new Trading Post.

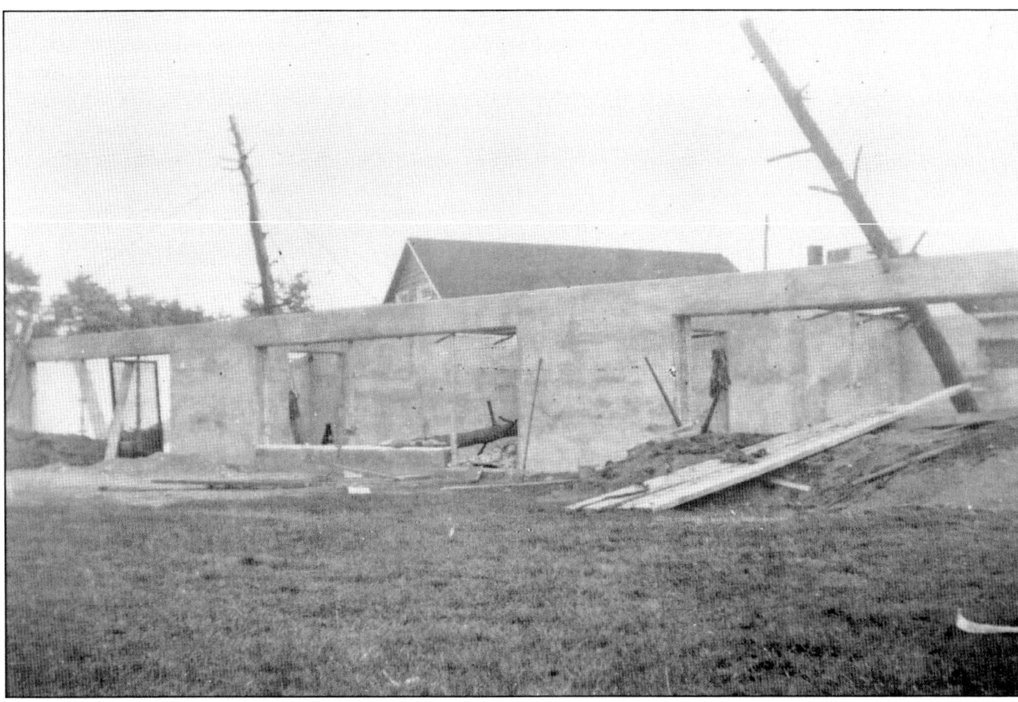

Edward was concerned the high concrete walls of the enclosures would block the public's view of his bear "road stoppers" and he would lose business. He had hemlock trees felled and the branches snubbed off, and erected them in the center of each enclosure for the bears to climb—where they would be visible to passing motorists. (Photograph by Gordon Stevens.)

The bears showed no interest in climbing the trees. Eleven-year-old Murray filled his pockets with crab apples and climbed the tree with Woggle, doling out crab apples as he went to keep her climbing. Later, platforms were added so the bears could rest or sit comfortably at the top, and a new tradition was born, a road stopper that continues to this day. (Photograph by Aria Roberts.)

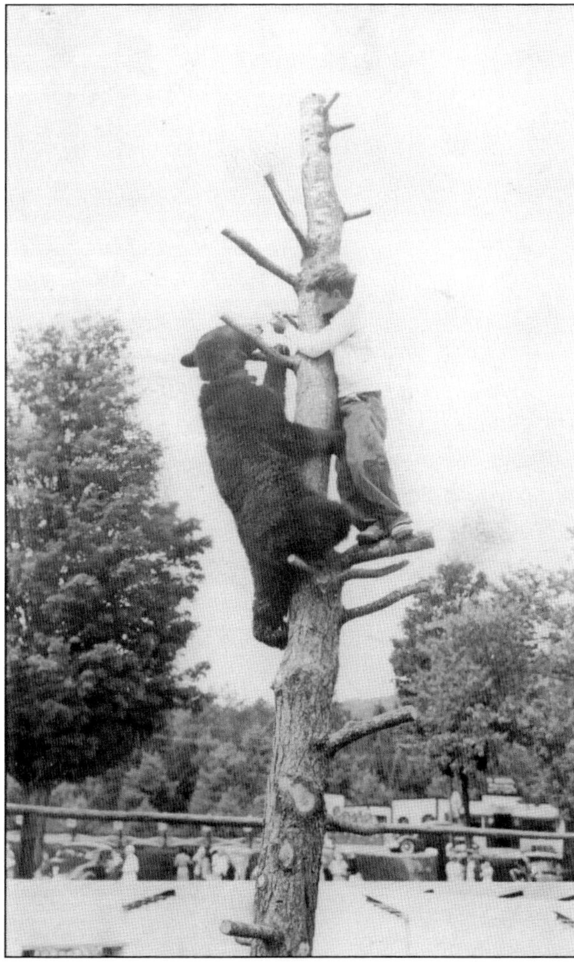

The bear pens appear in the foreground in this c. 1939 photograph. The "Arena" for sled dog demonstrations is on the left, and the dog pens can be seen in the background. One of the girl guides Edward hired to show visitors around can be seen at center right wearing her sombrero, identifying her as a guide.

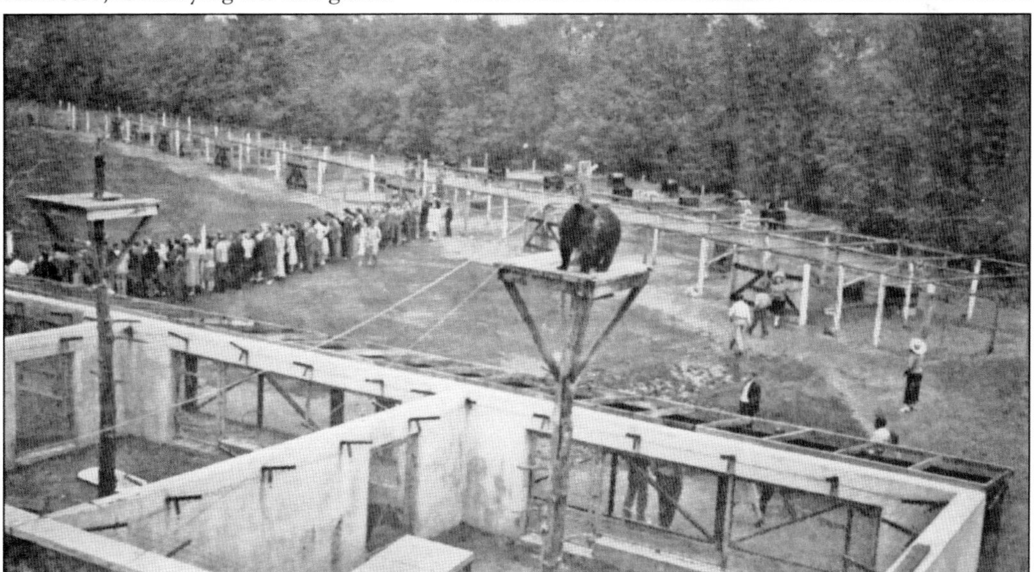

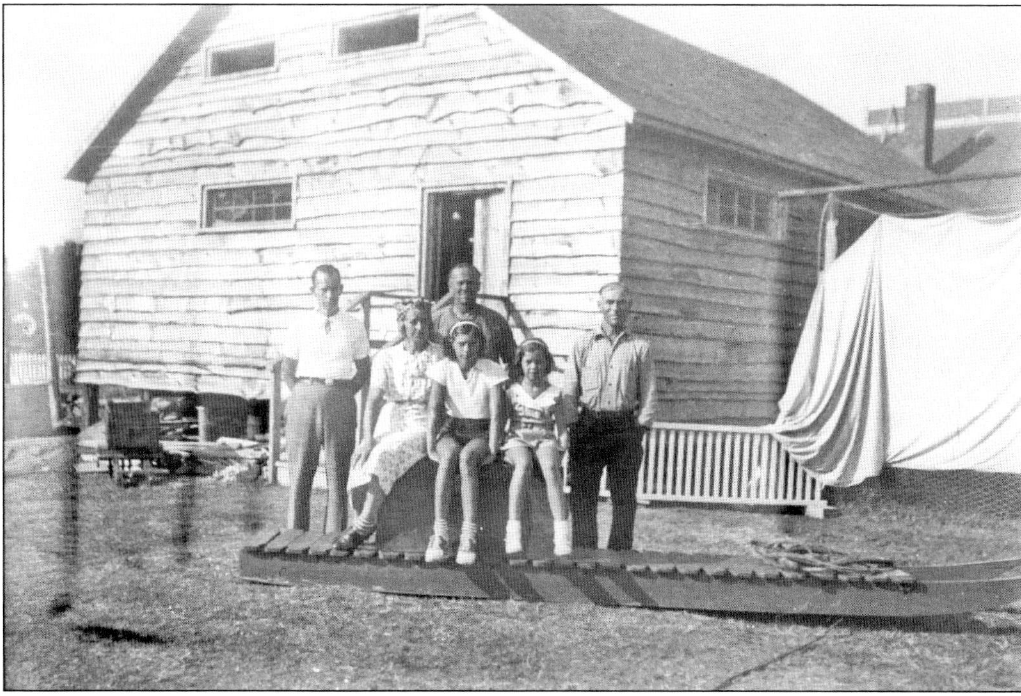

Pictured in front of the newly finished 1937 gift shop are, from left to right, Toddo Haviland, his wife and children, and Jim Martin. Edward Clark stands behind them. The structure was built for $500, including the roof.

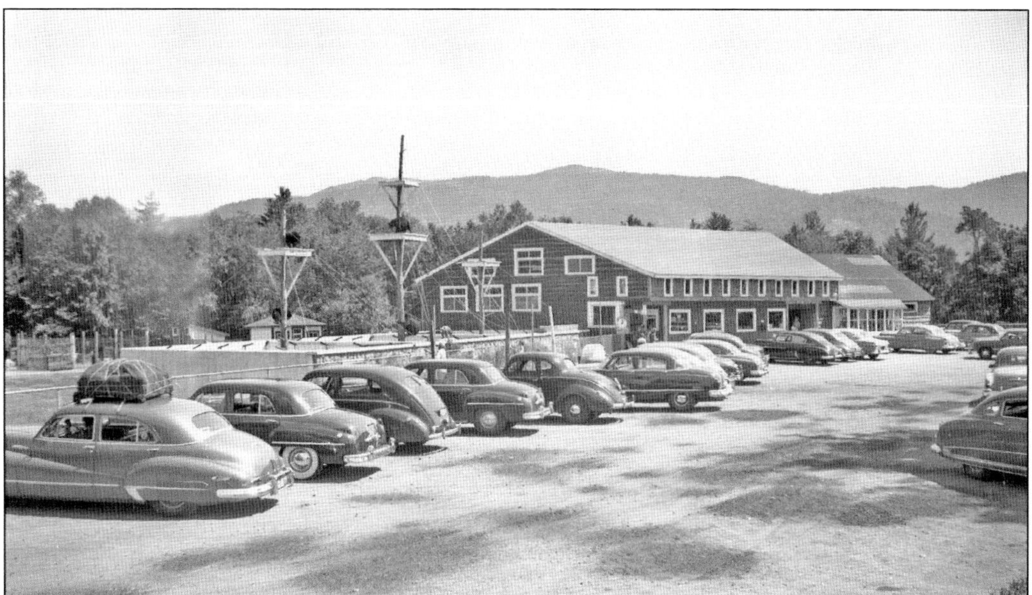

The 1937 gift shop has had more than one life. With construction of the north end of a new gift shop in 1948, it was moved back and attached at the south end of the new structure, as seen here.

Three

Clark's Trading Post

By 1940, the boys were assuming increasing responsibility for the business, and Florence felt they deserved more recognition. Speaking with Edward, she suggested that with the entire family involved, the name of the business should reflect that. Edward agreed, and the name was changed to Clark's Trading Post.

With the coming of World War II, the federal government approached Florence and Edward to inquire about supplying Eskimo sled dogs for the war effort. The offer came at an opportune time, as gas rationing had caused tourism to drop precipitously. The dogs were to be delivered to Reykjavik, Iceland, to the Norwegian Army. There was general agreement that someone from the family needed to oversee delivery, but with Edward and Florence in poor health, the only logical candidate was 18-year-old Ed Clark. Ed and the dogs boarded the SS *El Coston* in Boston, and the ship headed into the Atlantic—a very dangerous place in the summer of 1942. During his time in the outside world, Ed discovered a love of engineering and steam locomotion, and upon returning home from Iceland, decided to join the US Merchant Marine. Whenever home on leave, he spent a great deal of time with Joyce Avery. They fell in love and were married in 1944.

A few months after Ed left for Europe, the government once again came calling, asking for more dogs to be shipped to Glen Feshie, Scotland. It was 15-year-old Murray's turn for an adventure. Pulled out of school, Murray went first to Manitoba to procure the needed dogs and then to Scotland, turning 16 three days before embarking for Europe. Upon his return, he graduated from high school and joined the Navy, attending officer training at Brown University in Providence, Rhode Island.

Between the Depression and the war, the Trading Post languished. When the boys returned, there was a great deal of rebuilding to be done.

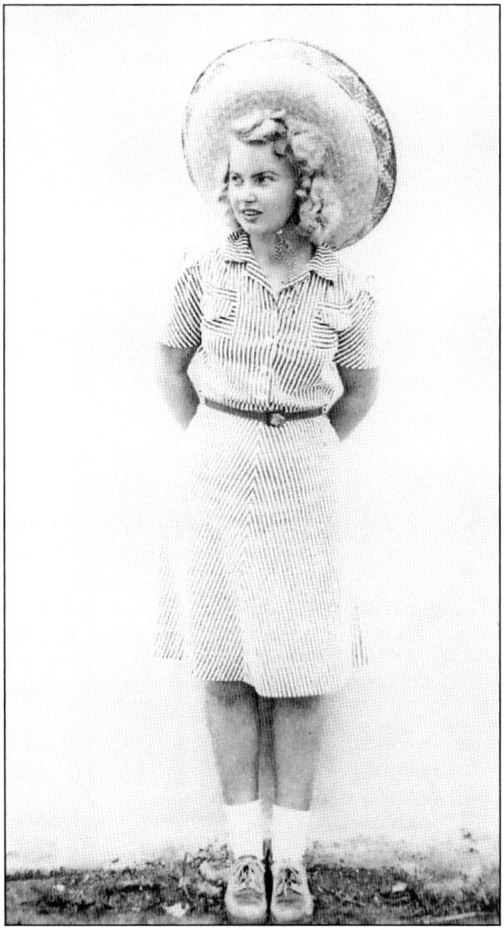

Joyce Avery, shown here wearing her sombrero, worked at the Trading Post as a girl guide. As part of her job, she would conduct tours, show visitors curios from the far north, and give the history and names of the dogs. Once, while guiding guests, Joyce realized that the actress Bette Davis, who owned a home in nearby Sugar Hill, was in the crowd.

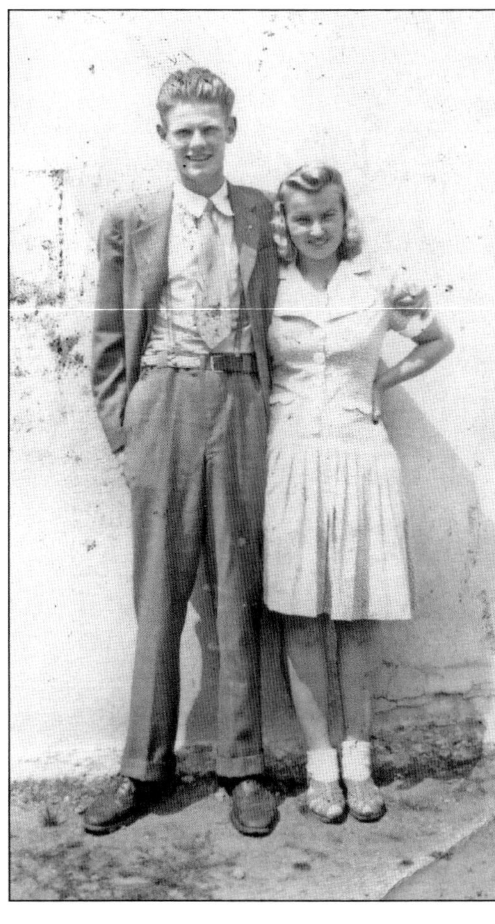

When the carnival came to town in 1939, Ed Clark and Joyce Avery, both 15 years old, became stranded together at the top of the Ferris wheel. It was the start of a long connection between the two families and a long romance between Ed and Joyce. In this picture taken around 1941, Ed is wearing a suit of his grandfather's that Florence had altered to fit him.

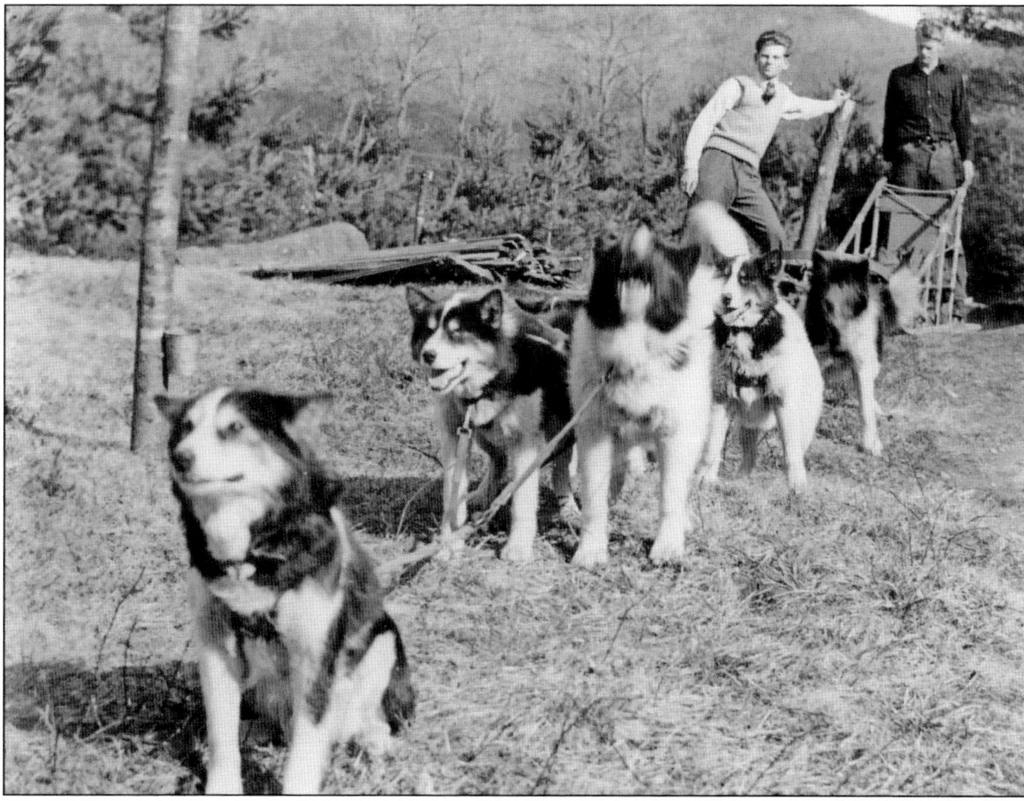

Murray (left) and Ed are shown with six of the pups who were taken to Iceland in the summer of 1942 as part of the war effort. Kyak, their mother, is the lead dog. Ed insisted on remaining with the dogs until he could train the men who would be working with them—a difficult task, as there were no sleds.

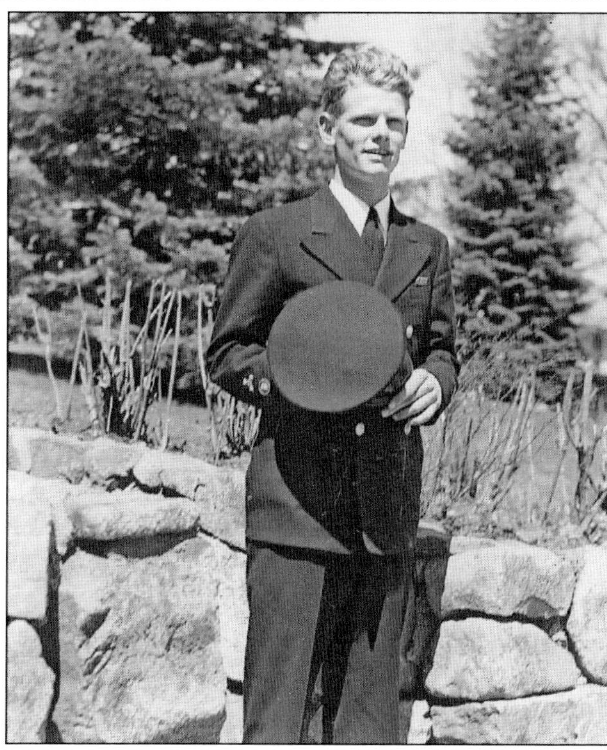

Ed fell in love with steam locomotion on his voyages across the Atlantic, and soon after returning home from Iceland, realized he wanted to see more of the world. Florence and Edward were not happy about this. However, Ed was clearly fascinated by steam engines and the sea and he received his parents' blessing to join the US Merchant Marine. He eventually saw action on Omaha Beach. He is pictured in his Merchant Marine uniform.

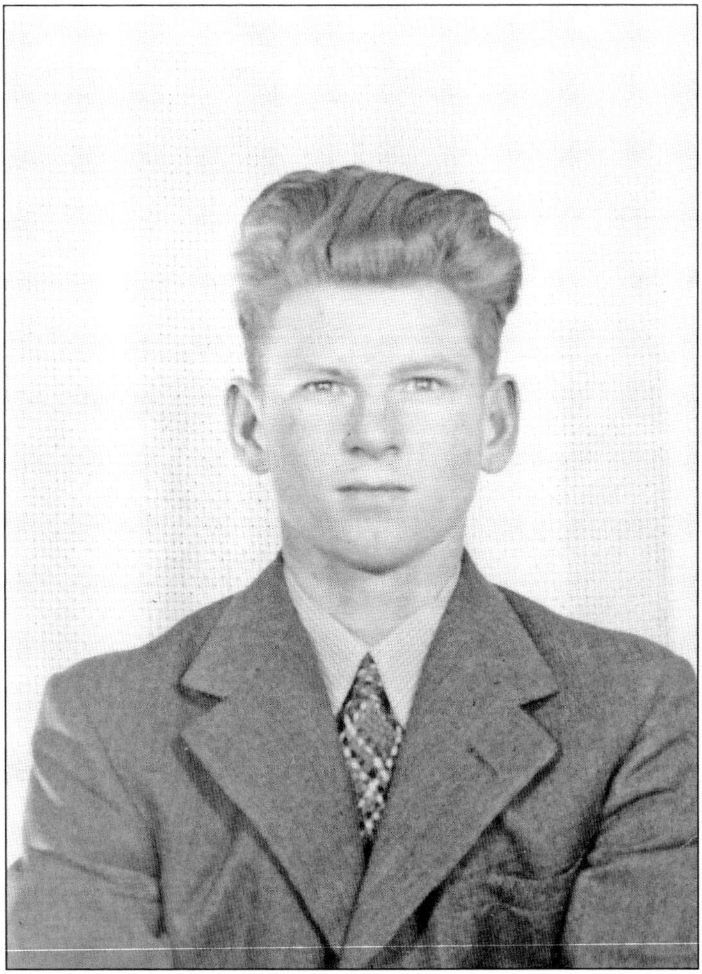

This is 15-year-old Murray Clark's 1943 passport photograph. He and the dogs boarded ship in New York for the trip to Scotland. His trip coincided with his brother's return from Iceland, and it is likely their ships passed at sea.

With both boys and most of the dogs away for the war effort, the Trading Post must have seemed hauntingly empty. Edward was suffering from severe arthritis, and Florence, ill herself, did her best to run the stand, but tourist traffic was almost nonexistent due to gas rationing, and there was little money to be made.

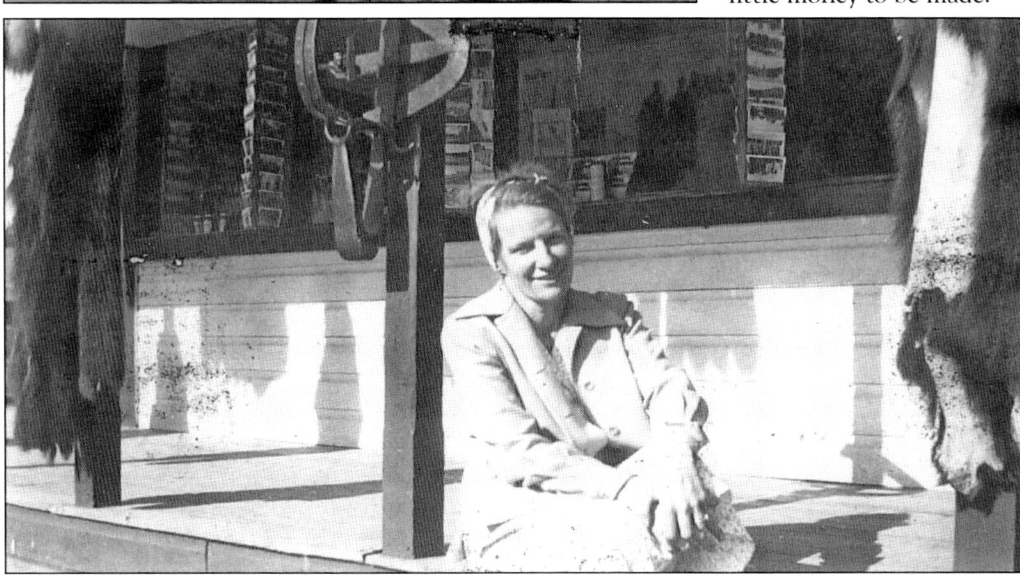

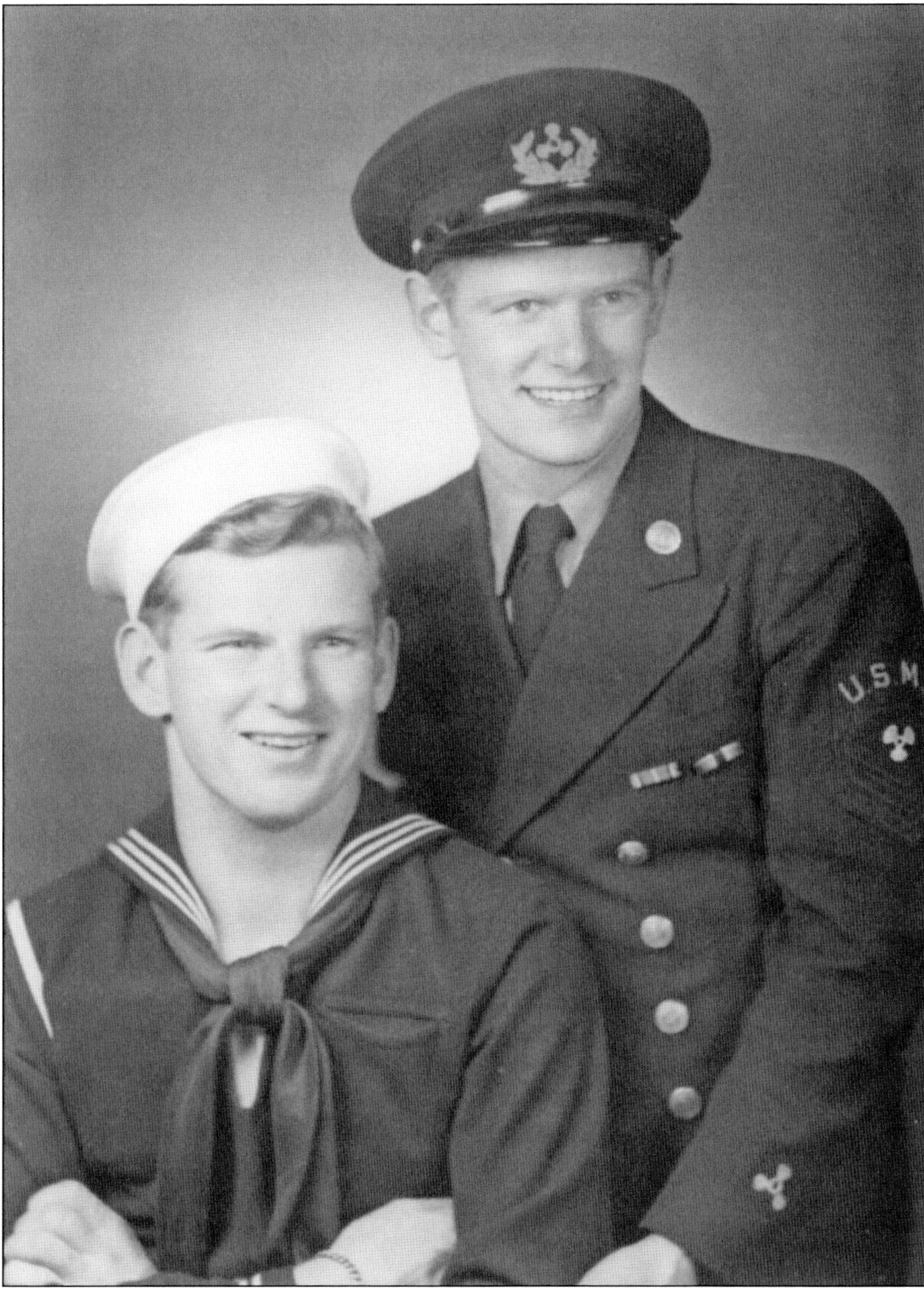

Murray (left) was in officer training at Brown University in Providence, Rhode Island, with the US Navy, and Ed was serving in the engine room on a fast freighter with the US Merchant Marine. The brothers met in the port of New York for this portrait, taken around 1944–1945. (Photograph by Richards Studios of New York.)

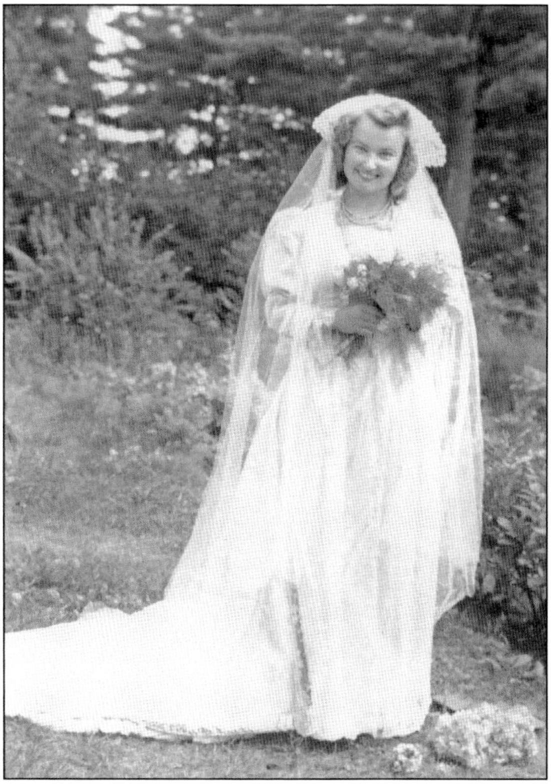

Joyce Avery and Ed Clark were married in the summer of 1944. Joyce wore the gown belonging to Ed's grandmother, Eleanor Pullman Clark. Among the items Ed brought home as souvenirs of the war were German C-rations he picked up from Omaha Beach after the D-Day invasion. The men in the crowd enjoyed sampling them at the reception.

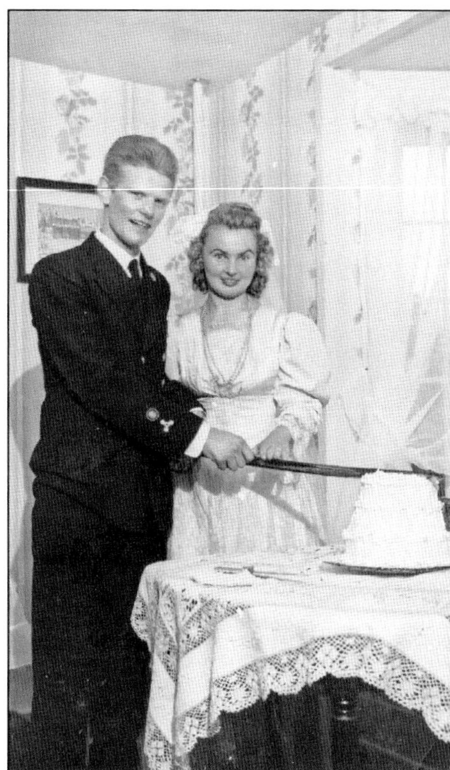

It was young Ed's intention to make the Merchant Marine his career. Florence told him she and Edward would like him to stay at the Trading Post, since they had worked most of their lives to build something for their sons. Ed and Joyce agreed to remain, but Ed would go back to sea many times over the next 30 years whenever money was tight. He always said that while he had been around the world many times, "All roads lead to Lincoln."

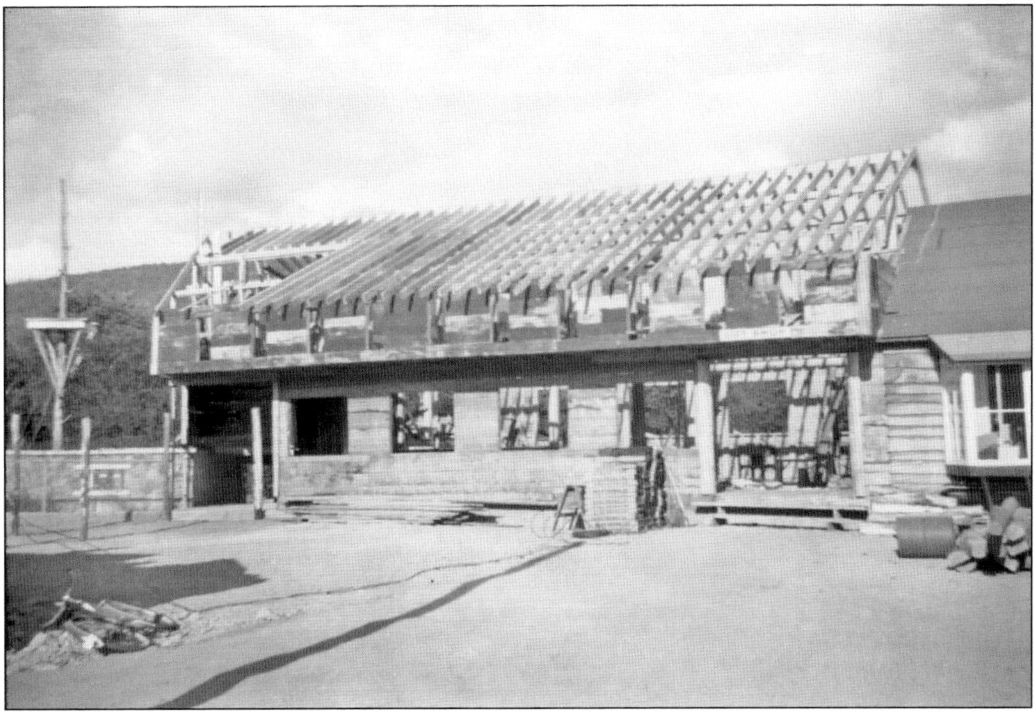

In 1947, Ed, always creative, designed a new gift shop resembling a blockhouse from bygone times. He included a four-foot overhang in the plan to shelter people from rain. The overhang is visible above, as is the first bear pen to the left of the structure. Construction of the new building began in the spring of 1948. In the photograph below it is evident why, on busy days, more parking space was necessary.

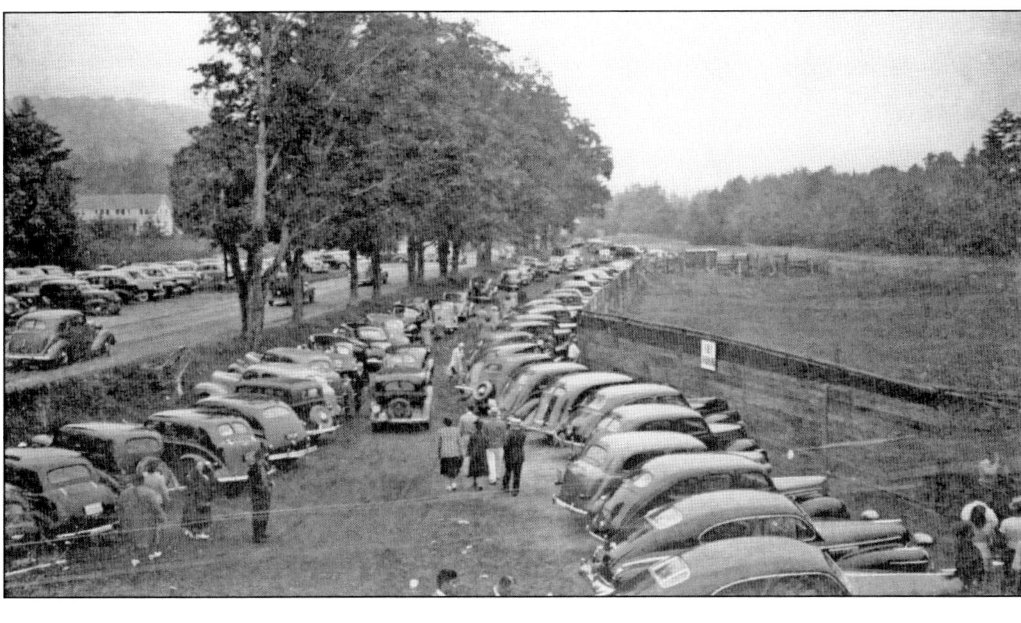

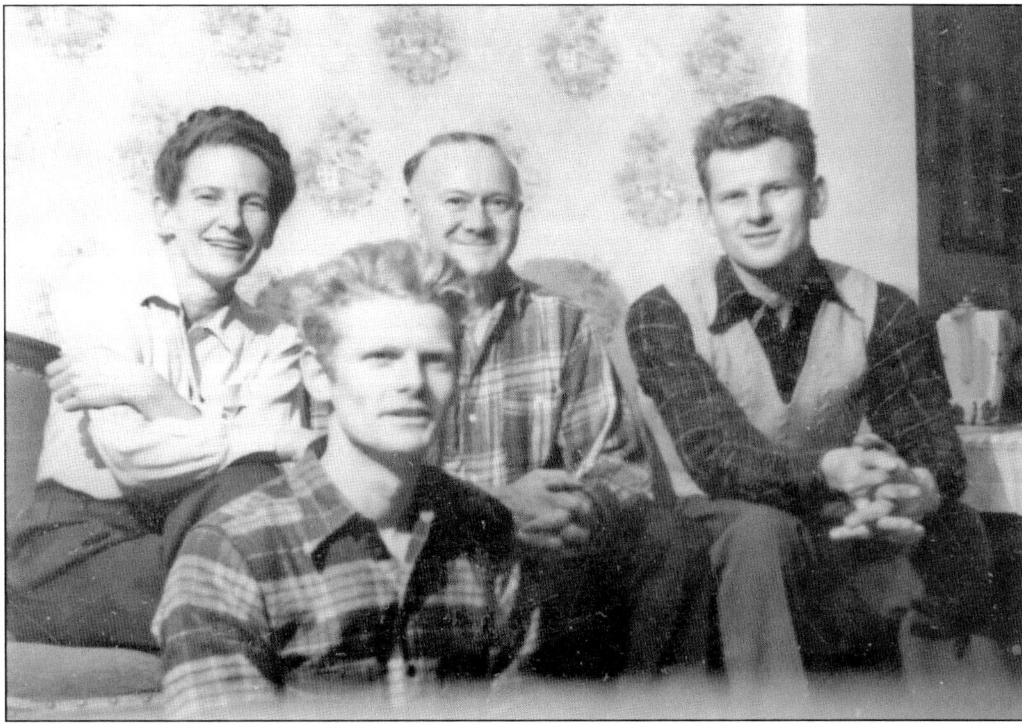

Taken during the Christmas season of 1948, this is the only known Edward Pullman Clark family portrait. From left to right are (first row) Edward M. Clark; (second row) Florence Clark, Edward P. Clark, and W. Murray Clark. (Photograph by W. Murray Clark using a self-timer.)

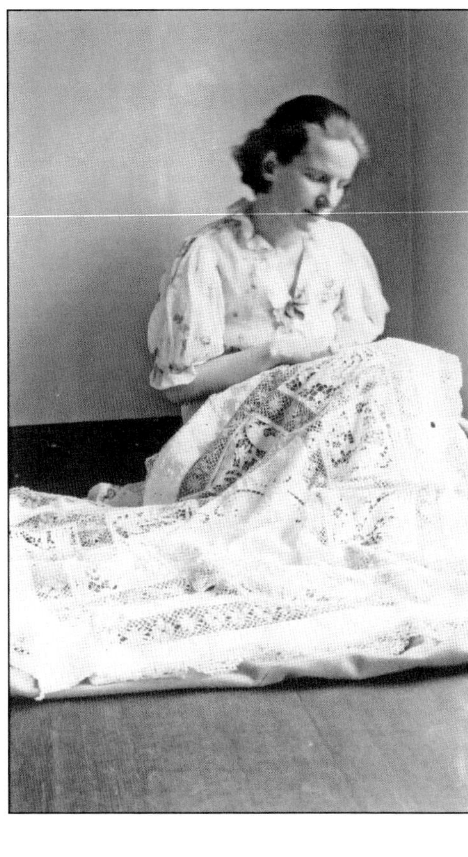

By the fall of 1949, Florence was so ill that she returned to the Glencliffe Tuberculosis Sanatorium. She was just two months shy of her 50th birthday when she succumbed to the disease. She is seen here during an earlier stay in the sanatorium working on a fairy tale tea cloth depicting Mother Goose tales and Aesop's fables in cutwork squares. It is difficult to imagine how hard it must have been for such a vital and active woman to be confined in the sanatorium. Her friend Bob Monahan wrote, "Mrs. Clark reached the end of her trail last week at the State Tuberculosis Sanatorium on the south slope of Mount Moosilauke. She would rather have ended life's journey while straddling the runners of her dog sled, but Fate decreed otherwise." Murray later said it was his mother's spirited nature and willingness to embrace life in the country that enabled the young couple to survive. Her strength in the face of adversity was crucial.

Four

Gold Standard Entertainment

"Use it up, wear it out, make do, or do without" is an old Yankee saying that could have been written to describe the philosophy of young Ed and Murray Clark. In 1949, with the war over, optimism was increasing in the country, and tourist travel was on the rise. With Edward and Florence in poor health, responsibility for long-term decisions and the day-to-day running of the Trading Post fell increasingly on the brothers.

It was still a hardscrabble existence. Ed and Joyce now had two children, and the Trading Post was not generating enough income to support three generations of the family. In addition to running the Trading Post, the brothers hauled gravel in the summer and pulpwood in the winter. To make ends meet, Murray built and ran a sawmill and Ed often went back to sea with the Merchant Marine. Edward Pullman Clark was diagnosed with leukemia in the mid-1950s and passed away in 1957.

Murray married Barbara Avery (Joyce's sister). There was little money for expanding the business, and ingenuity, imagination, and creative recycling often replaced hard cash. Artifacts the brothers collected from bygone days now ended up in new entertainments at the Trading Post.

The goal was always to provide the public with "Gold Standard Entertainment." Joyce and Barbara ran the gift shop, helped with office work, and assisted in acquiring the collections that ended up in the museums. The Clark children began working as bear helpers as early as the age of five or six and moved onto more responsible positions as they grew older. Ed and Joyce's oldest boys, Eddie and David, were expected to devote most of their spare time to the business. David recalls, "It was 'get home from school, change clothes, and get down to the project,' whatever the project might be. You'd work until dark, then go and take care of the dogs. They had to be cleaned, watered, and fed before you could have supper." His words carry an eerie echo of his father's and his uncle's descriptions of their own youth.

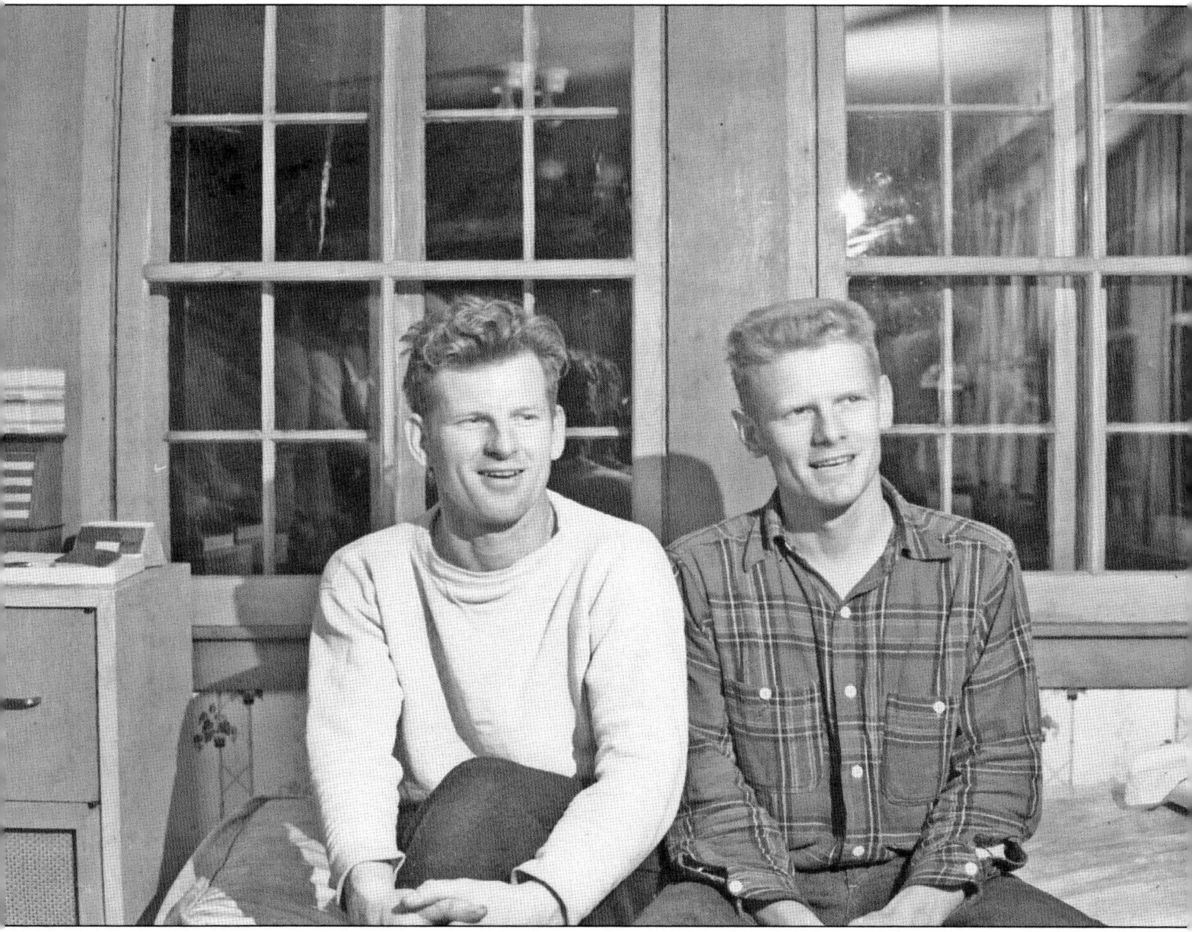

This picture of Murray (left) and Ed was taken in the late 1940s or early 1950s. Young, seasoned by hard work, and undaunted by challenges, Ed and Murray between them possessed all the qualities necessary to make a success of the Trading Post. Ed was a visionary; supremely confident in his ability to accomplish whatever he attempted. Murray was the more practical, ensuring that whatever was started could be completed. Murray's daughter Maureen described the brothers this way: "My uncle had his foot on the gas pedal all the way to the floor, while my father was pressing just as hard on the brake." While it made for a mercurial relationship at times, both personalities were essential to shaping the Trading Post into what it is today.

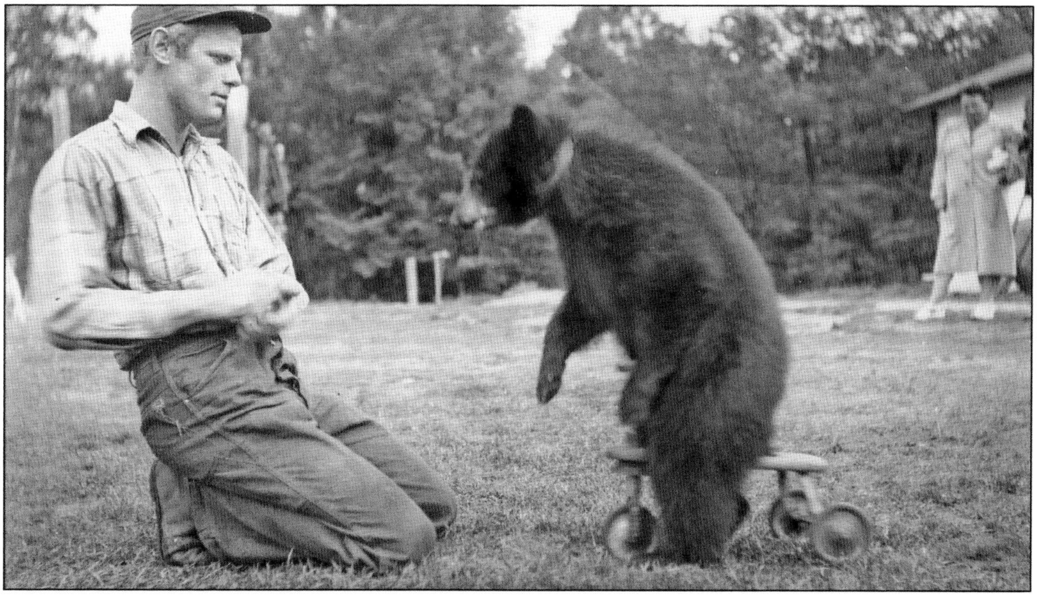

In 1949, Edward P. Clark and Ed traveled to Benson's Animal Farm in Hudson, New Hampshire, and purchased two young black bears, Ebony and Midnight. Ed and Murray began training the cubs, and the first season of regularly scheduled bear shows launched that summer. In this picture, Ed is working with Ebony, the more capable cub. Through trial and error, the daily shows became better and more sophisticated, introducing props such as Ebony's tricycle.

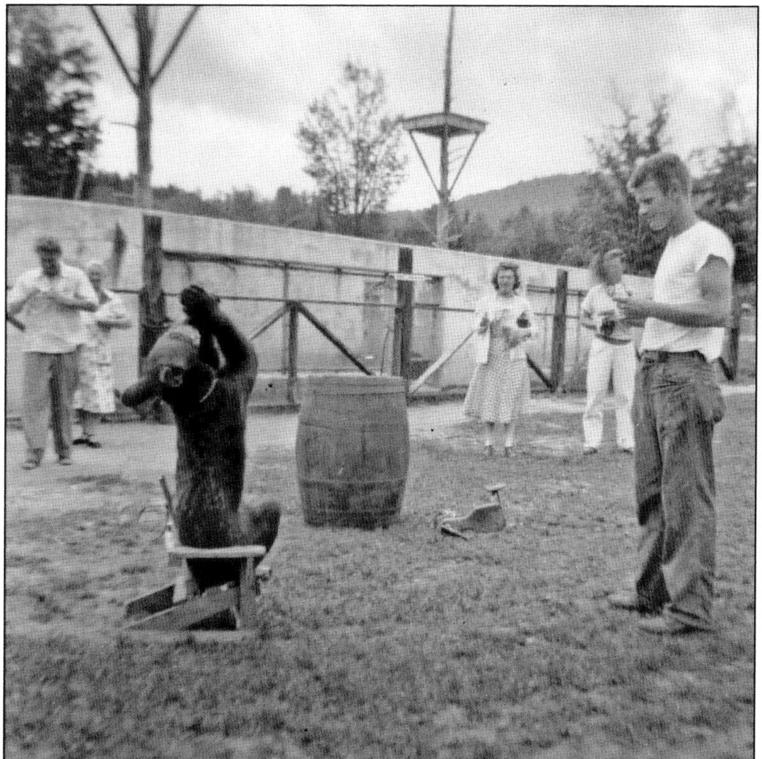

Shows were performed in the open, with the bear often unleashed. All the techniques the brothers acquired while training dogs were now transferred to bear training. Guests would form a circle around the props, within which Ebony would perform. Occasionally, she would bolt through the back door of the gift shop, creating chaos, her trainer seconds behind her. The Clark women working there would keep treats handy to entice her back outside.

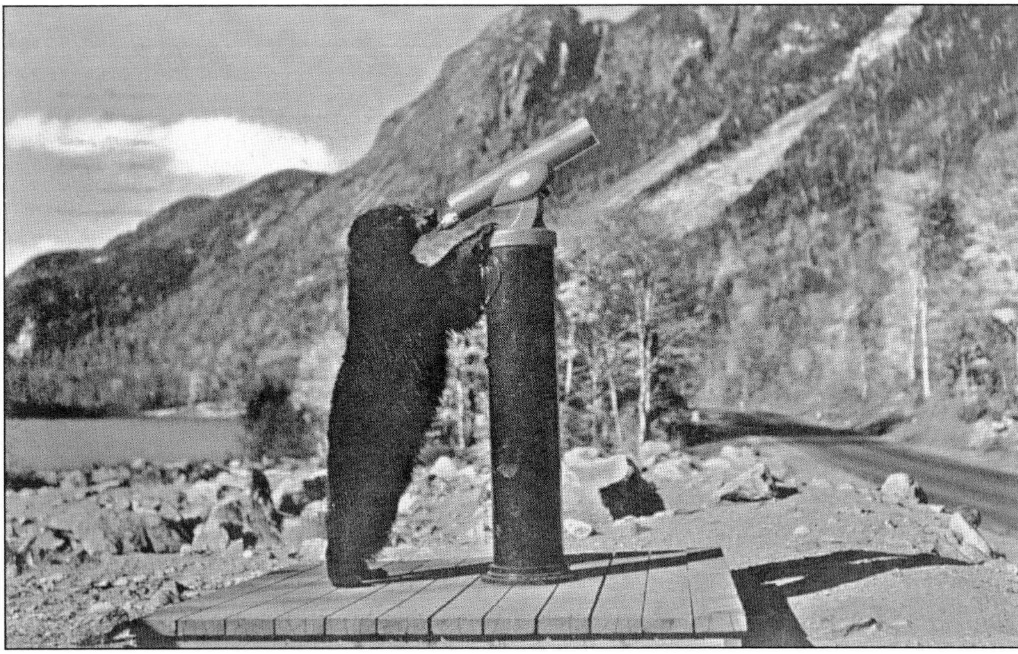

A massive landslide in 1948 buried US Route 3 through Franconia Notch. This is a picture from a postcard of Ebony checking out the slide. Murray was an accomplished photographer, but how he and Ed managed to transport Ebony and his photographic equipment to the site, set up the shot, take it, and return Ebony to the Trading Post without causing a public riot is a mystery.

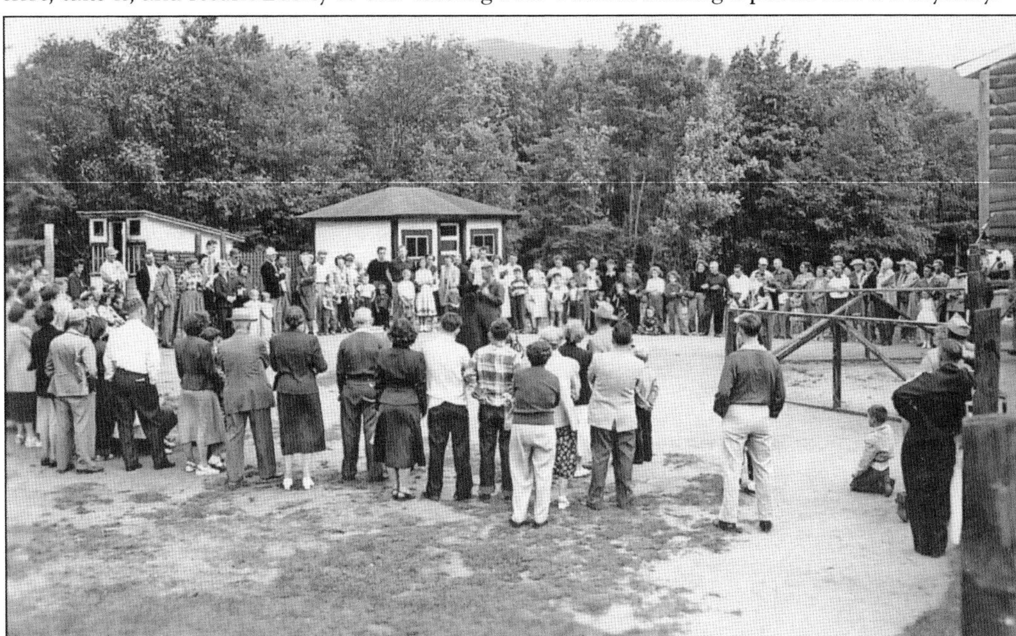

The size of the audiences for the bear shows had increased dramatically by 1951. Here, Ed is performing with Midnight in the center of the crowd, having led her from her pen. Part of the gift shop is visible on the right, and the cookhouse, used for preparing dog food, is in the center background. (Photograph by W. Murray Clark.)

Barbara Avery is seen here in front of Clark's Trading Post around 1951 in her colorful striped skirt. Barbara served as a girl guide, and after Florence died, often helped out at the house, cleaning and cooking for Murray and his father. (Photograph by W. Murray Clark.)

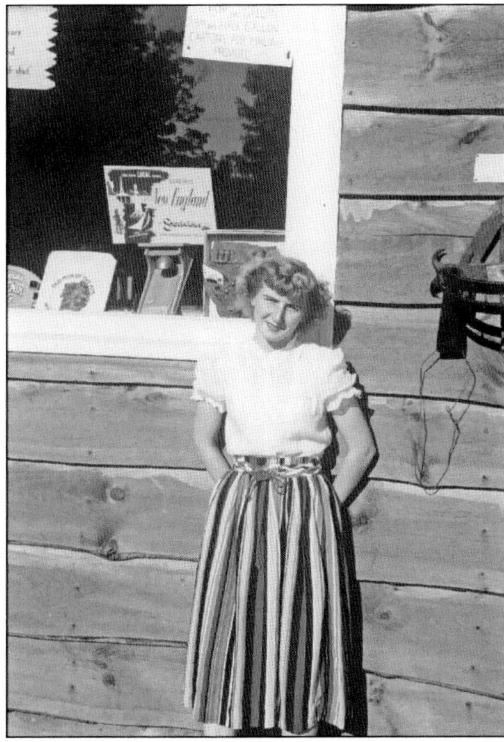

Barbara and Murray fell in love and were married in October 1952, after the summer season ended. Since the Clark brothers married the Avery sisters, the two couples' children are often referred to as "double cousins." From left to right in the doorway are Art Ives, Ed Clark (his brother's best man), and Otis Howe. (Photograph by Charlie Trask.)

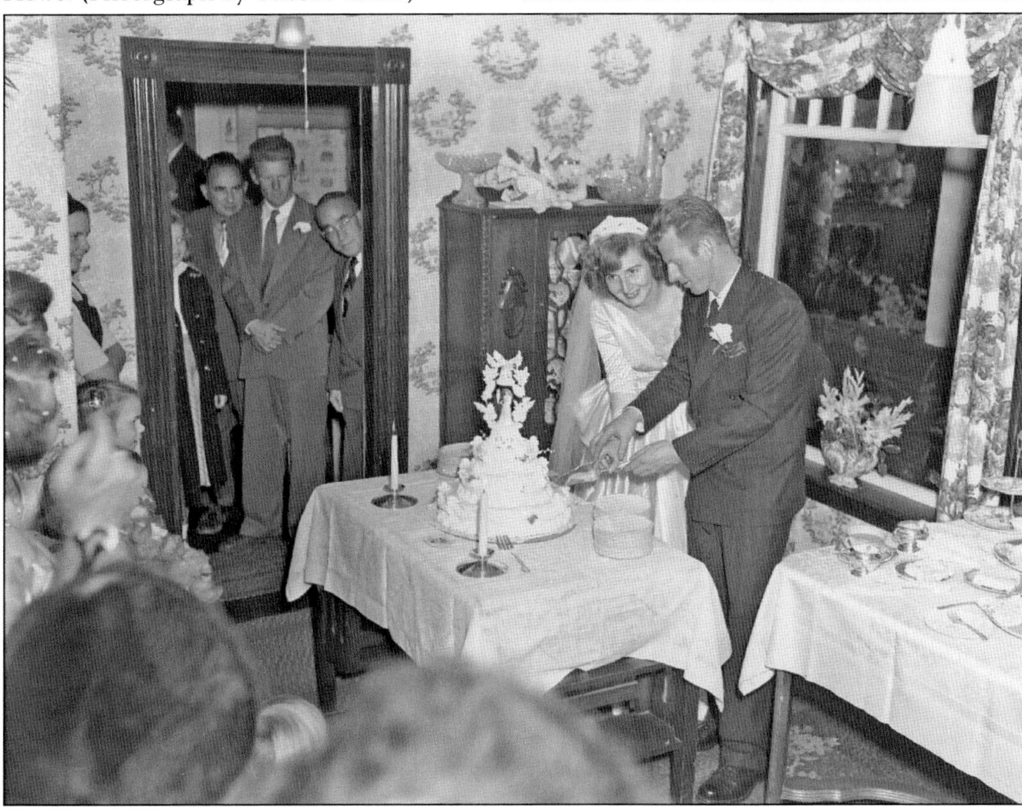

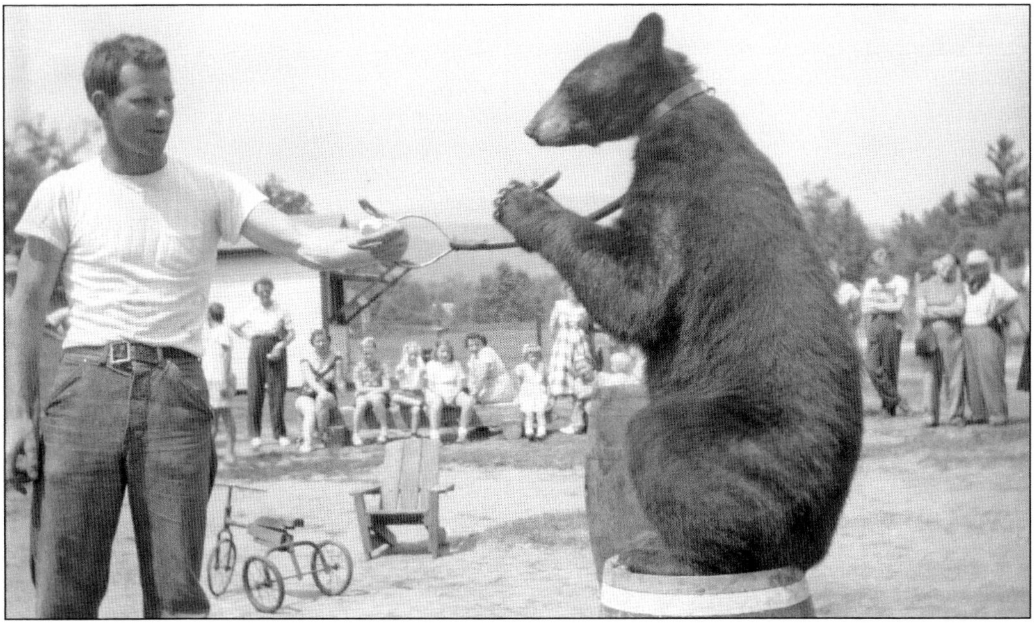

Murray and Ebony are seen here in the early days of the bear show. The brothers alternated shows, performing every 40 minutes. Murray made it a point to explain that all training was done with love, kindness, and rewards. It was never done with weapons, fright, or punishment. Such training methods were far ahead of their time, and the same successful principles are the bedrock of bear training at the Trading Post today.

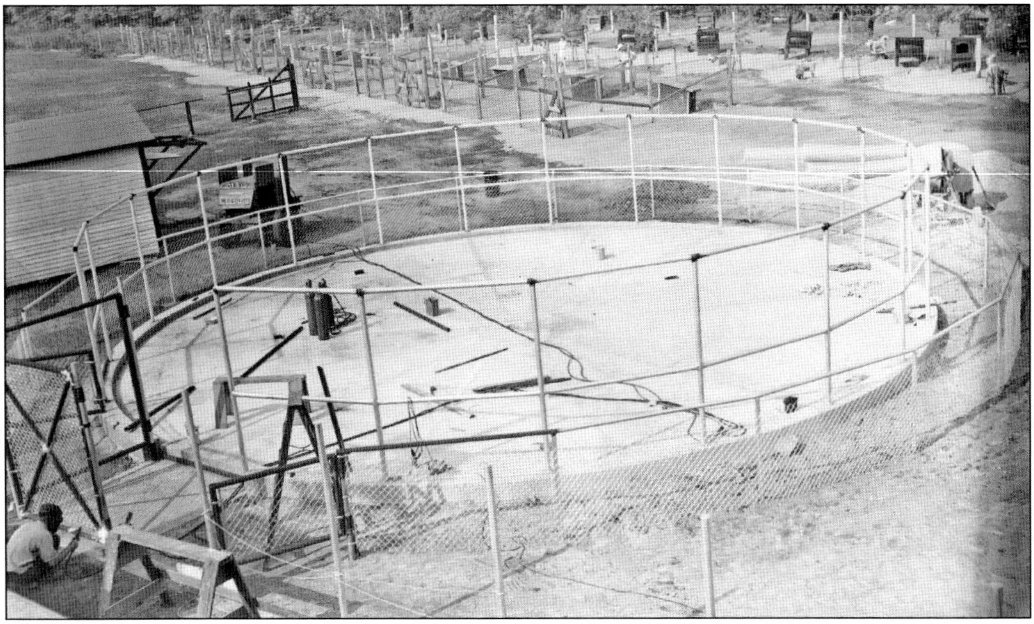

The pipes used to construct the bear performance ring in 1954 came from Mount Lafayette. They originally brought fresh water to the Profile House, one of the grand hotels in the White Mountains, which was destroyed by fire in 1923. The Clarks dug out the pipes and used them to construct the bear ring, the dog team merry-go-round, and new dog pens. In 1969, a second level was added to the ring. Ed can be seen welding at lower left. (Photograph by W. Murray Clark.)

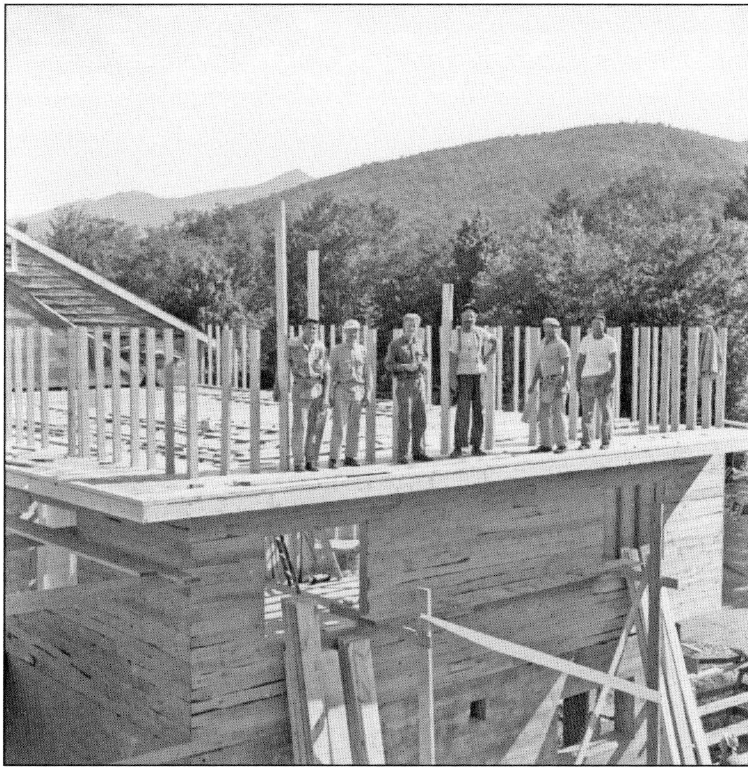

Construction of the southern end of the gift shop began in 1957. Third from the left is Ed Clark; the other men are unidentified. (Both photographs by W. Murray Clark.)

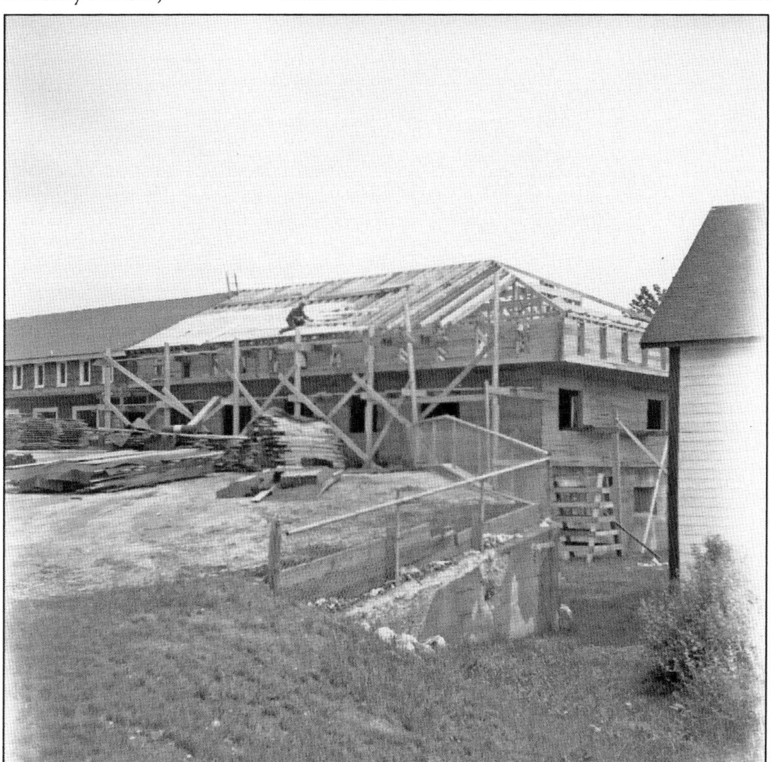

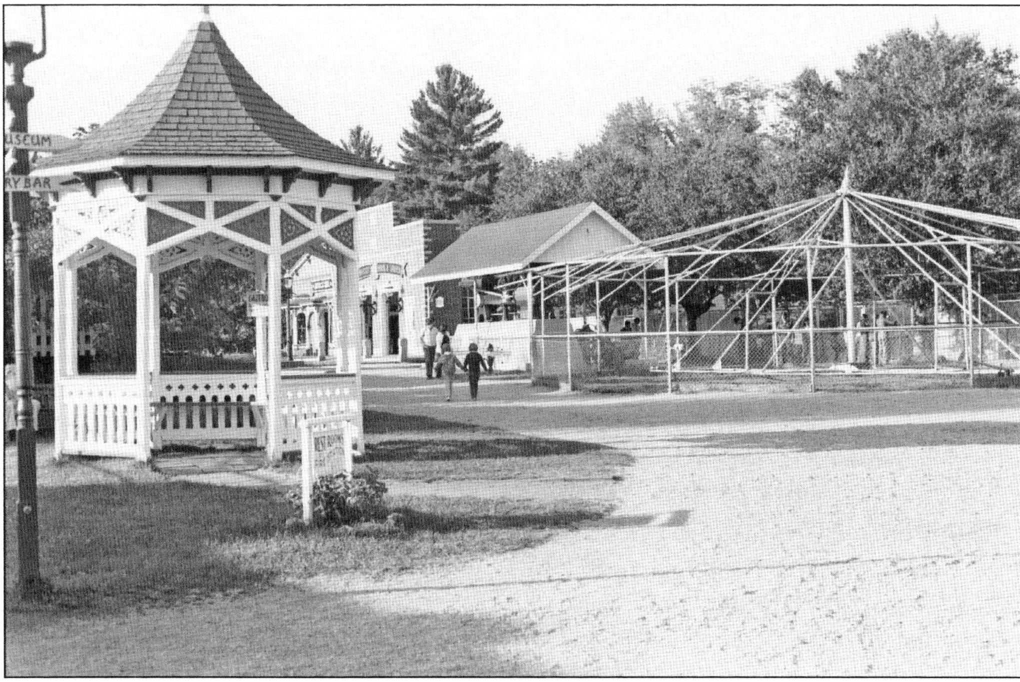

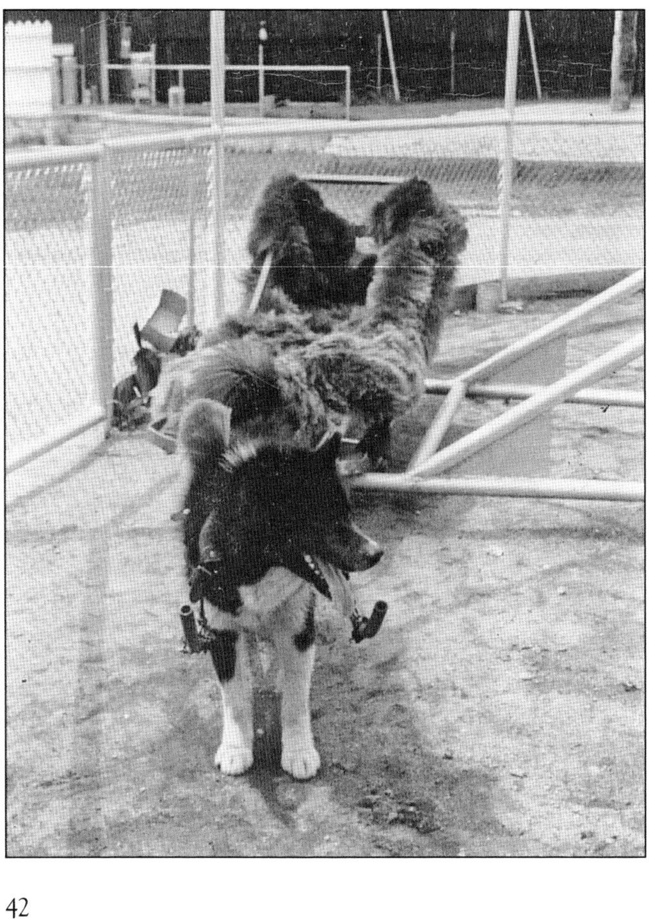

Designed to exercise the dogs and provide guests with a semblance of a dog team ride, the dog team merry-go-round, seen here, could accommodate two dogs and sleds at a time.

Ellesmere, one of the Eskimo sled dogs, is harnessed to a fur-covered dog sled on the merry-go-round. He is waiting patiently for a guest to take a ride around the ring.

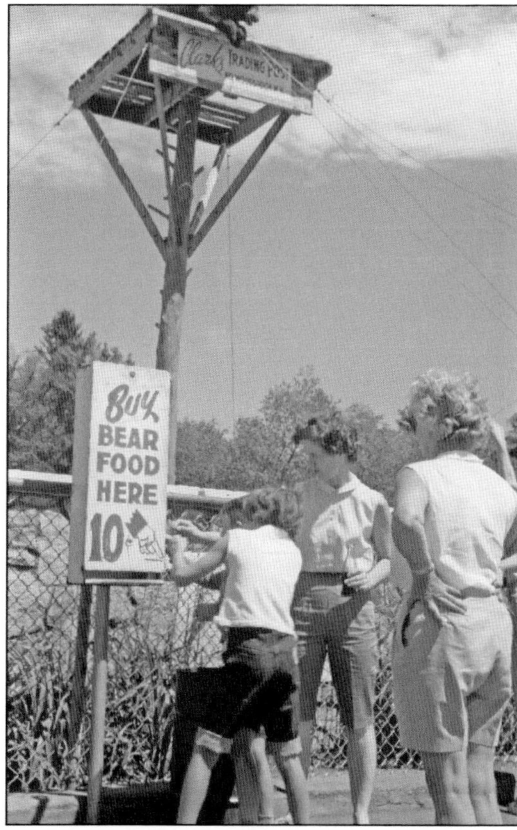

Inspired by the Aerial Tramway at Cannon Mountain, Murray designed a "tramway" for the bears using twine, nails, and an old baby carriage wheel. Each of the three bear enclosures had a trolley line strung to a pole below. A treat could be placed in a cup; perched high on the platform above, the bear could pull up the cup and collect his reward. Machines were created that for a modest fee would dispense dog chow, which the public could feed to the bears. All the bears were expert at working the "chow lines." (Both photographs by W. Murray Clark.)

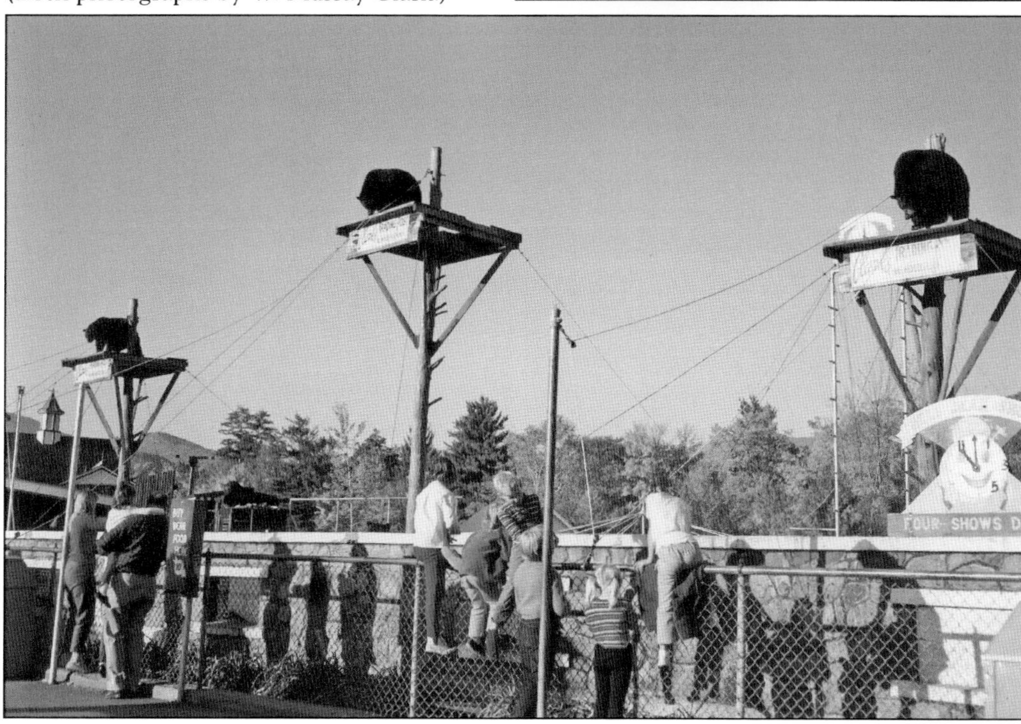

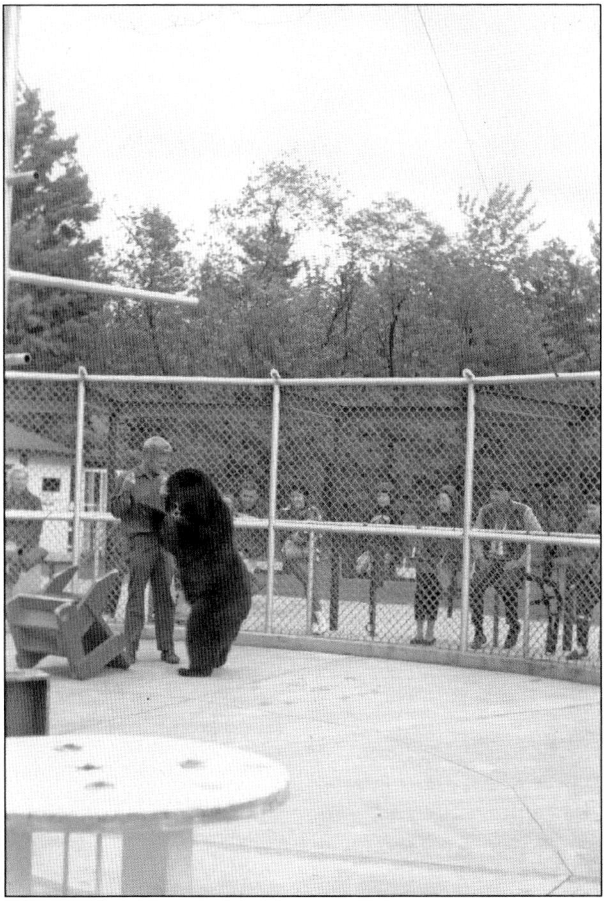

Ed is inside the ring performing with Midnight in the fall of 1966. Both brothers often worked with multiple bears at a time, and it made for a lively show, but it required keeping several bears occupied at all times and increased the risk to the trainer. Ed used to say, "These are just a couple of old New Hampshire bears. Just think what they could do if they came from Massachusetts or Connecticut." (Photograph by Dick Hamilton.)

This is an early family of Clark bears posing in the ring. From left to right are Rufus, Ebony, Rastus, and Midnight. Rufus and Rastus were Ebony's sons. Of the four, Ebony was by far the best show bear. Rufus, known as "Old Fella," lived to be almost 38. That is likely an all-time record for a North American black bear and far exceeds the average lifespan of a black bear in the wild. (Photograph by W. Murray Clark.)

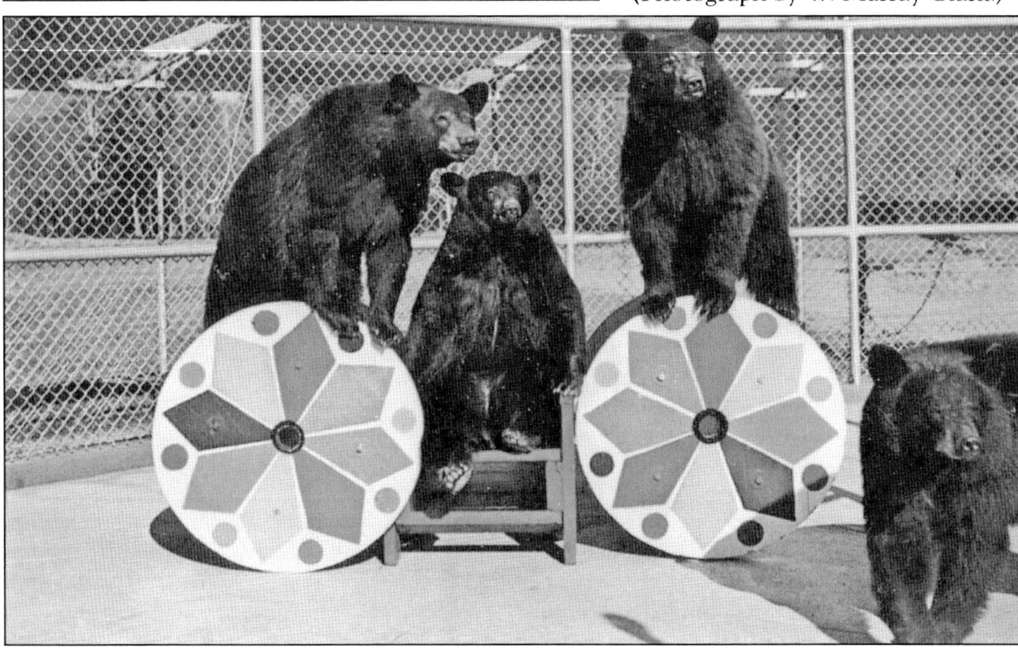

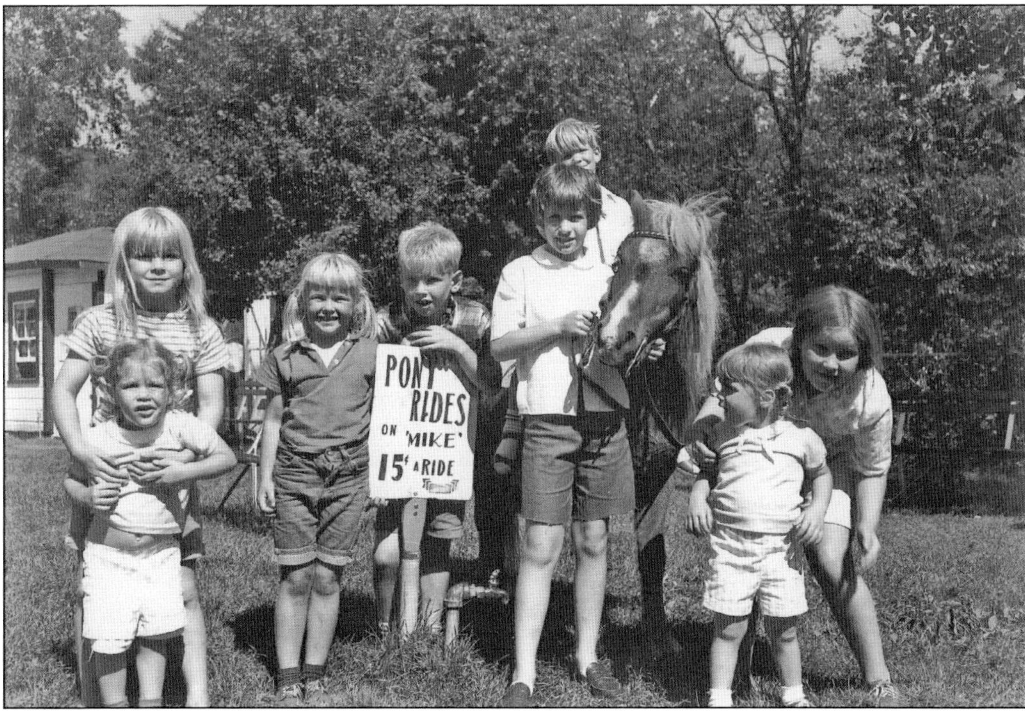

Mike the pony had his own bank account. For 15¢ a ride, one of the Clark children would lead him, with a guest on his back, three times around the loop. All the money earned went to Mike's account to pay for his feed and upkeep. From left to right are (first row) two unidentified; (second row) Maureen Clark, Anne Clark, Tom Clark, Debbie Moody, unidentified on Mike's back, and Nola Clark.

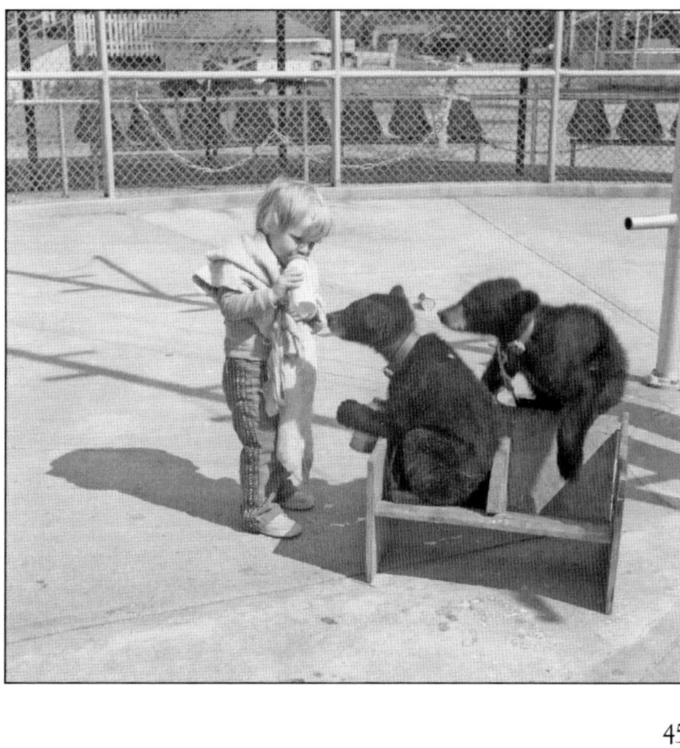

In this photograph from June 1971, Murray Avery Clark, son of W. Murray Clark, is sharing a breakfast snack with Saphire and Pearl, two cubs in training who also have their baby bottles. (Photograph by W. Murray Clark.)

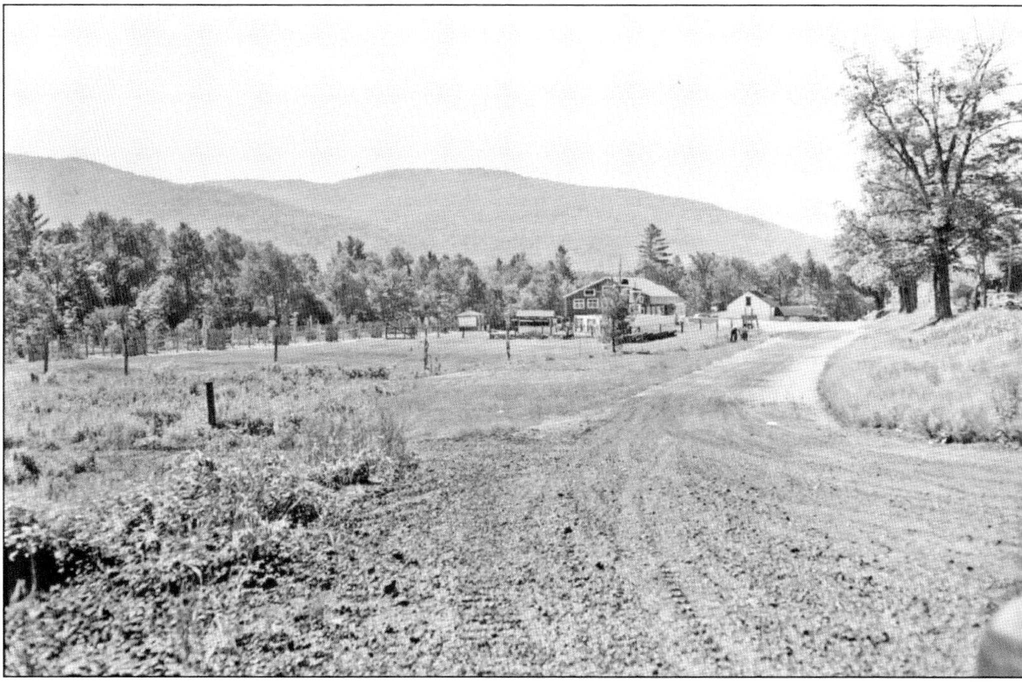

Taken around 1948 from the north end of the property, this photograph shows that while the north end of the gift shop has been completed, there is little else beyond the dog pens and bear enclosures. It is a very tranquil scene with US Route 3 just visible on the far right.

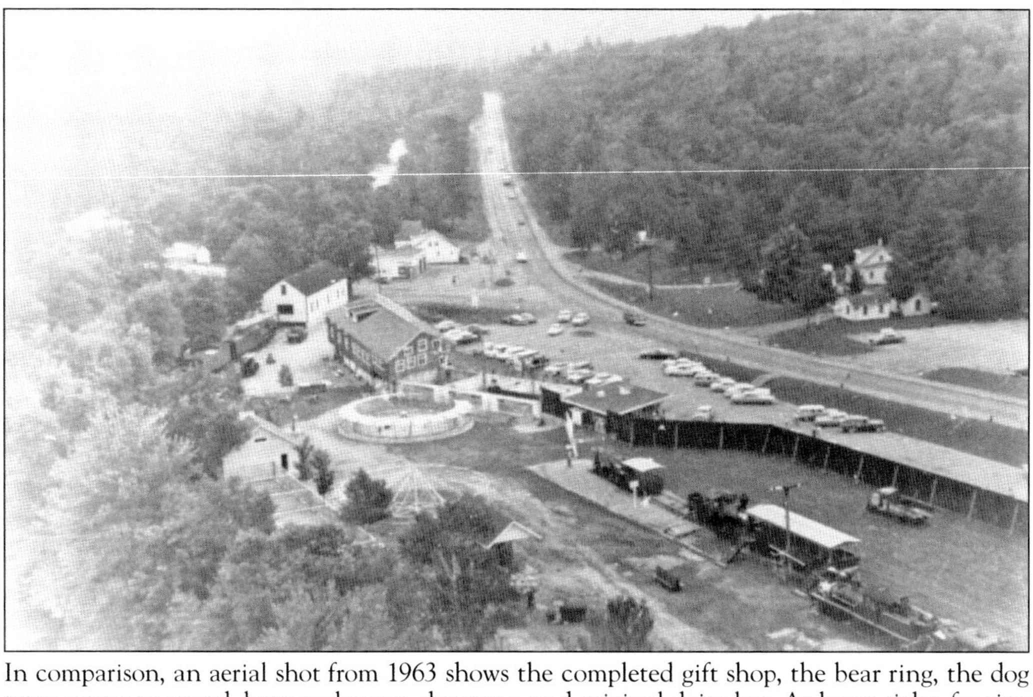

In comparison, an aerial shot from 1963 shows the completed gift shop, the bear ring, the dog team merry-go-round, bear enclosures, dog pens, and original dairy bar. At lower right, fencing shields the vacant space where the railroad station will be erected and provides mystery to entice visitors to pay their admission and come inside.

Five

White Mountain Central Railroad

The White Mountain Central Railroad was built with a great deal of hard work, heart, and sweat. It was created from secondhand parts and equipment from other railroads, with family and friends volunteering their time and expertise, laboring over a period of many years to bring the grand vision to completion.

Edward P. Clark purchased a local paper mill's deactivated Climax 50-ton logging locomotive, and enough rails and ties to set it on, as a gift for young Ed. The display was named the White Mountain Central Railroad and began acquiring additional rails whenever possible. Steam engines were purchased as they became available, so that by 1958, they had collected enough rolling stock to realize Ed's dream of "green pastures for iron horses." By then they had also purchased and laid enough track to allow visitors to enjoy a short train ride, and an open-air excursion car had been constructed to carry them. When more cars were needed, they converted caboose chassis into the passenger cars still used today.

But the ride was short—they needed a bridge to cross the Pemigewasset River and extend the line to land the Clarks had leased from the state of New Hampshire. A covered bridge in East Montpelier, Vermont, that was no longer in service was purchased. Granite abutments were located on the Connecticut River. After dismantling, transporting, and reassembling the abutments on either side of the Pemigewasset, they turned to the task of disassembling the bridge in the fall of 1963, with a crew consisting of Ed's sons (Eddie, 17, and David, 16) and their friend Peter Thompson, 16. It was a cold, hard, miserable job that took months to finish. Another year was required to reassemble the bridge in Lincoln. In 1965, it was finally pulled across the river onto the stone abutments. Two more years were required to lay enough rail for the first passenger train to travel across the bridge. Over the ensuing years, additional rail was laid to reach the current end of the line.

Today, the White Mountain Central Railroad is a treasured and beloved part of the Trading Post experience. Visitors love smelling the wood smoke, hearing the steam whistle, and being chased by Wolfman.

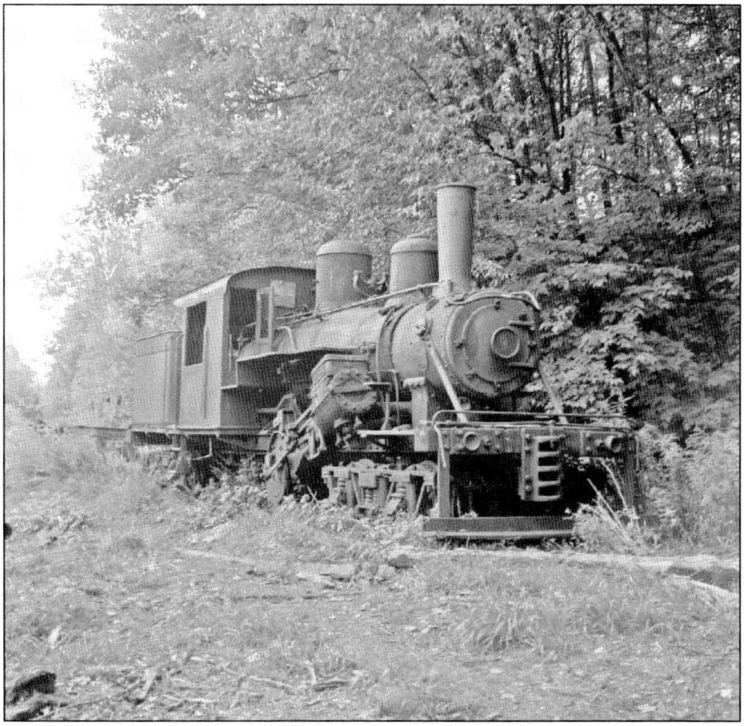

While the bears were popular, the brothers realized they needed more to sustain the interest of guests. Here, the Climax locomotive is pictured just out of storage. Extensive renovation was required, and it did not enter regular service on the White Mountain Central Railroad until 1977. (Photograph by W. Murray Clark.)

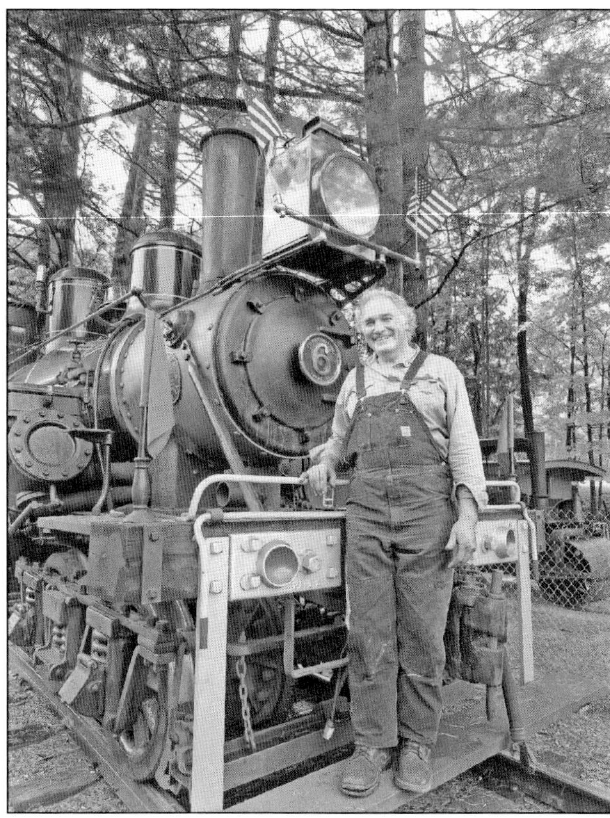

Leon Noel, a longtime White Mountain Central engineer, poses with the Climax as it appears today. Known as "Queen of the Rails" at the Trading Post, she was built in 1920, purchased new by the Beebe River Lumber Company in Campton, New Hampshire, and later sold to the Parker Young Paper Mill in Lincoln. (Photograph by Maureen S. Clark.)

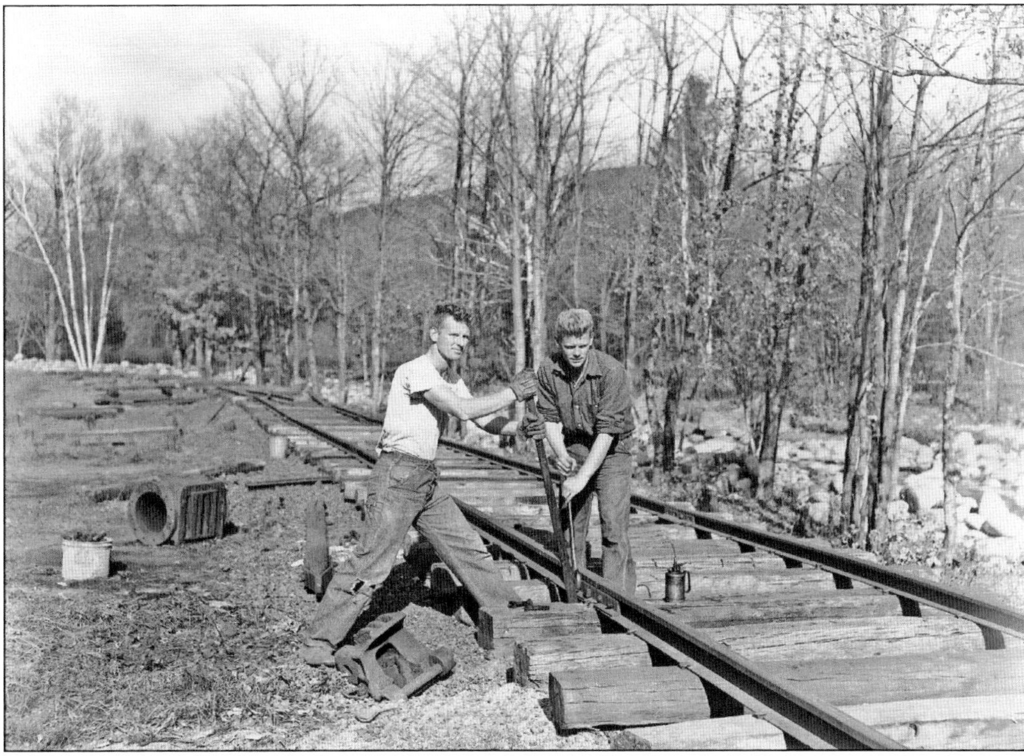

The first "section crew" for the White Mountain Central Railroad, Murray (left) and Ed, are laying rail. The brothers continued to find secondhand rail wherever they could. Once home, the rail had to be laid—a back-breaking, dirty job. By 1958, they had laid enough track to allow guests a short excursion. (Photograph by W. Murray Clark with a self-timer.)

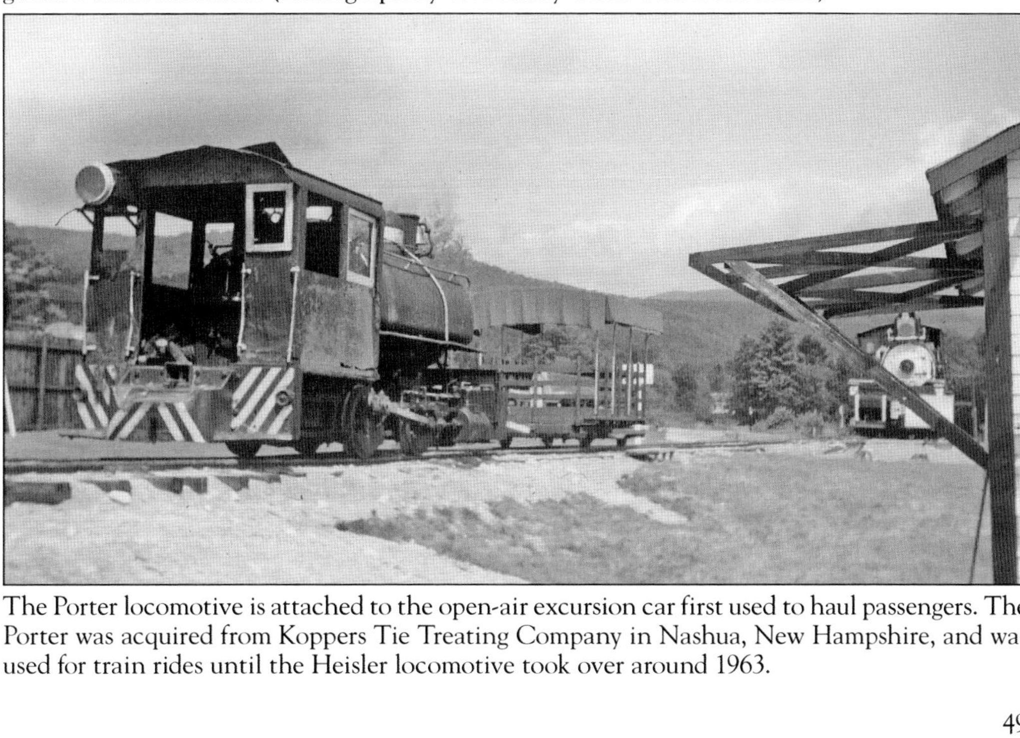

The Porter locomotive is attached to the open-air excursion car first used to haul passengers. The Porter was acquired from Koppers Tie Treating Company in Nashua, New Hampshire, and was used for train rides until the Heisler locomotive took over around 1963.

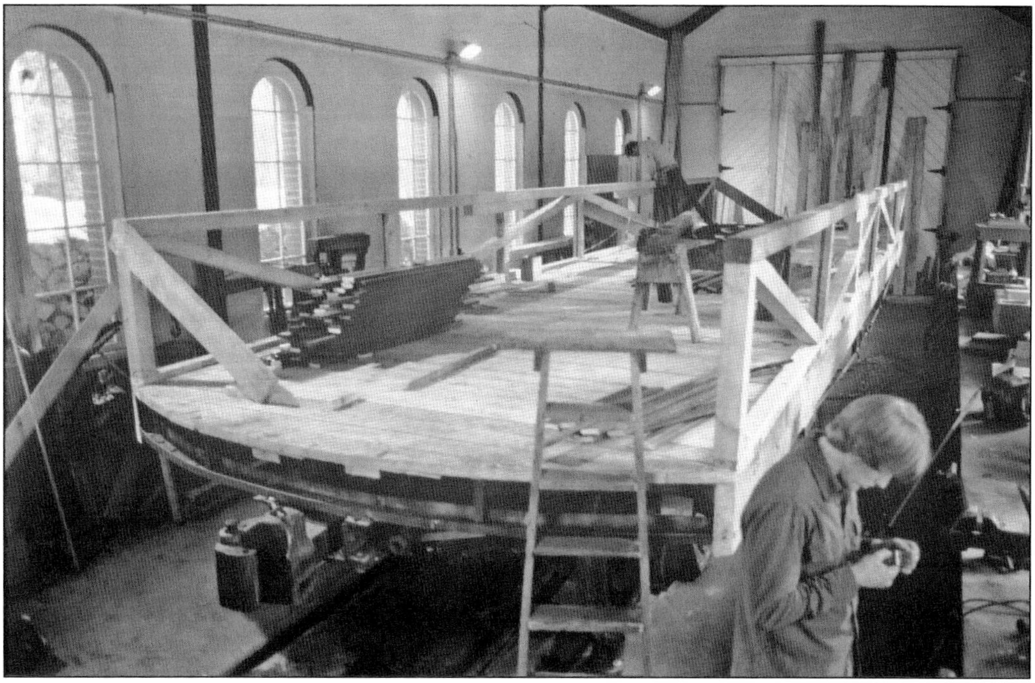

When it became clear that more cars were needed to haul passengers, the brothers decided to convert caboose cars. They stripped off the housing and added flooring, benches, and a canopy roof. These cars are still in operation today. Eddie Clark (left) and Jeff Ingalls are working on a new excursion car. (Photograph by Maureen S. Clark.)

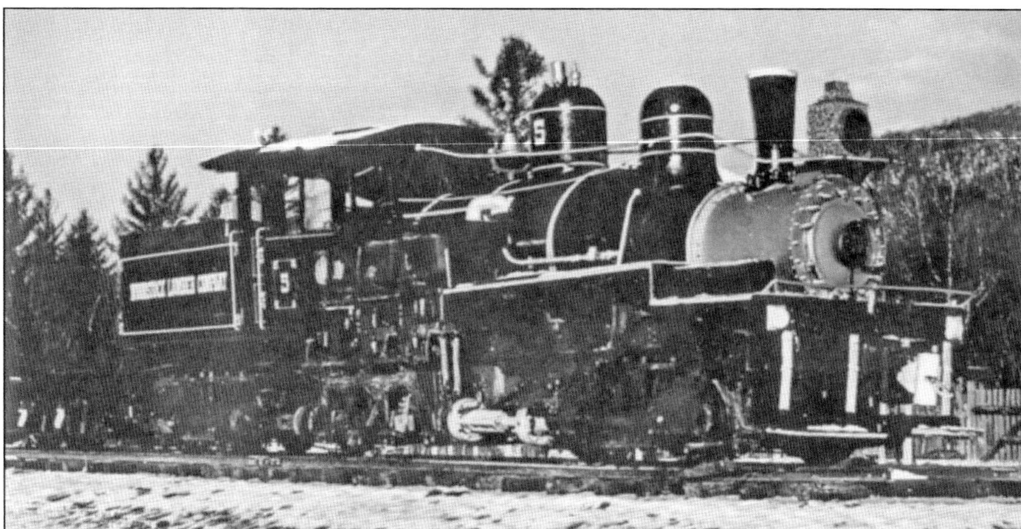

The Lima Shay locomotive was designed to haul heavy loads over poor rail beds. It was used in the White Mountains from 1919 through 1952, when the Parker Young Company retired it. The Clarks purchased it in 1953. It never saw any active service on the White Mountain Central Railroad but completed Ed's wish to acquire one geared locomotive from each of the three companies manufacturing them: the Climax Locomotive and Machine Works, the Heisler Locomotive Works, and the Lima Locomotive Works.

A source of water is essential when running steam locomotives. The Clarks purchased their water tower from the Franconia Paper Corporation in Lincoln for $10. It had been dormant for years and was starting to collapse. The Clarks dismantled it, brought it home, and refurbished it. David Clark (left) and Peter Thompson wave from atop the ongoing restoration project. (Photograph by W. Murray Clark.)

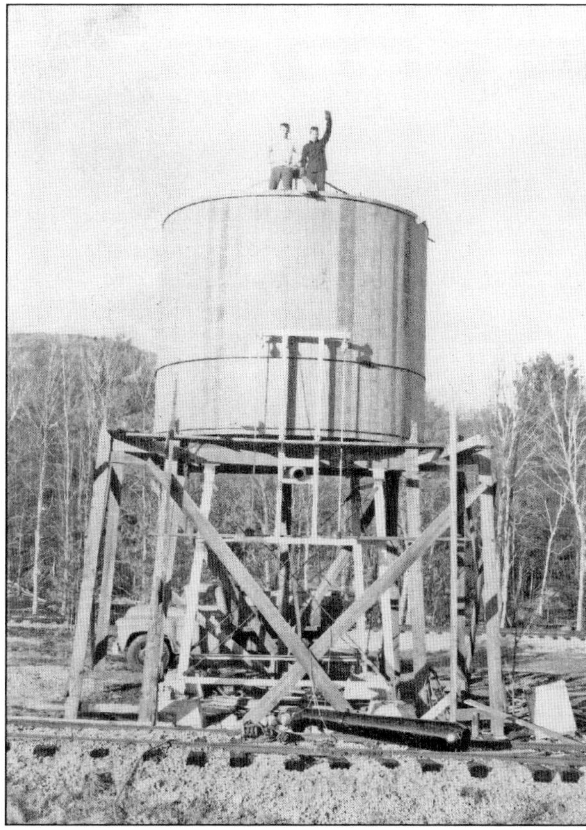

Bob Henderson is posing with the Clark family's four Buffalo Springfield steamrollers. Ed purchased one of the steamrollers in Northfield, New Hampshire, and, lacking funds to truck it to Lincoln, simply steamed it home at four miles per hour, arriving two and a half days later. While helping build the Kancamagus Highway, one of his steamrollers developed a steam leak. Ed poured in cooked dog chow, which plugged the leak, and kept on steamrolling. (Photograph by Jon P. Lasseigne.)

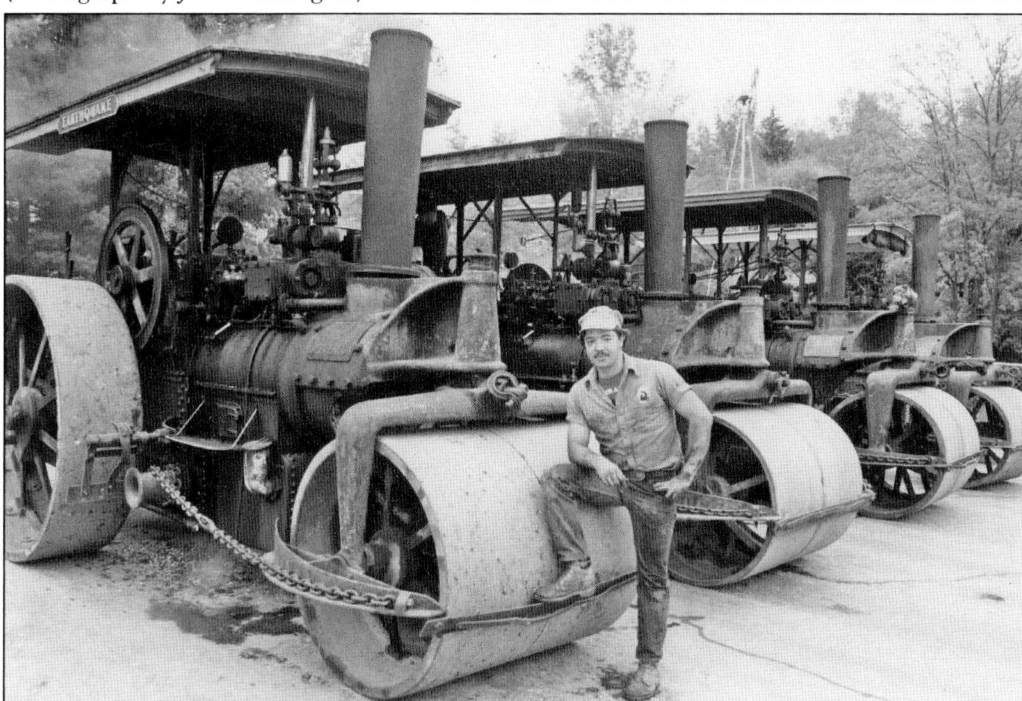

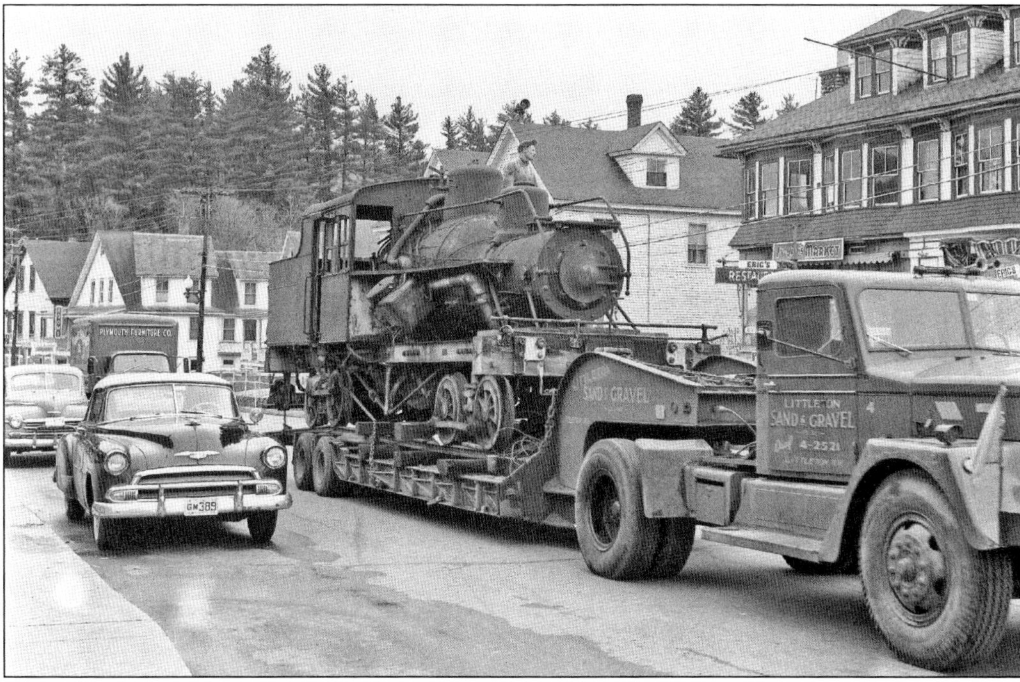

The Heisler locomotive was purchased in 1958 and shipped by rail from West Virginia to Lincoln, New Hampshire. In this picture, Ed is on top, ready to lift wires if necessary, as it is trucked from the Lincoln railroad station up Main Street in North Woodstock to the Trading Post. After restoration, it hauled passengers on the White Mountain Central Railroad until 1977, when the Climax, its refurbishment complete, entered service. (Photograph by W. Murray Clark.)

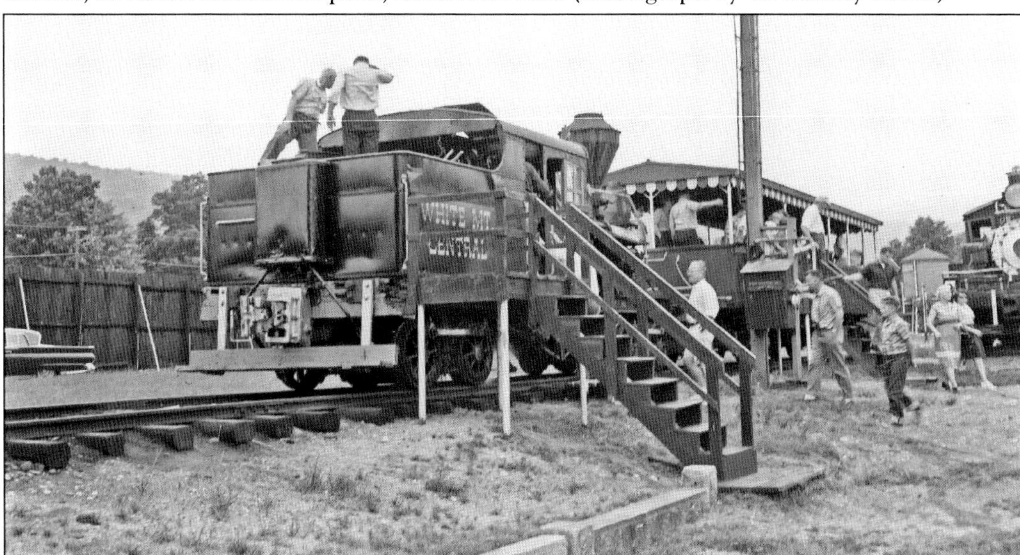

The Heisler was a workhorse for the White Mountain Central Railroad and carried many guests in its time. In this picture, note the stairs for boarding the passenger cars. Prior to installation of stairs on the cars themselves, engineers had to line up the cars with the stationary stairs at trackside. This often required backing up and trying more than once, depending on the skill of the engineer.

All of the Clark children were expected to help out wherever needed. When her brother David enlisted in the US Army during the Vietnam War, 15-year-old Carol found herself at the throttle of the Heisler. As soon as the train ride ended, she would hop down and give rides on the dog team merry-go-round. (Photograph by Alan Thomas.)

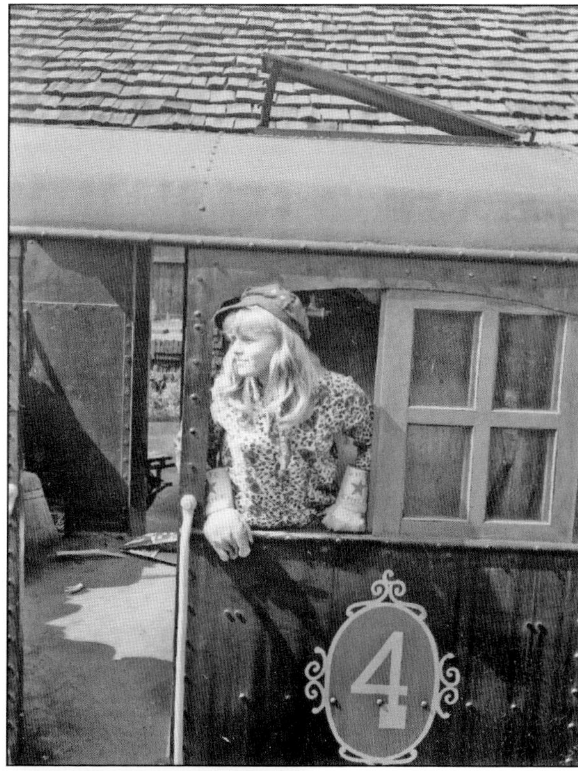

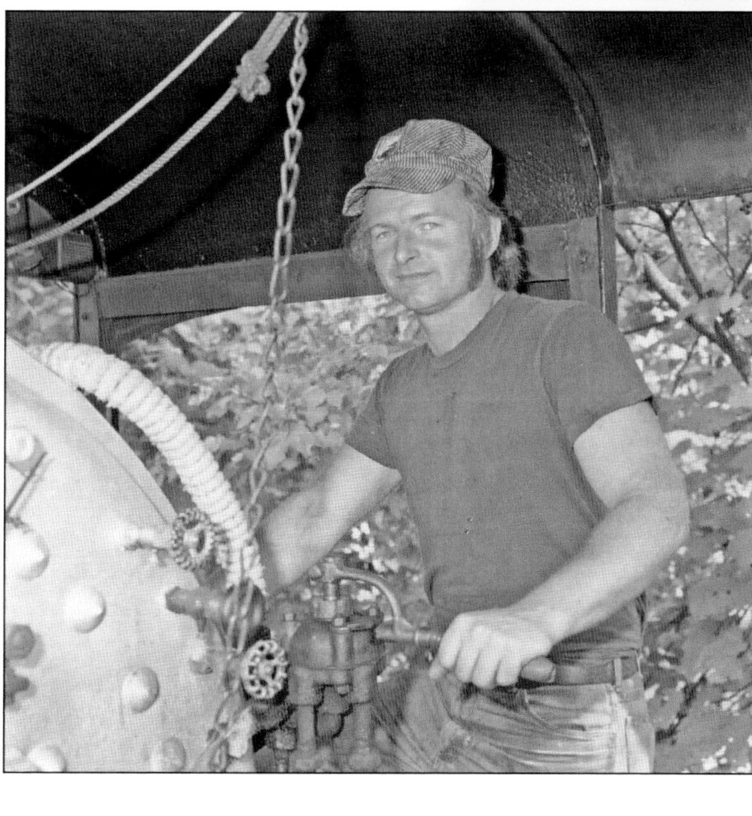

David Clark has been part of the work crew for nearly every major reclamation and expansion project at the Trading Post. He has an encyclopedic knowledge of all things pertaining to the White Mountain Central Railroad. Now semiretired, David still oversees all steam-related projects. He is seen here in the cab of the Heisler. (Photograph by Maureen S. Clark.)

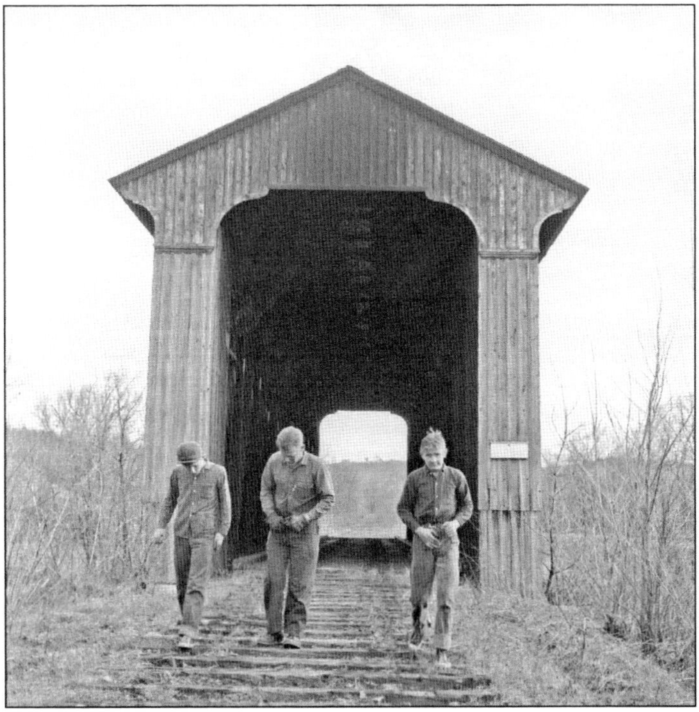

From left to right, David Clark, Ed Clark, and Eddie Clark wonder what they have gotten themselves into. In an effort to create a longer, more scenic excursion, the Clarks wanted a covered bridge. One was found spanning the Winooski River in Vermont, and Ed and Murray made a trip with two of Ed's sons, Eddie and David, to inspect it. A deal was struck to buy the bridge for $1,000 and the body of a 1910 Ford Model T. (Photograph by W. Murray Clark.)

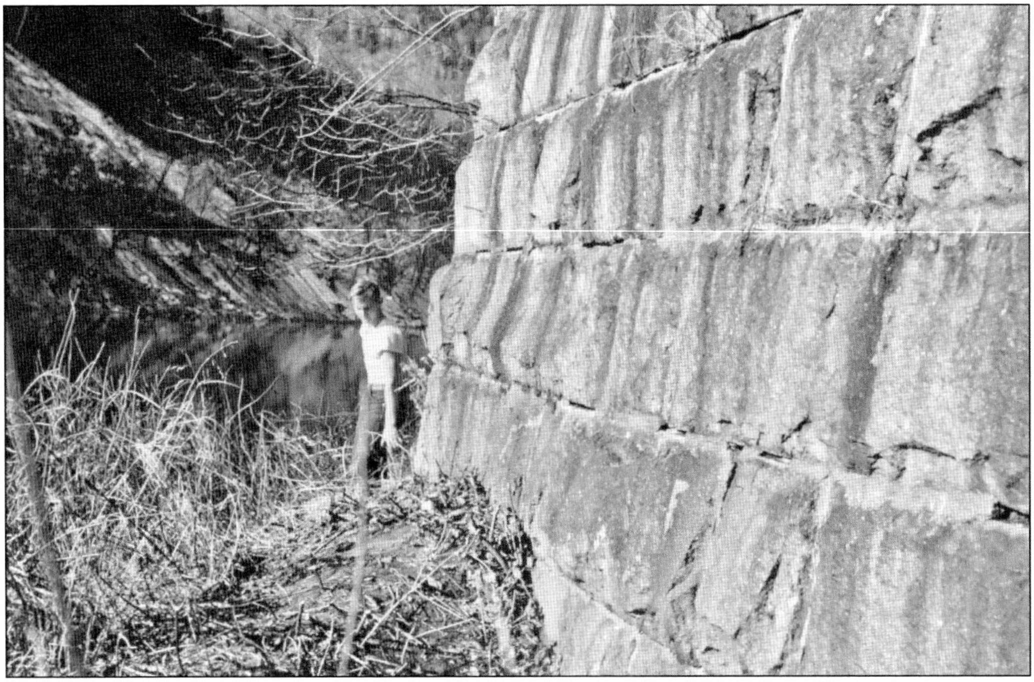

Having purchased a bridge, granite abutments for it to rest upon on either side of the river were needed. Ed found them on the Connecticut River and, with his crew of two young sons and their friends Allan Pommer and Bernie Dowland, marked all the stone layers, disassembled them, and transported them home for reassembly. Here, young Eddie is checking the numbering. (Photograph by W. Murray Clark.)

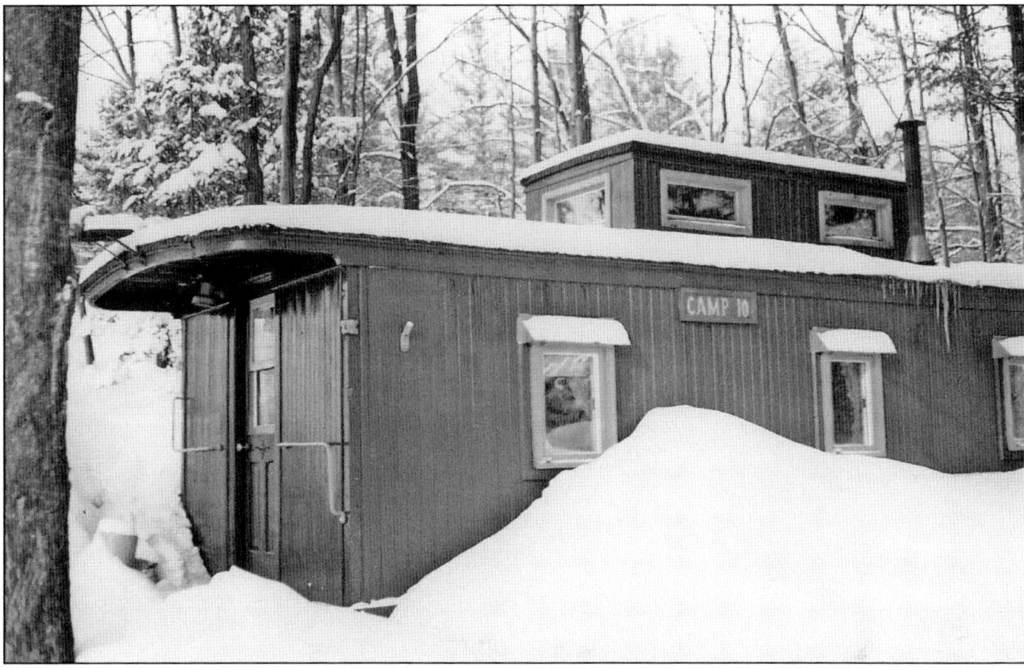

A caboose was purchased and positioned at the covered bridge site as living quarters for the young disassembly crew during the long, harsh winter. A small woodstove was installed, but it did little to keep the caboose warm. It was still so cold that a bottle of tonic placed next to the stove would be frozen by morning. Eskimo dogs supplied both companionship and warmth as they snuggled with the crew on bitterly cold nights.

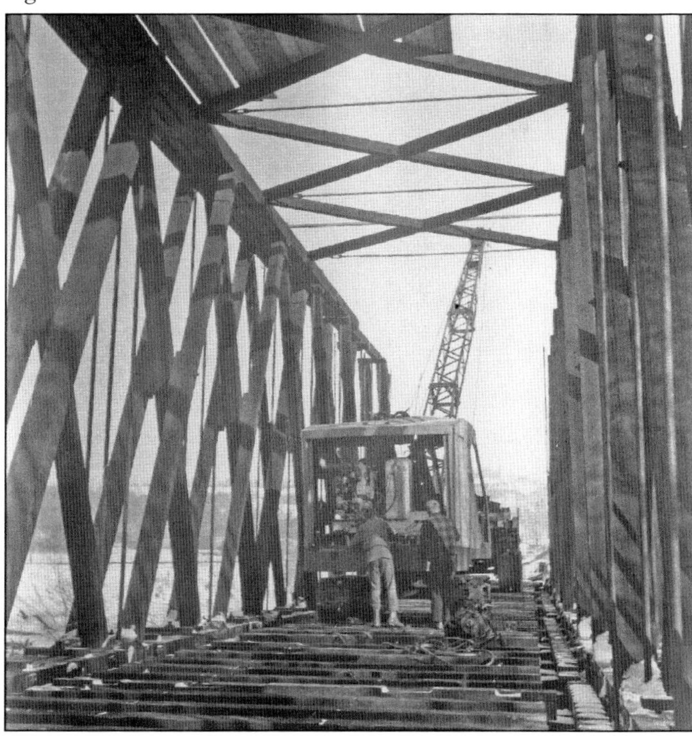

Ed gathered his very capable teenage crew consisting of sons Eddie and David, Peter Thompson, and Bernie Dowland, and tasked them with dismantling the bridge. They numbered all 3,500 pieces and trucked them back to the Trading Post in the dead of winter. It took four cold, hard months to bring the entire bridge back to Lincoln.

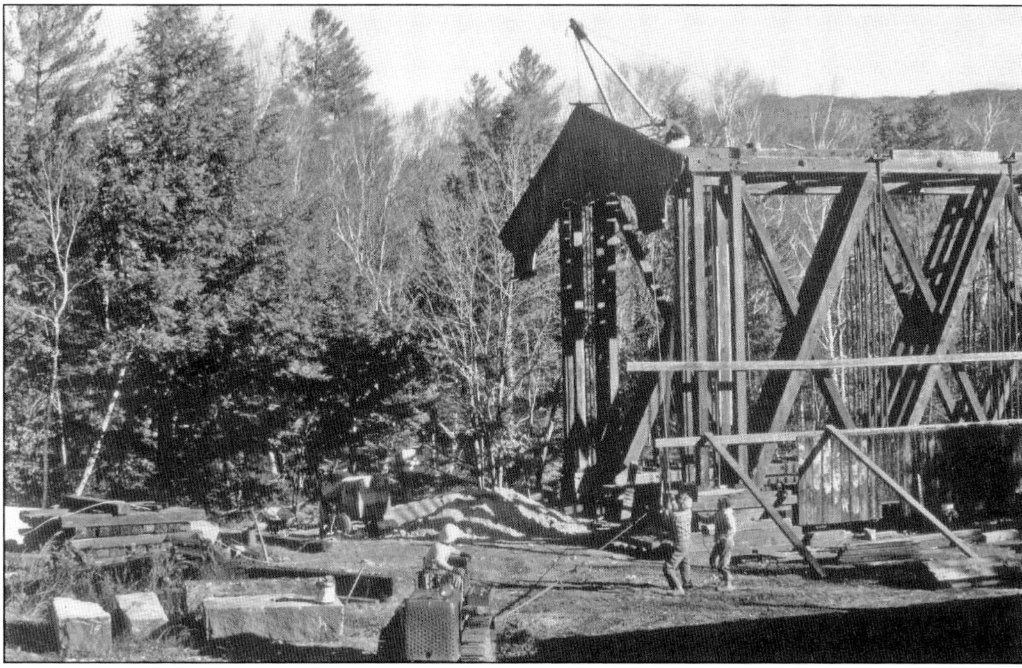

Once all the numbered pieces were back in Lincoln, it took another year to reassemble the giant wooden puzzle—something the boys referred to as "playing bridge." The scope of the project becomes more daunting when one realizes that both disassembly and reassembly of the abutments and the bridge were accomplished using extremely antiquated equipment. From left to right are Peter Thompson, Ed Clark, and David Bickford.

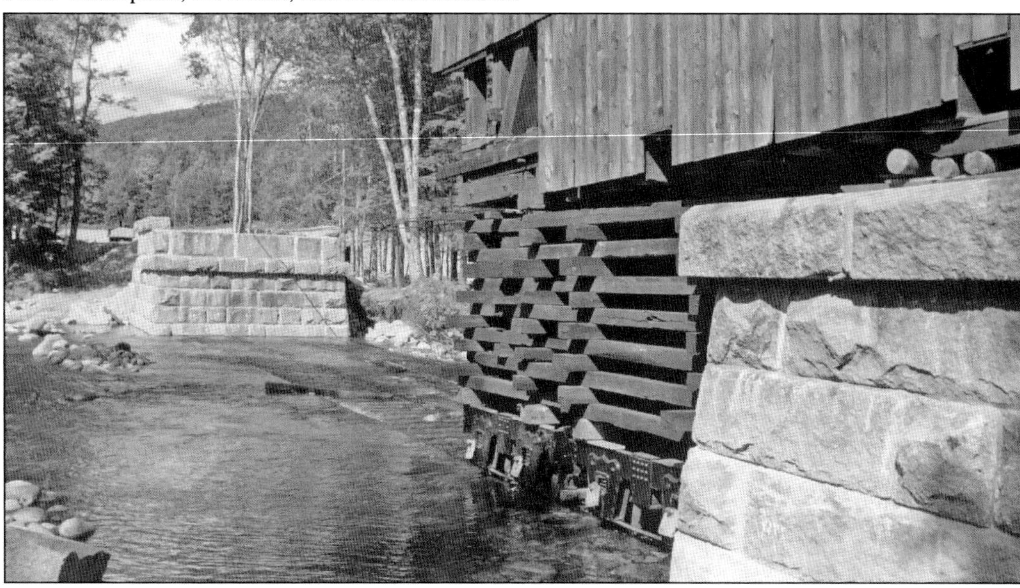

After the bridge was reassembled, it had to be moved across the river. Railroad tracks were laid in the riverbed, and railroad tie cribbing, mounted on log trucks, was used to support the front end of the bridge while the other end was rolled across on hard wood rollers. An ancient Linn half-track truck was hooked to the front end by cable to pull the bridge into place. (Photograph by W. Murray Clark.)

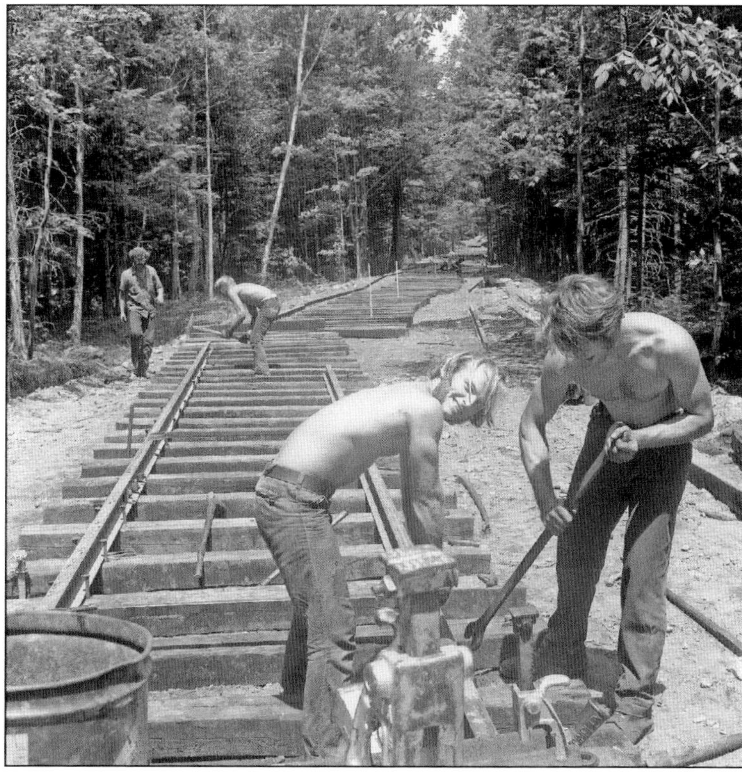

Even with the bridge in place, no train could cross the river without additional track. The brothers continued to buy used rail, and Ed's young work crew continued to lay it. From left to right are (front) David Clark and Leon Noel; (back) Bill Castlebury and Don Hedenburg. (Photograph by W. Murray Clark.)

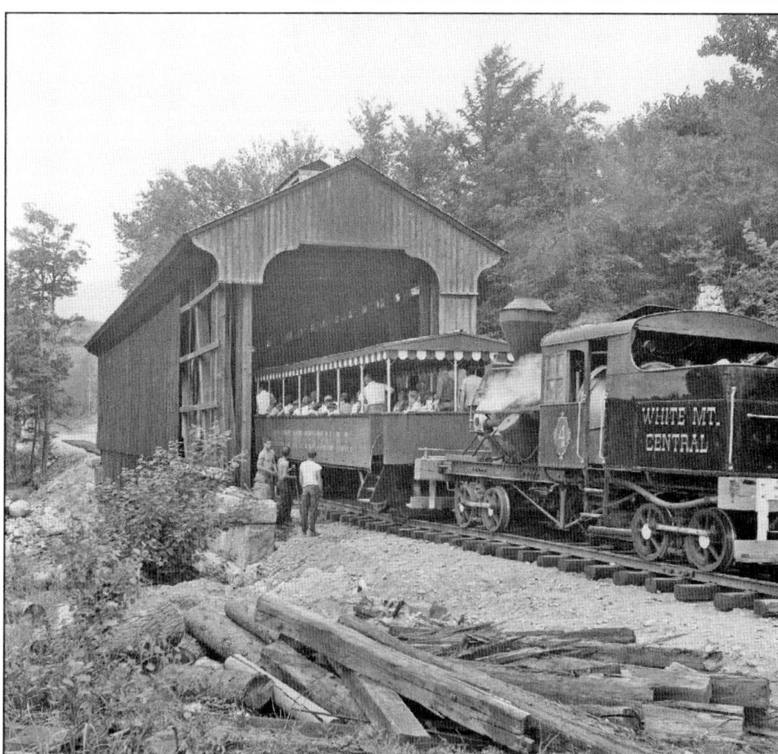

The Heisler locomotive hauls passengers on the first trip through the newly assembled covered bridge. It was approximately two years after completion of the bridge before the first trip was possible, as it took that long to acquire and lay sufficient track for the excursion over the river and through the woods. (Photograph by W. Murray Clark.)

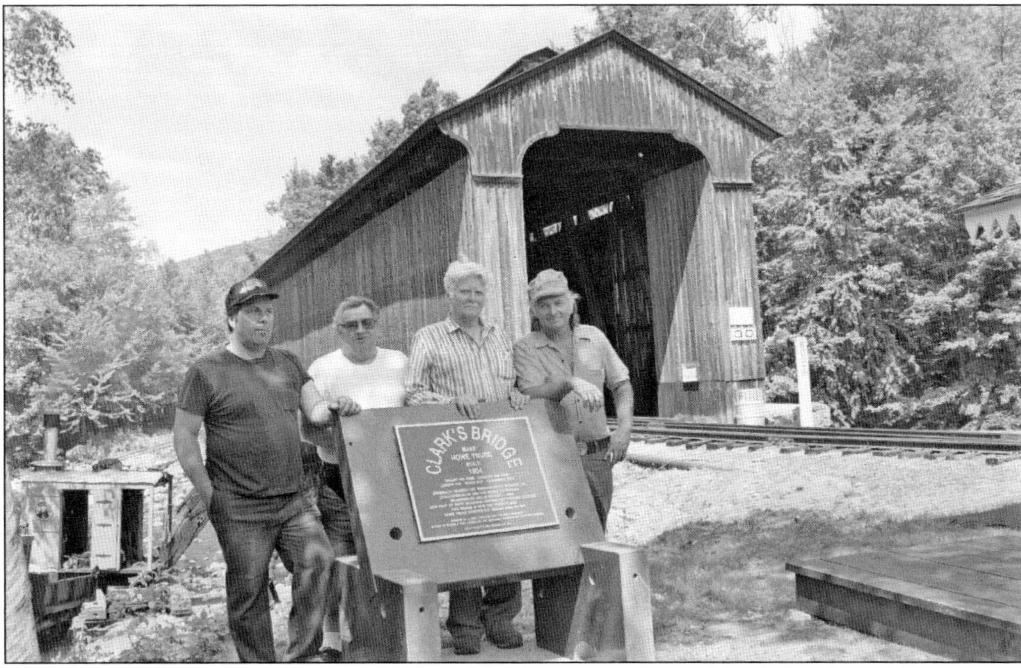

From left to right, Peter Thompson, Bill Duguay, Ed Clark, and David Clark pose at the dedication of the railroad covered bridge. (Missing from the original crew are Eddie Clark, Quinten E. Mulleavey, and others.) Originally built in 1904, the bridge is now the world's last Howe truss railroad covered bridge still in use. It is eligible for listing in the National Register of Historic Places and is officially known as New Hampshire Bridge No. 64.

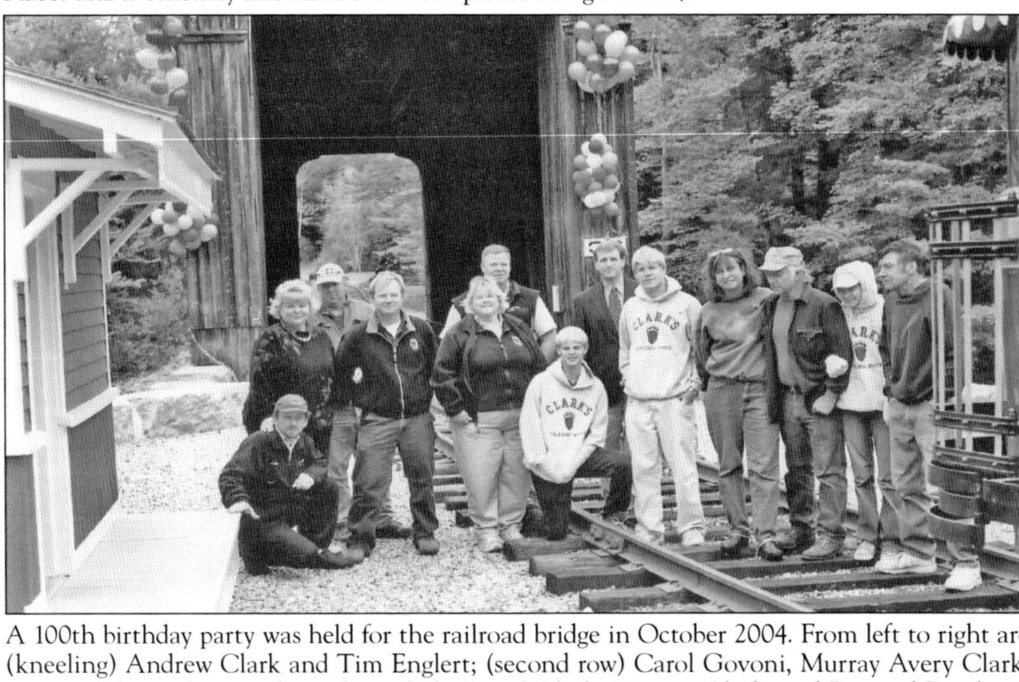

A 100th birthday party was held for the railroad bridge in October 2004. From left to right are (kneeling) Andrew Clark and Tim Englert; (second row) Carol Govoni, Murray Avery Clark, Anne Englert, Chris Englert, Elise Clark, David Clark, Morgan Clark, and Bernard Dowland; (third row) Tom Clark, Fred Englert, and Ben Clark.

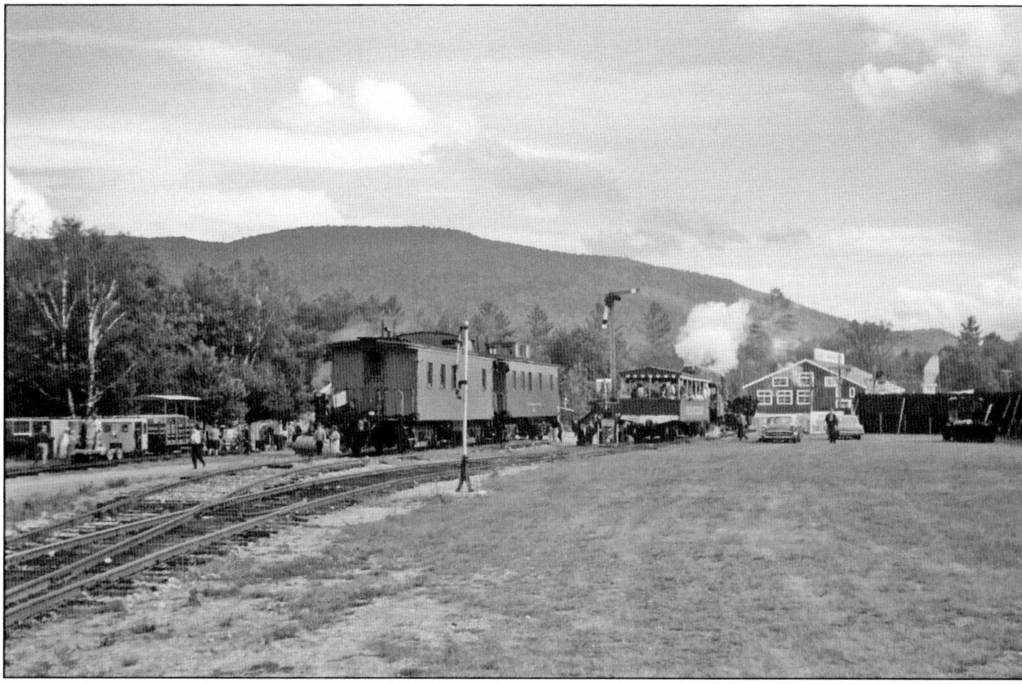

Taken in 1964, the photograph above shows a busy day for the White Mountain Central Railroad with the Heisler locomotive under steam. At far left, the original excursion car can be seen. The 1962 view below shows where the future railroad station would be erected. The bear performance ring at center had yet to receive its second seating deck. (Above, photograph by George Povall; below, photograph by W. Murray Clark.)

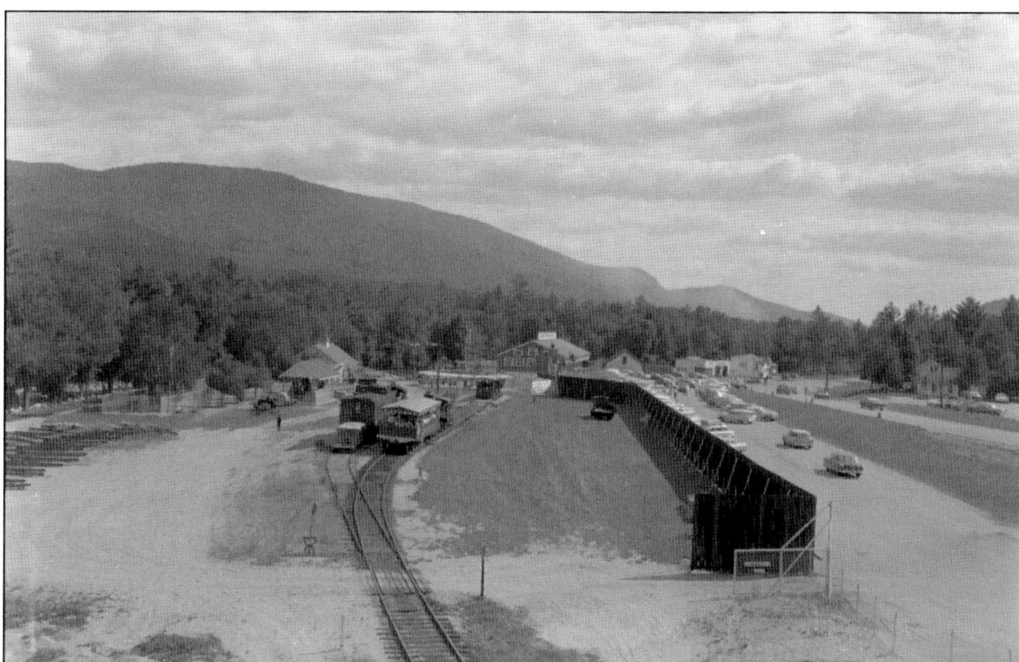

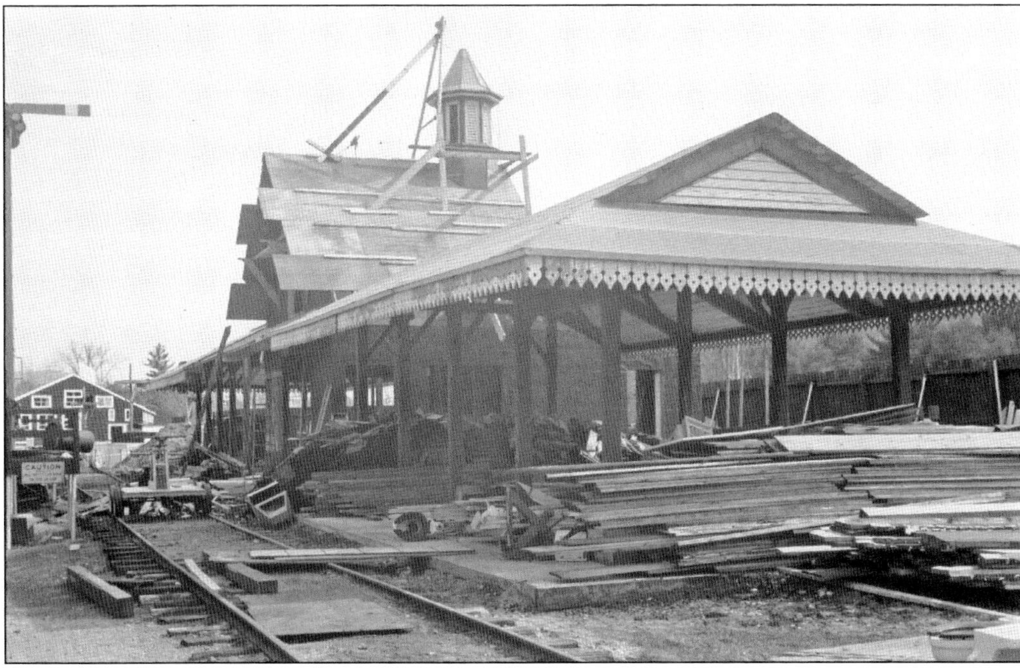

In 1965, Freedomland, USA, an entertainment complex in the Bronx, went bankrupt and everything was put up for sale. The Clarks acquired an enormous amount of salvaged material, including buildings, lamps, bricks, and seating. By far the most significant purchase was a version of the Chicago railroad station. The Clarks dismantled the structure, transported it home, redesigned it, and reconstructed it. Today, it serves as the entrance to the Trading Post grounds. Refurbishment of the Littleton National Bank yielded a pair of antique teller windows with grillwork that now serve as ticket windows. The Poli Movie Theater in Hartford, Connecticut, provided a walnut fireplace mantel for the interior. (Both photographs by W. Murray Clark.)

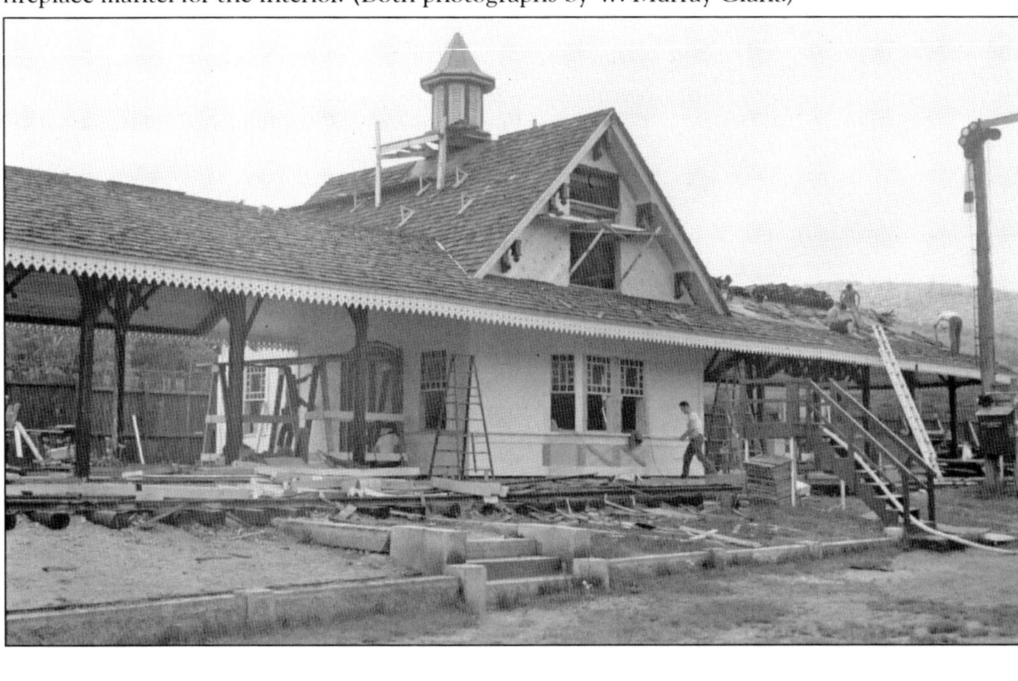

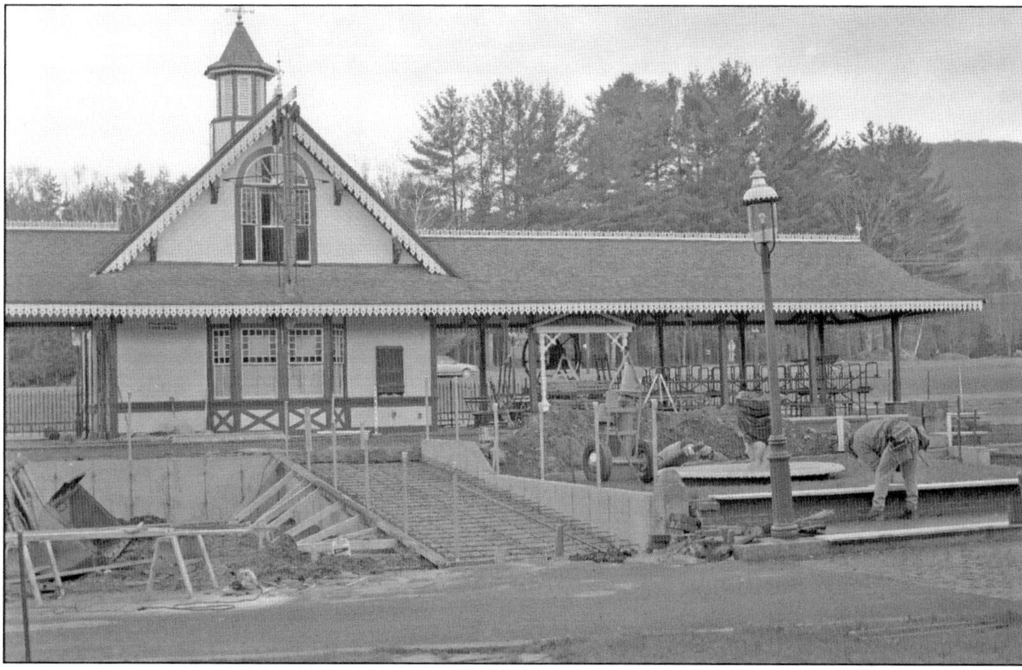

Construction of a ramp leading to the railroad tracks from Main Street afforded guests a shortcut to the station.

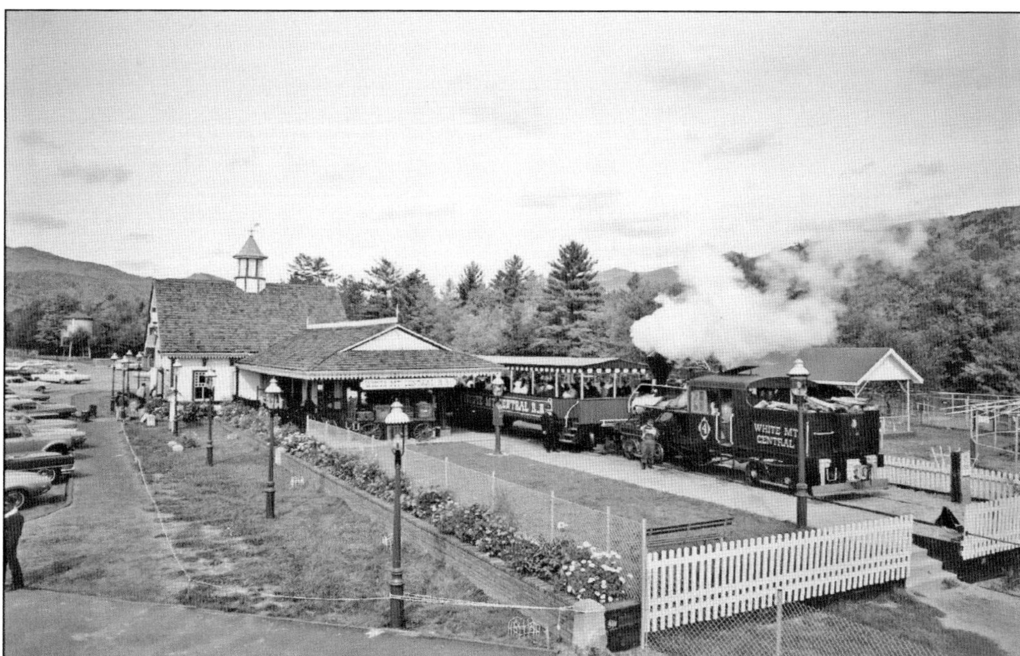

The completed railroad station is seen here, with the Heisler under steam and ready to transport guests on an excursion. The streetlights were another of the items obtained in the treasure trove from Freedomland, USA. This photograph was taken in the fall, sometime around 1968. (Photograph by W. Murray Clark.)

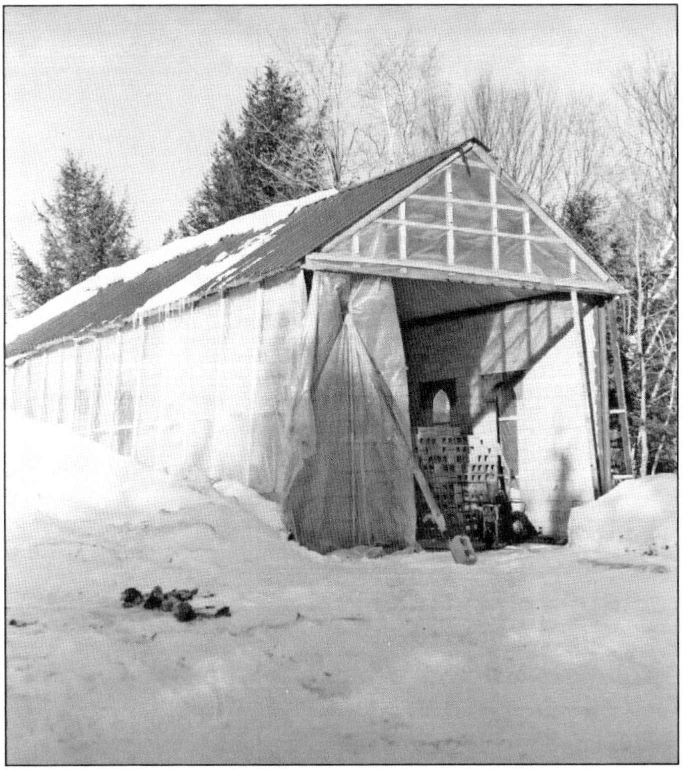

In 1972, refurbishment of the Climax began. By 1975, it was apparent that the locomotive had to be moved under cover to complete the job properly, and construction of an engine house began. The finished building is a replica of an 1848 gatehouse in Lowell, Massachusetts. It was an important addition for the White Mountain Central Railroad, allowing restoration, repair, and rebuilding projects to be carried out year-round. The granite blocks bearing the inscription "RR Department" were items Ed had salvaged years earlier from an old YMCA building slated for demolition in Concord, New Hampshire. (Left, photograph by Maureen S. Clark; below, photograph by John K. Eisenhart.)

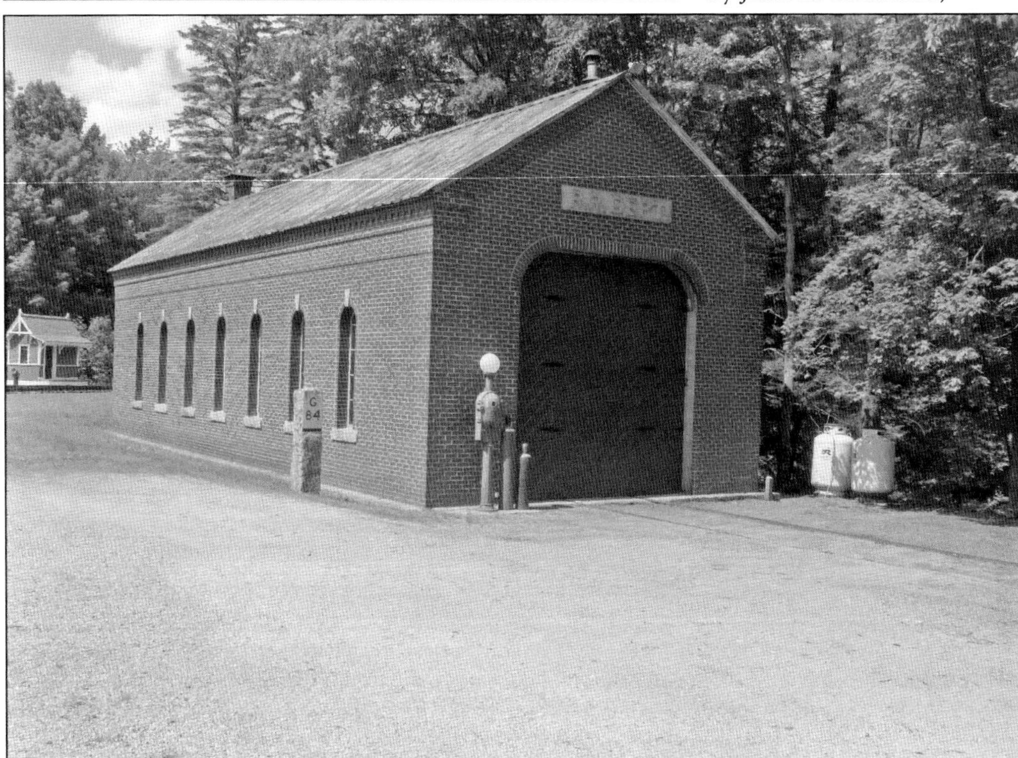

This c. 1976 photograph could be titled *Bad Boys of the White Mountain Central Railroad*. From left to right are Butch Gilbert, Leon Noel, David Clark, and Don Hedenburg posing in front of the Heisler. (Photograph by Maureen S. Clark.)

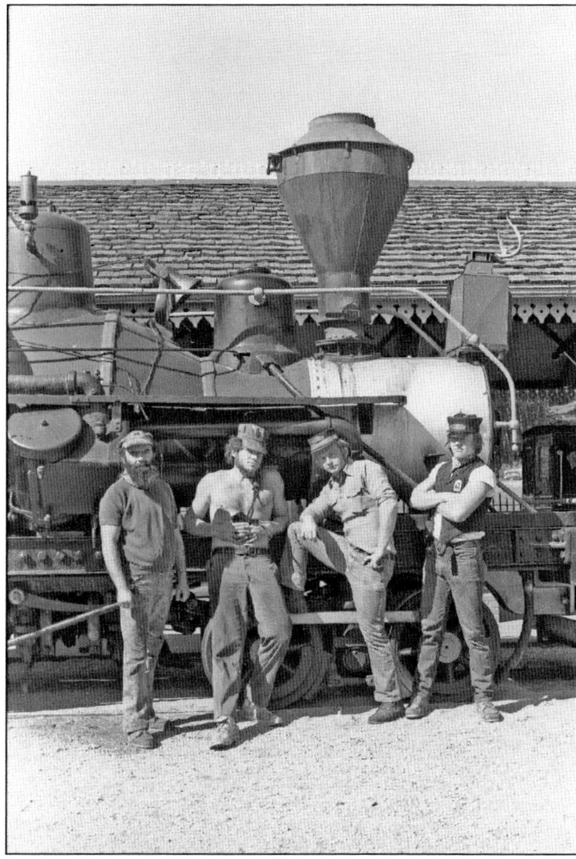

During the October 1976 Steam Meet, hosted by the White Mountain Central Railroad, Maureen came upon this scene and could not resist recording it for posterity. From left to right are David Clark, Eddie Clark, Tom Clark, Ed Clark, and Don Hedenburg in front of one of the Clarks' Buffalo Springfield steamrollers. (Photograph by Maureen S. Clark.)

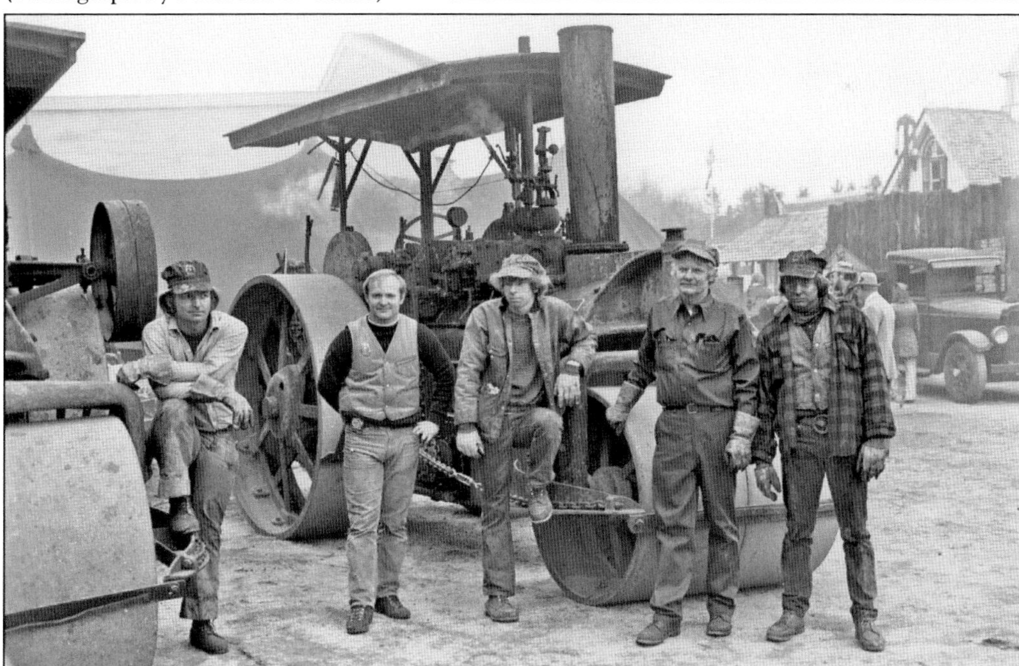

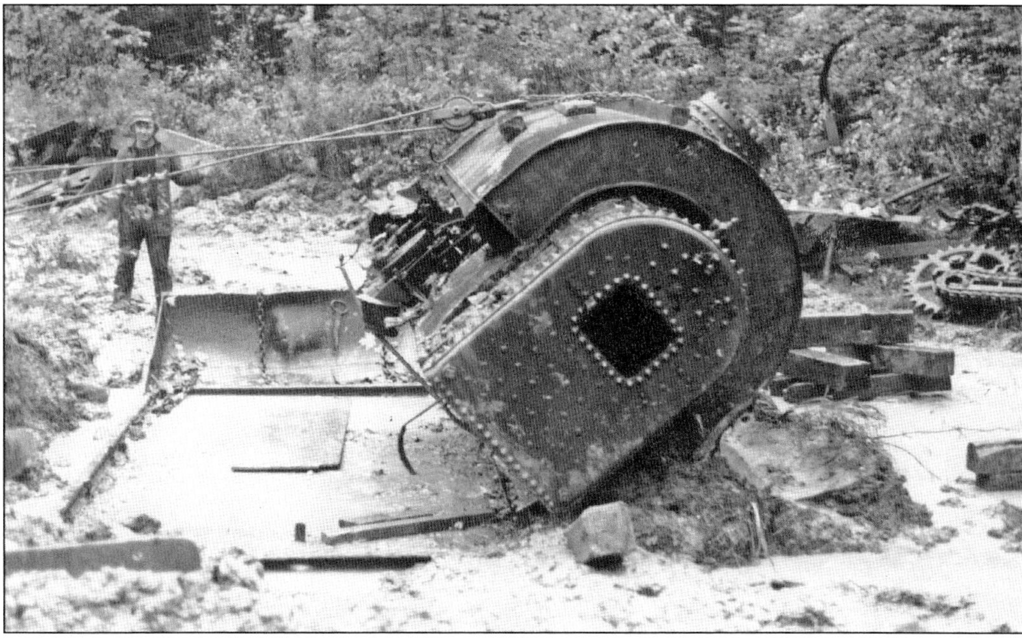

In 1976, the work crew headed to Maine to retrieve a Lombard log hauler, an unusual piece of equipment that is half tractor and half locomotive—a forerunner of today's snowmobile. When the men arrived, they found the parts had been bulldozed over and were buried in mud. They brought back what they could and spent years searching for missing pieces, fabricating what they could not find. David Clark is seen above as they are flipping the boiler onto a scoot to haul home.

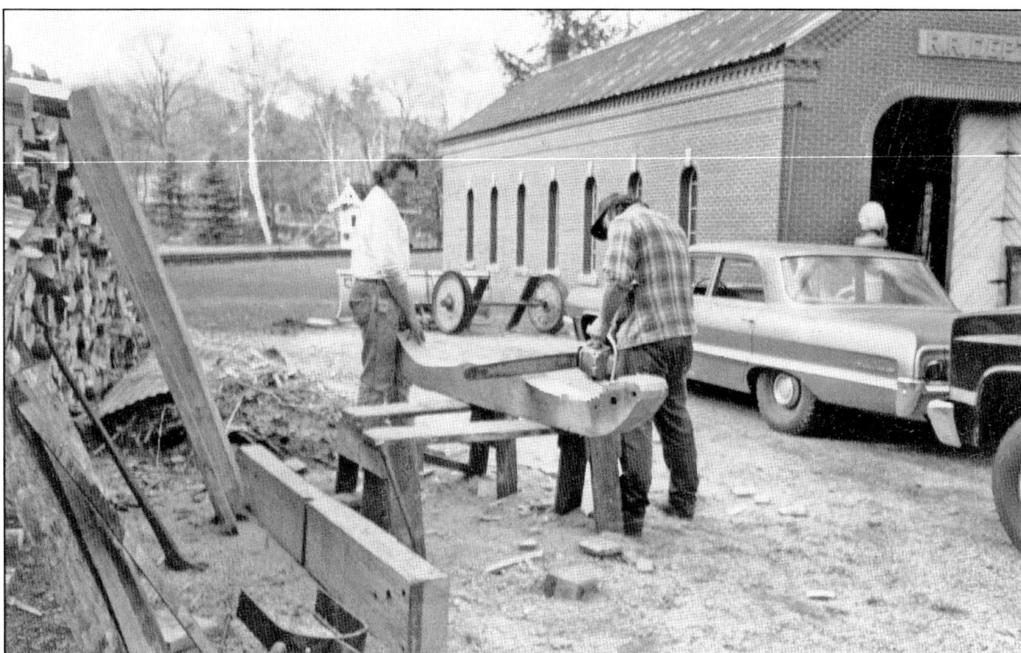

Leon Noel (left) assists Don Johnson to fabricate skis for the Lombard in 1989. The entire project took 13 years to complete, using parts from six different machines. It is exhibited in the carriage shed near the covered bridge. (Photograph by David A. Clark.)

The long restoration of the Lombard log hauler was completed in 1990. From left to right are Tom Clark, David Clark, Don Johnson, Ed Clark, and Leon Noel as the steersman. (Photograph by Maureen S. Clark.)

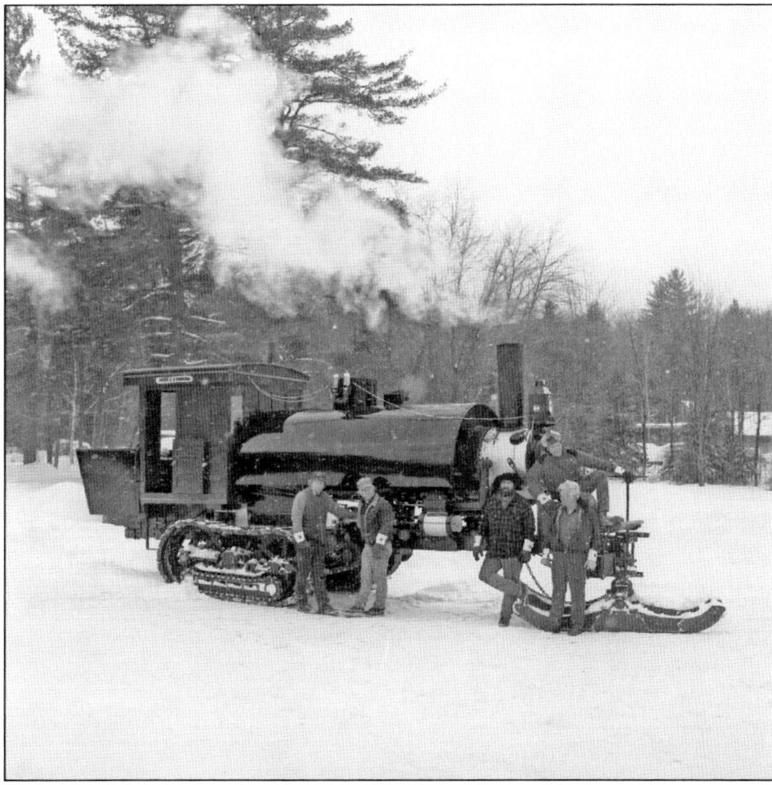

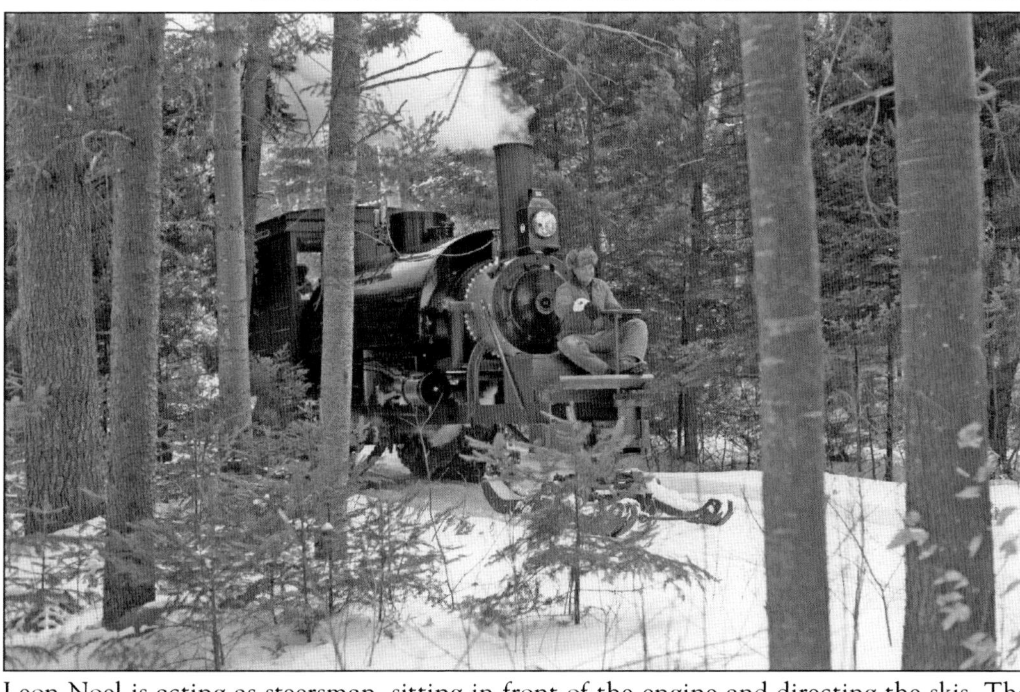

Leon Noel is acting as steersman, sitting in front of the engine and directing the skis. The Lombard requires three people to operate it: an engineer, a fireman, and a steersman. (Photograph by Maureen S. Clark.)

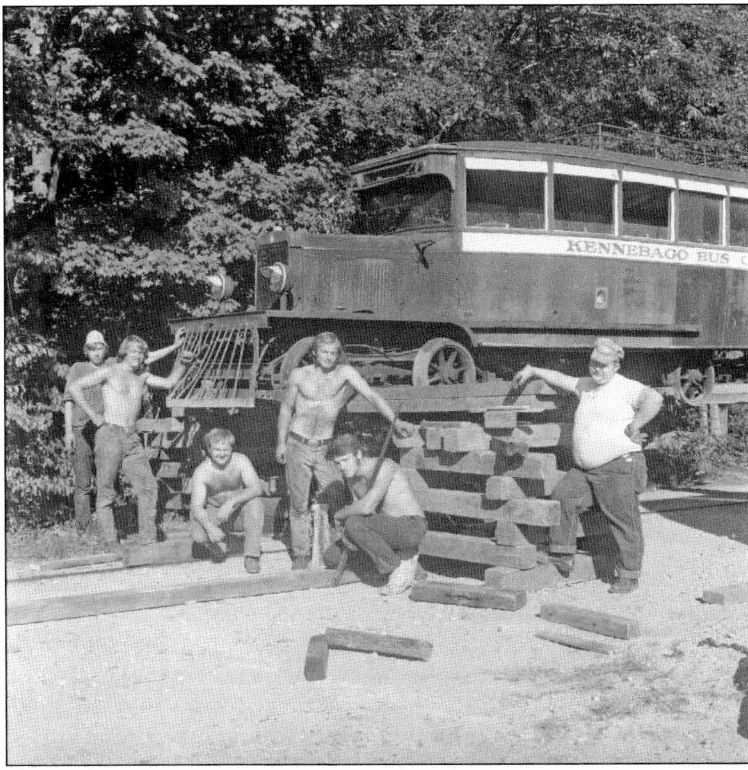

The 1930 Reo Speedwagon rail bus was acquired from the Starbird Lumber Company in Maine and is shown as it appeared when it first arrived at the Trading Post. It has undergone extensive renovation and now carries passengers for an occasional White Mountain Central Railroad Steam Celebration. From left to right are Tom Clark, Don Hedenburg, Eddie Clark, David Clark, Leon Noel (kneeling), and Bill Albrecht. (Photograph by Maureen S. Clark.)

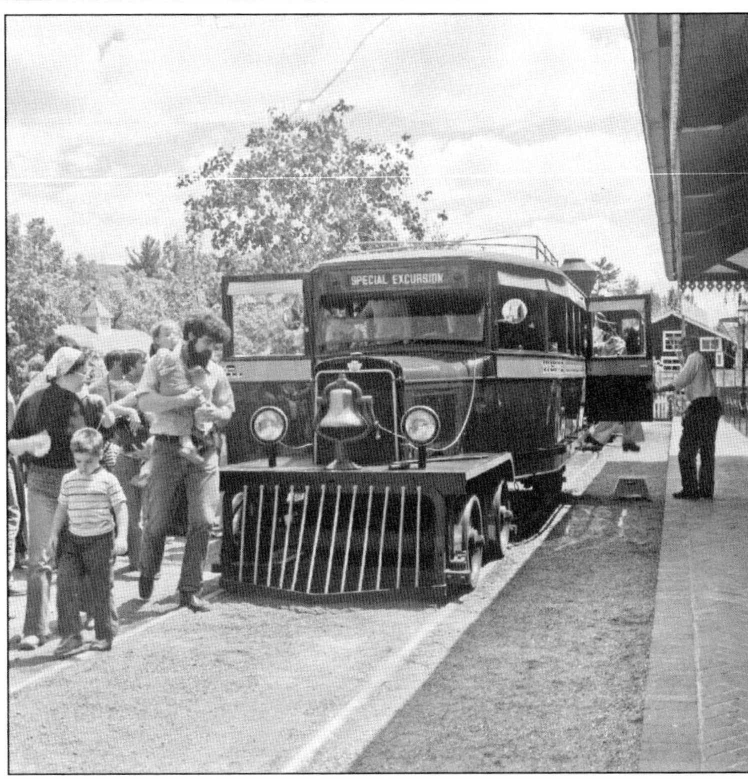

Passengers are seen exiting the refurbished Reo Speedwagon rail bus during one of its occasional outings. (Photograph by Maureen S. Clark.)

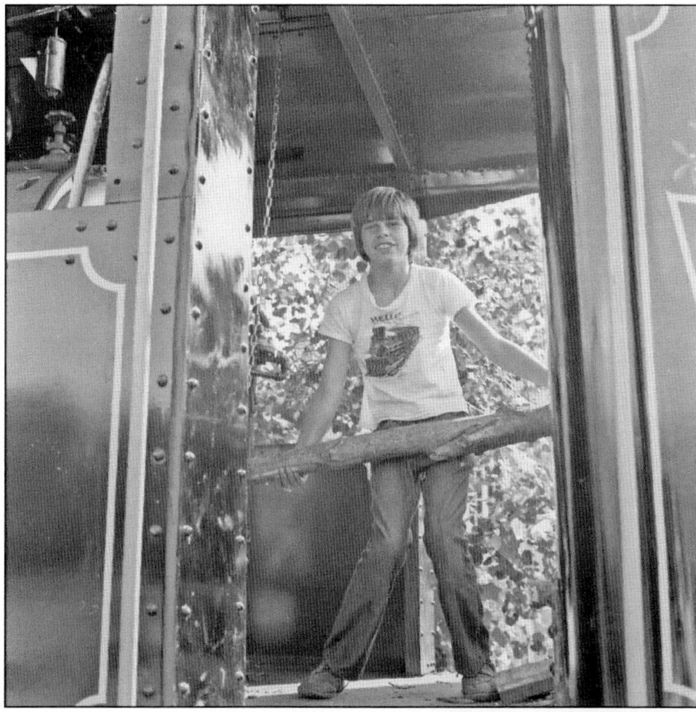

August 1977 heralded the first day of operation for the Climax after her long restoration. Lee Thompson is the fireman, building up pressure so there will be plenty of steam for her maiden trip down the rails. (Photograph by Maureen S. Clark.)

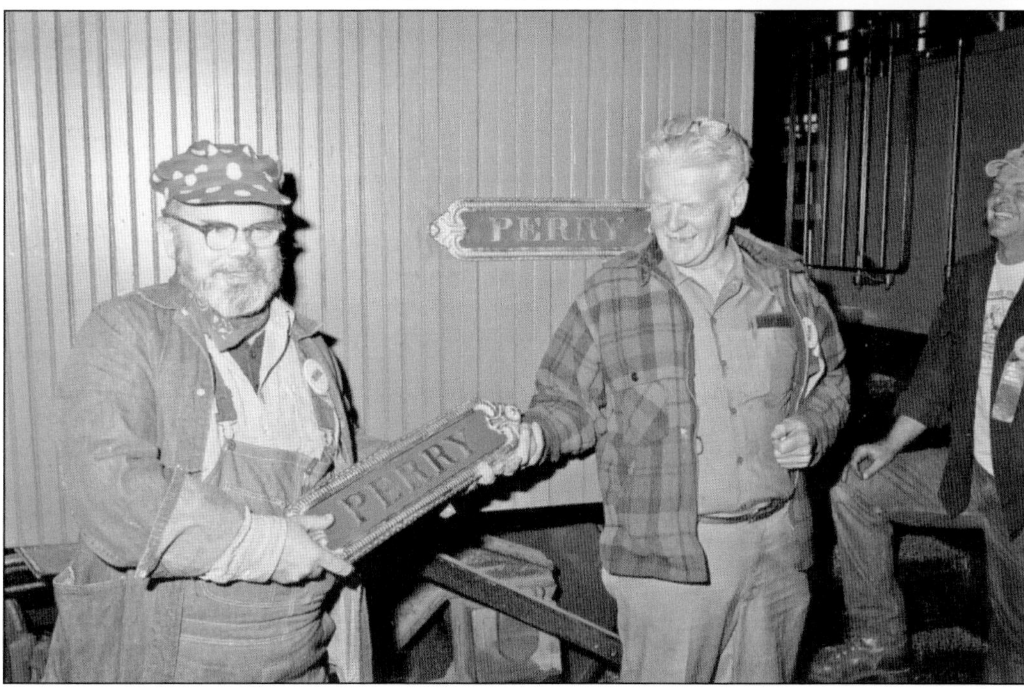

Brass name plates were attached to excursion cars to honor Ben Perry, Alan Thomas, Allan Wiswall, and Allan Pommer in recognition of their enormous contributions of time and effort in helping to build the White Mountain Central Railroad. In the early days, no pay and hard work were the norm, and they did it out of love of railroading. Here, Ben Perry is receiving his duplicate plaque from Ed Clark. David Clark is visible at right. (Photograph by Jon P. Lasseigne.)

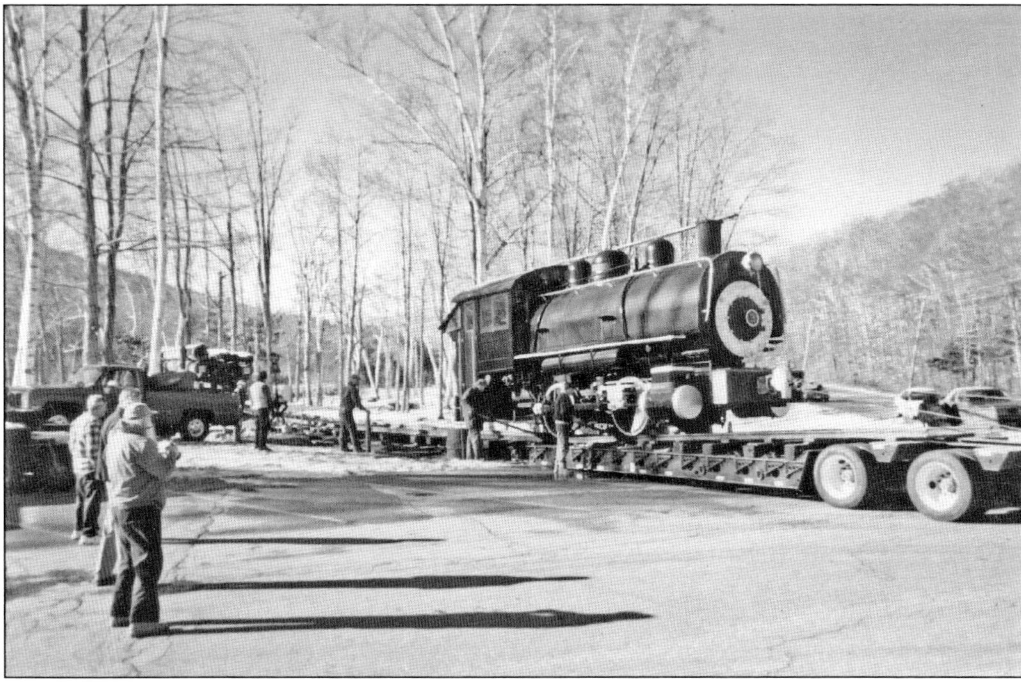

The Baldwin locomotive is being loaded for departure from Loon Mountain in Lincoln in December 1998. Loon Mountain resort had the non-functioning No. 5 Baldwin on display, and the men at White Mountain Central wanted to see if they could get it into operating condition. (Or, as Leon Noel expressed it: "See if the No. 5 could ever be hot again!") A trade brought the Baldwin to White Mountain Central and sent the refurbished Porter to Loon.

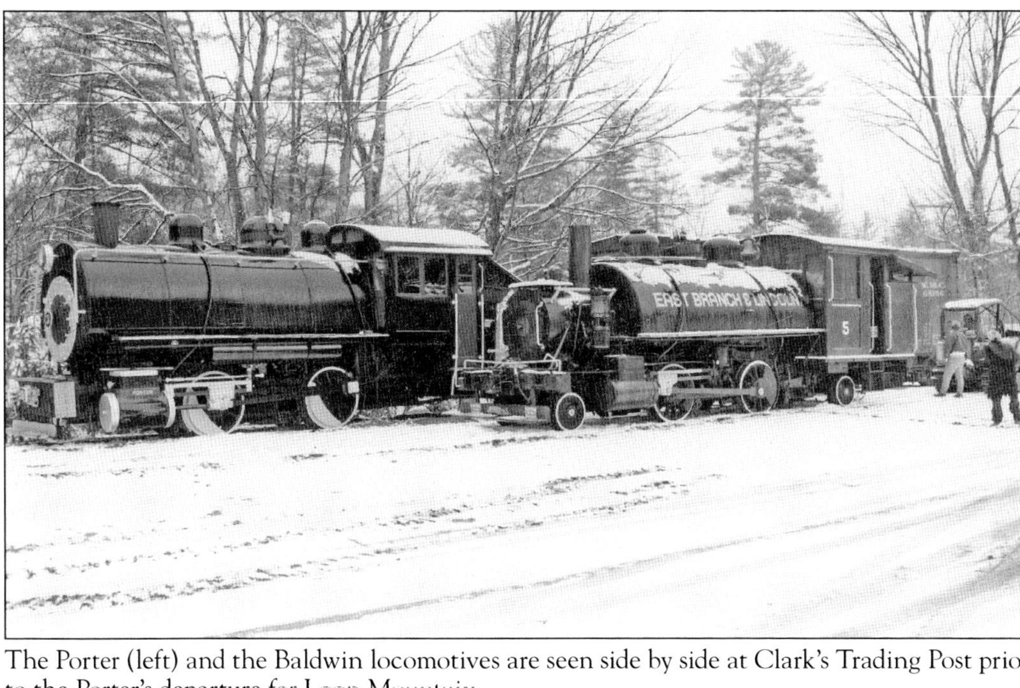

The Porter (left) and the Baldwin locomotives are seen side by side at Clark's Trading Post prior to the Porter's departure for Loon Mountain.

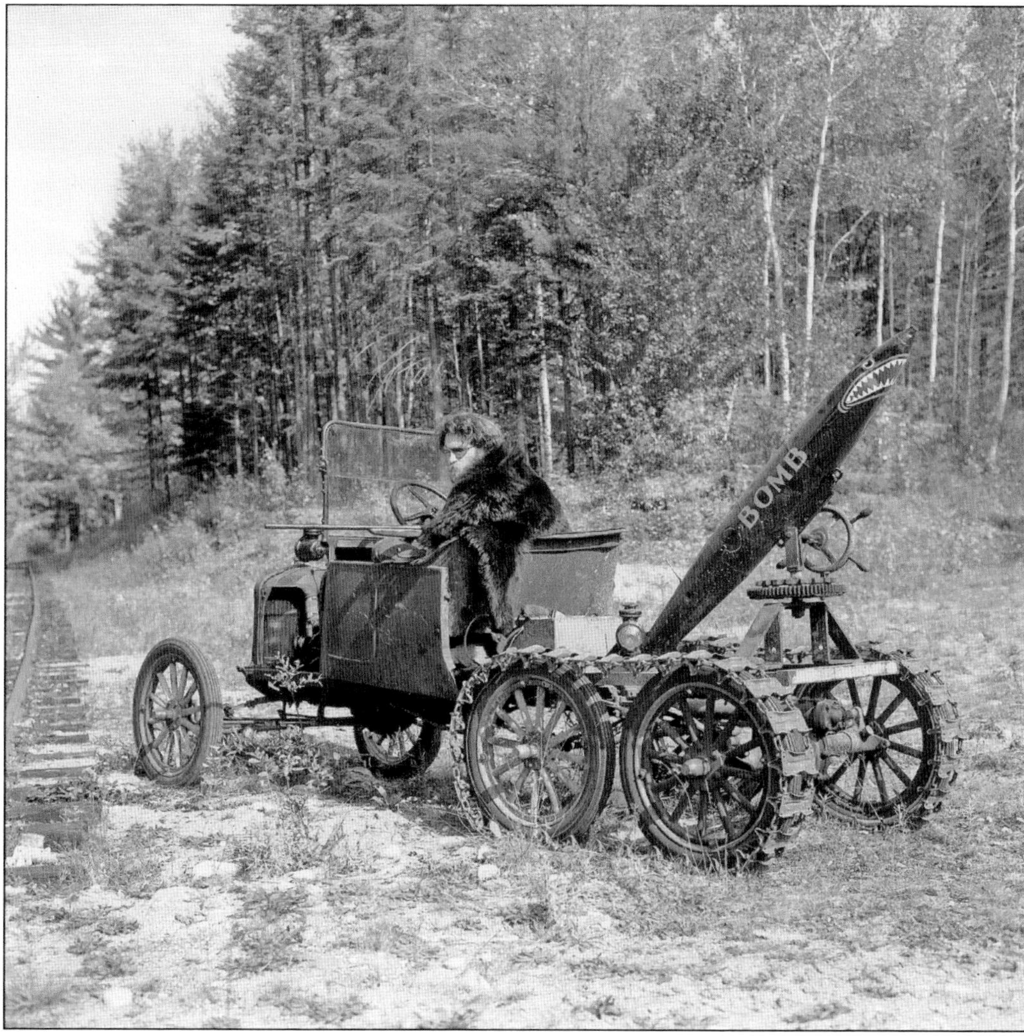

Wolfman was "born" in 1973, when illness sidelined Murray for a few days and bear shows were canceled. Leon Noel, attempting to fill the void, ran around in the woods yelling at passengers on the train to get off his property. What started as a temporary amusement to entertain guests became such a hit that it was established as a daily feature of the White Mountain Central Railroad. In this October 1982 photograph, Leon is seen in the role he created with the original "wolfcar," based on a Model T snow machine. Leon has been an honorary member of the Clark family since Murray hired him directly out of high school. His enthusiasm and sunny disposition make him a treasured goodwill ambassador—he loves interacting with the public, and the public loves him. For decades, he has been the smiling face of the White Mountain Central Railroad, beaming down from the cab of the locomotives. (Photograph by Maureen S. Clark.)

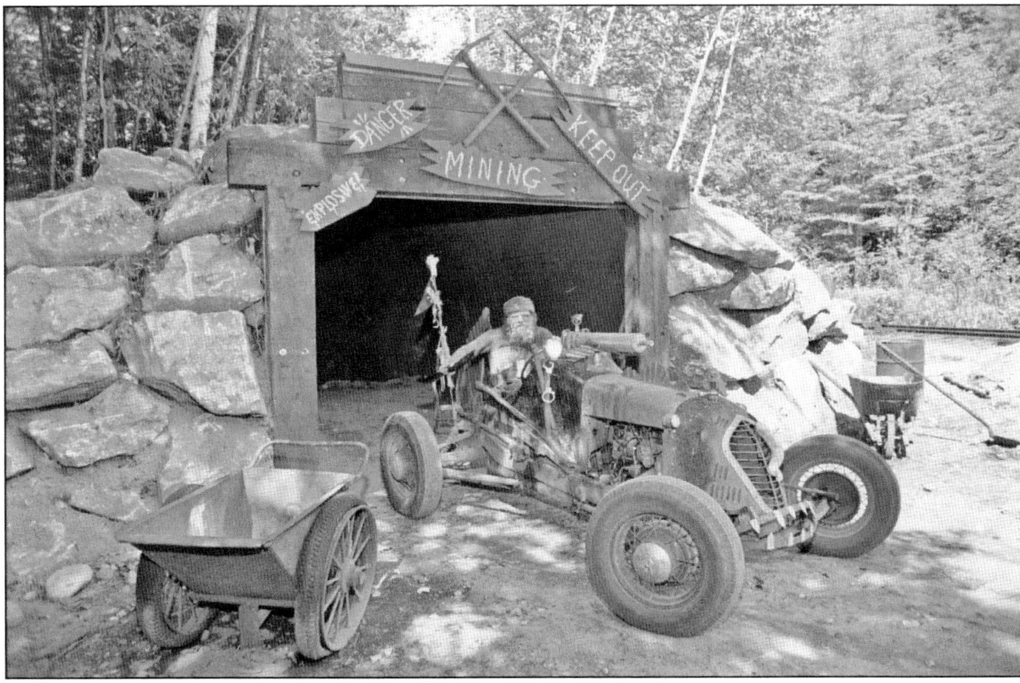

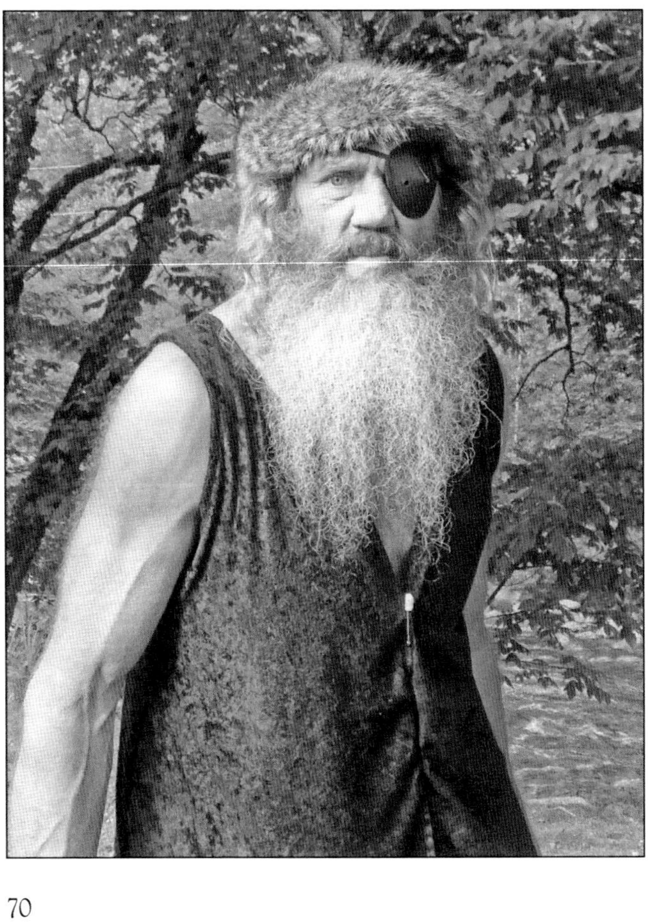

The character of Wolfman is a highly coveted position at the Trading Post, despite being a physically demanding role. Wolfman chases all trains and every Segway Safari, inspects the tracks for safety, and, at the end of the day, often takes his wolfcar to the front of the gift shop to greet guests. Bill Farrand, posing above in front of the "unobtanium mine," held the position for 15 years.

Tim Ryan (Wolfman Timber) held the position for seven years and had a devoted following. All the Wolfmen now use wolfcars built by David Clark. The cars are an exciting part of the sight of Wolfman racing out of the woods to chase the train. One has a machine gun mounted on the hood; both have a set of gnashing teeth on the front bumpers. (Photograph by Maureen S. Clark.)

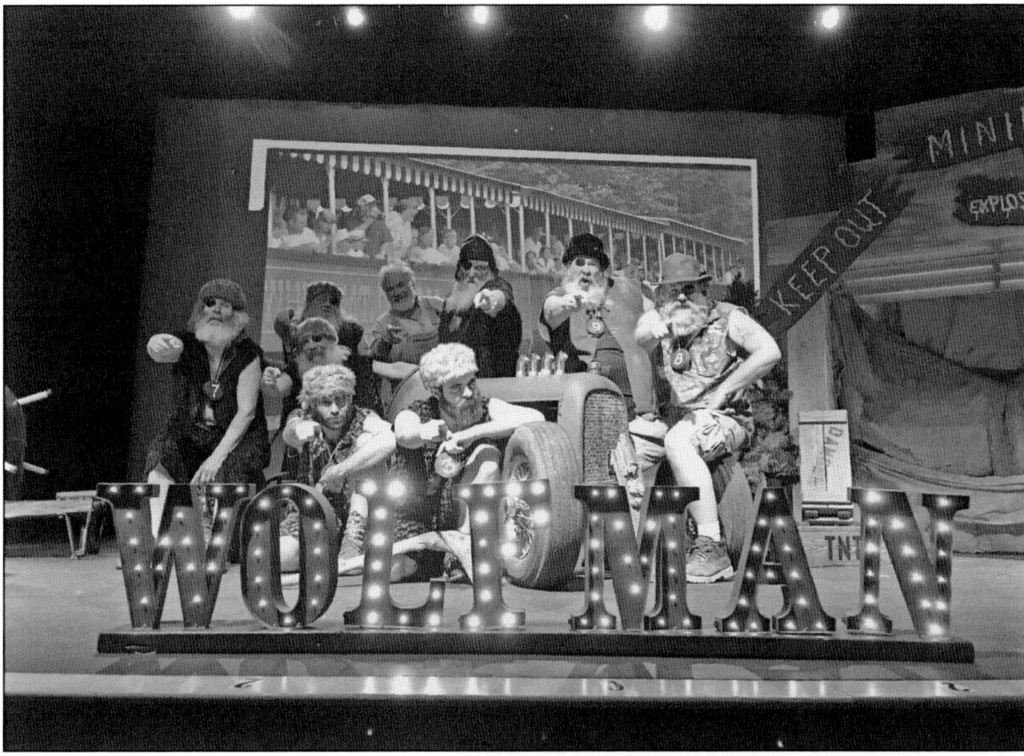

When Tim Ryan retired as Wolfman in 2016, the word went out that a new Wolfman was needed. Auditions were held at Jean's Playhouse in Lincoln in front of an enthusiastic, overflowing audience, and Larry Vigus (second row, fourth from left) was the overwhelming crowd favorite. Vern Gray (first row, second from left) was chosen as an alternate. (Photograph by Maureen S. Clark.)

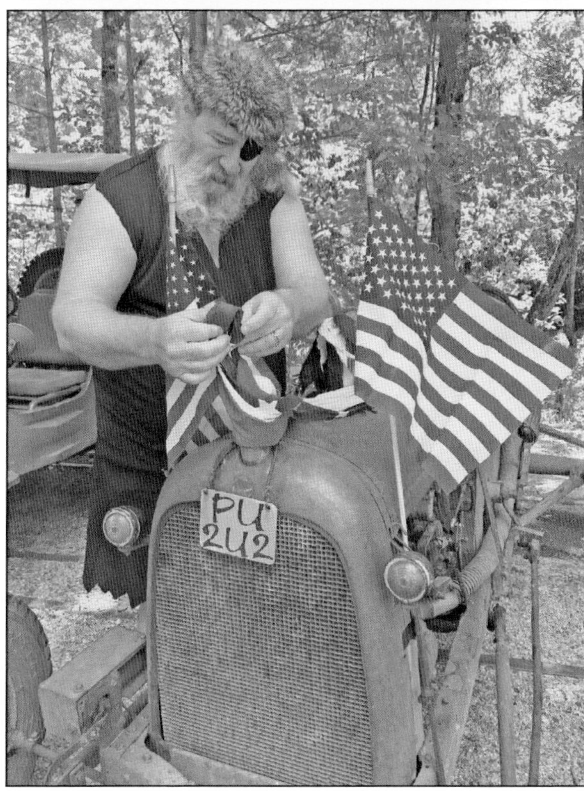

Wolfman Larry is decorating his wolfcar for the 2017 Fourth of July parade. The two wolfcars are based on old dirt-track racers with Chevrolet Iron Duke four-cylinder engines, Ford Model A suspension parts, and automatic transmissions. (Photograph by Maureen S. Clark.)

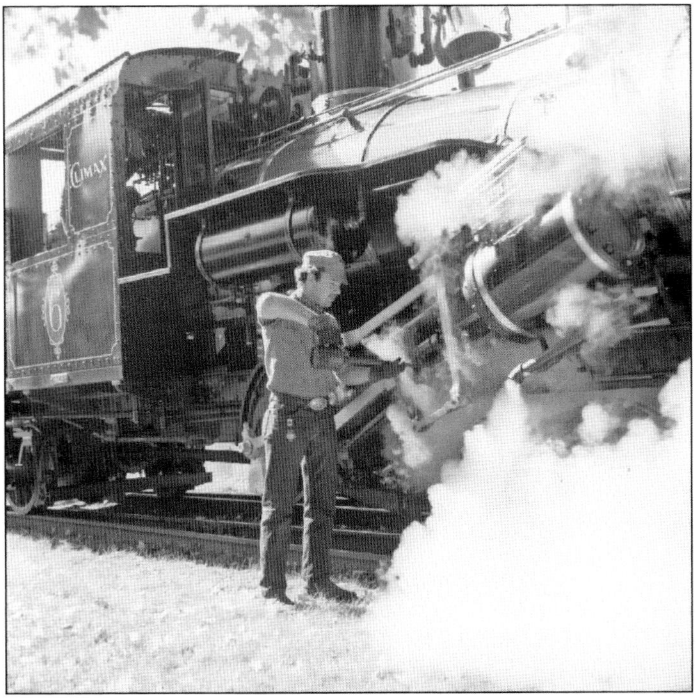

Bob Henderson, seen here tending to the Climax, has been with the Trading Post since he was volunteering at 13, giving Tuttle's Rustic House tours. He joined the staff officially at 14 and served as conductor on the steam locomotives by the time he was 15. He is an invaluable presence at the Trading Post, capable of filling in anywhere and fixing almost anything. He knows where everything is, why it is there, and how it works. (Photograph by Priscilla Carton.)

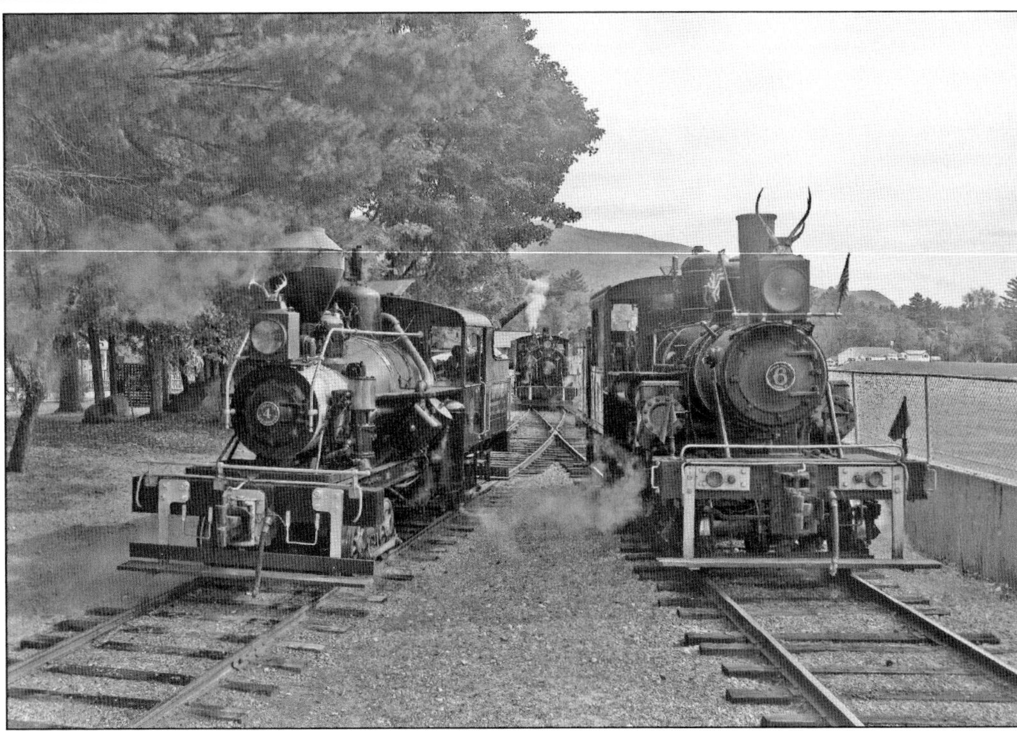

This joyous depiction of the proud, hard-earned heritage of the White Mountain Central Railroad was captured on film during a 2006 White Mountain Central Railroad Days Celebration. From left to right, the locomotives are the No. 4 Heisler, the No. 5 Baldwin, and the No. 6 Climax. (Photograph by Nola Grant.)

Six

SQUARE YOUR SHOULDERS

"Square your shoulders" was a favorite expression of Ed Clark. It means to brace yourself and tackle whatever job is at hand, however difficult. During the 1970s, the Clarks removed dog pens and constructed the Americana Museum and the Pemigewasset Hook and Ladder Fire Station. Tuttle's Rustic House, the Peppermint Saloon, Kilburn's Photo Parlor, and the Maple Cabin all opened. Windows, doors, and other assorted material salvaged from various sites including the Corbin Lock Factory in New Britain, Connecticut, were repurposed in many of the buildings. Vintage bricks from a factory floor would eventually be laid to create Main Street. The Climax steam engine refurbishment was completed, and she replaced the Heisler.

By 1969, David Clark had returned home from the Army, Leon Noel had been recently hired, and Eddie Clark and Peter Thompson rounded out the core crew. "The boys" did everything from grading ground and burying water pipes to repairing locomotives and putting up buildings, learning and figuring it out as they went.

In 1972, Murray was elected state representative for his district, a position he held with distinction for 10 years. Ed, a man of many interests, left the Trading Post to follow his passion for steam engines, spending time as general manager of the Cog Railway, operating freight railroads, and resurrecting dormant hydroelectric plants. Murray was left to manage the business, train the bears, and do the bear shows throughout the summer.

Construction projects and maintenance took place during the off-season, ensuring that the core group of family and employees had year-round employment and that return guests would have new attractions to entertain them.

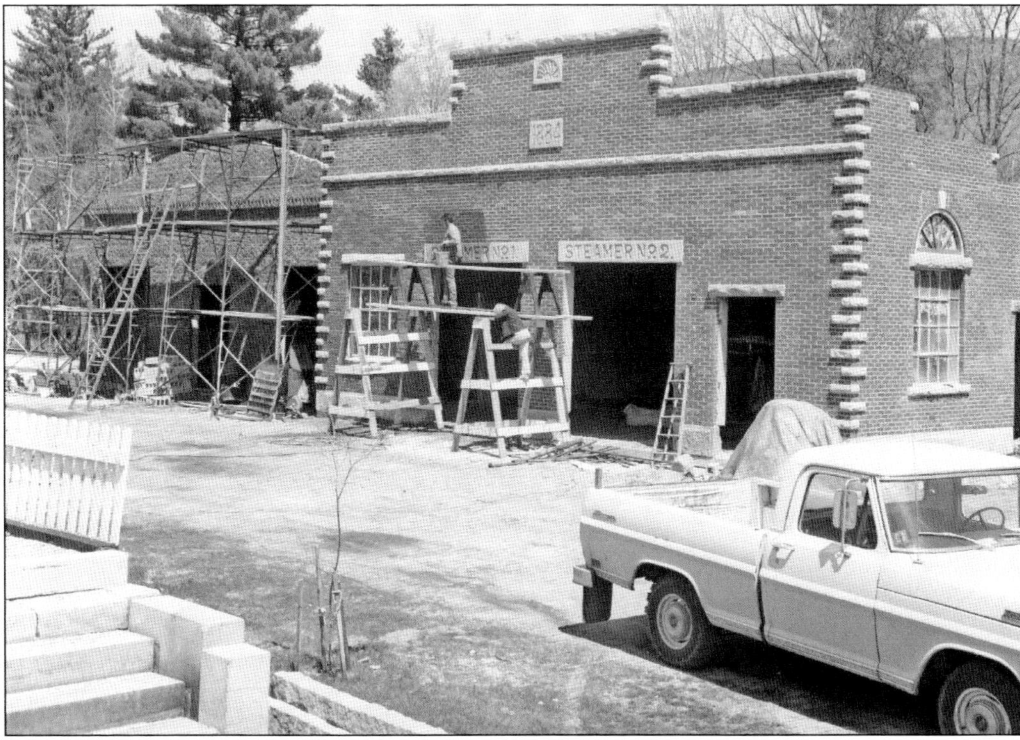

The Americana Museum and the Pemigewasset Hook and Ladder Museum were built to house the family's growing assortment of collectibles and horse-drawn and steam-powered fire-fighting equipment. Building the Pemigewasset Hook and Ladder Museum provided Ed the opportunity to use two granite blocks incised with "Steamer 1" and "Steamer 2," which had been acquired years before. (Photograph by W. Murray Clark.)

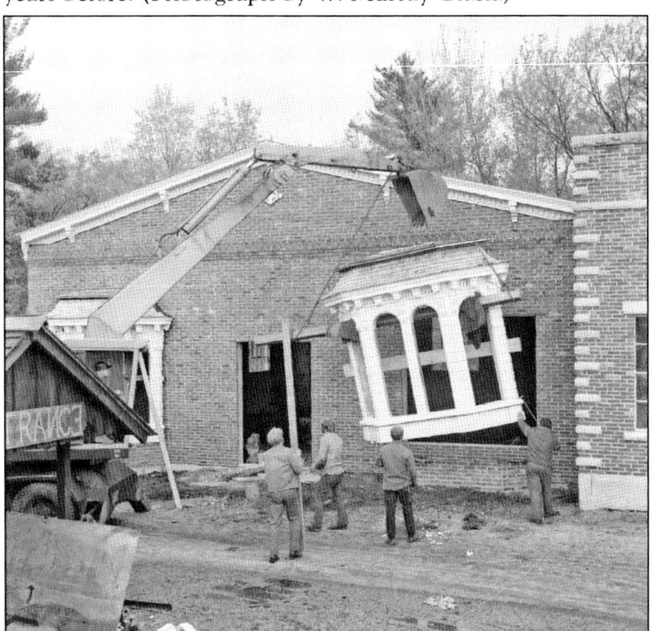

From left to right, Ed Clark, David Clark, Eddie Clark, and Bill Duguay are lowering a bay window into place on the Americana Museum in 1971. The windows were repurposed from a private residence in Plymouth, New Hampshire, and the entry doors were salvaged from the Lowes Poli Theater in Hartford, Connecticut, which shut down in the 1960s. (Photograph by W. Murray Clark.)

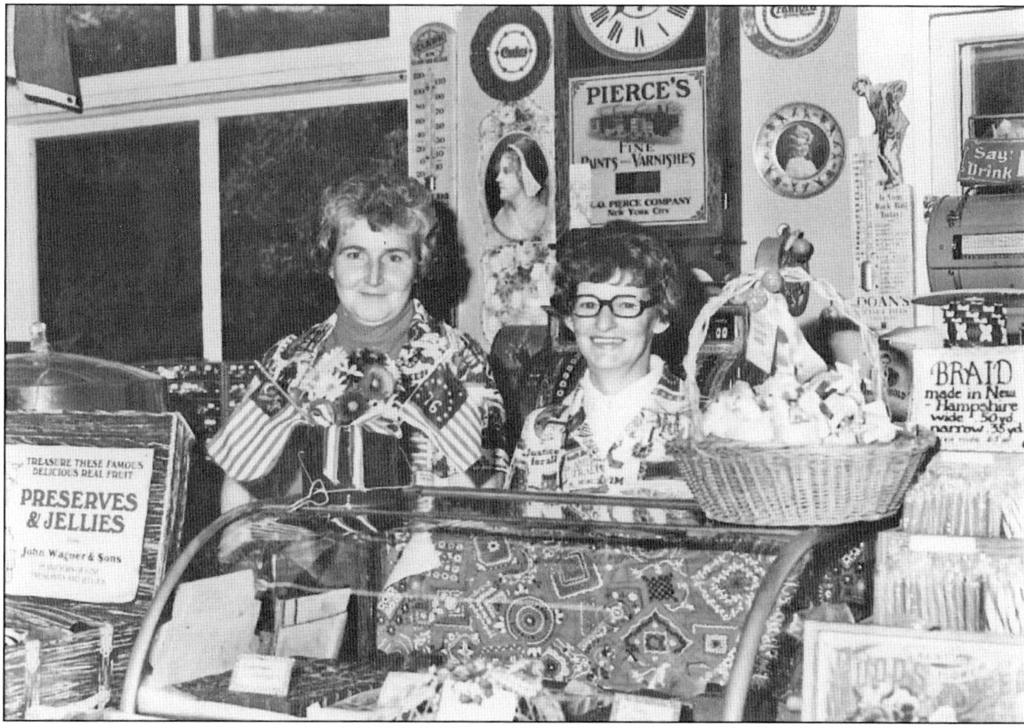

Barbara Clark (left) and Barbara Moody are seen behind the candy counter of the gift shop in 1976. Many of the antique artifacts on the wall are still there, although the fudge counter has expanded, selling as much as 9,000 pounds in a season. (Photograph by Maureen S. Clark.)

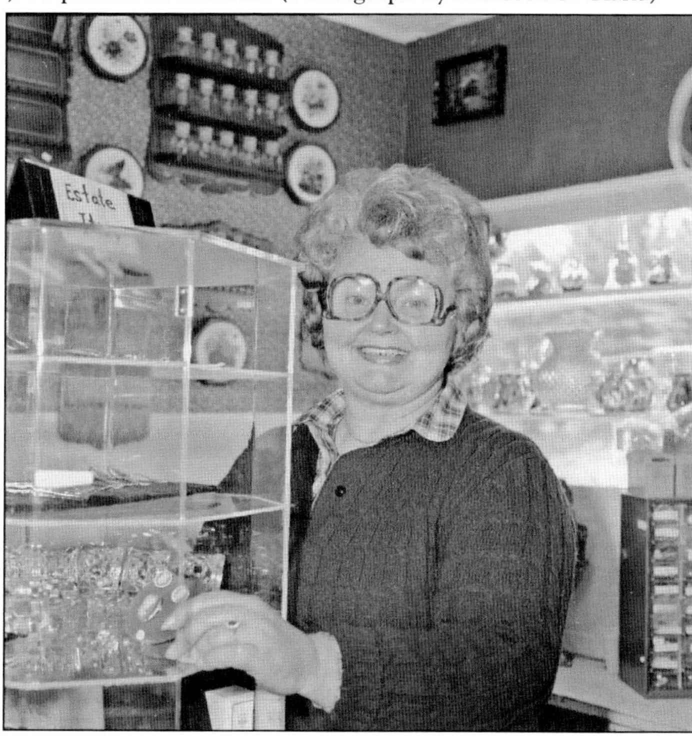

Joyce Clark is seen here at the jewelry counter. Barbara and Joyce worked just as hard as their husbands and deserve a great deal of credit for the success of Clark's Trading Post. By making the gift shop profitable, they provided a steady flow of income to support expansion of the entire business. (Photograph by Maureen S. Clark.)

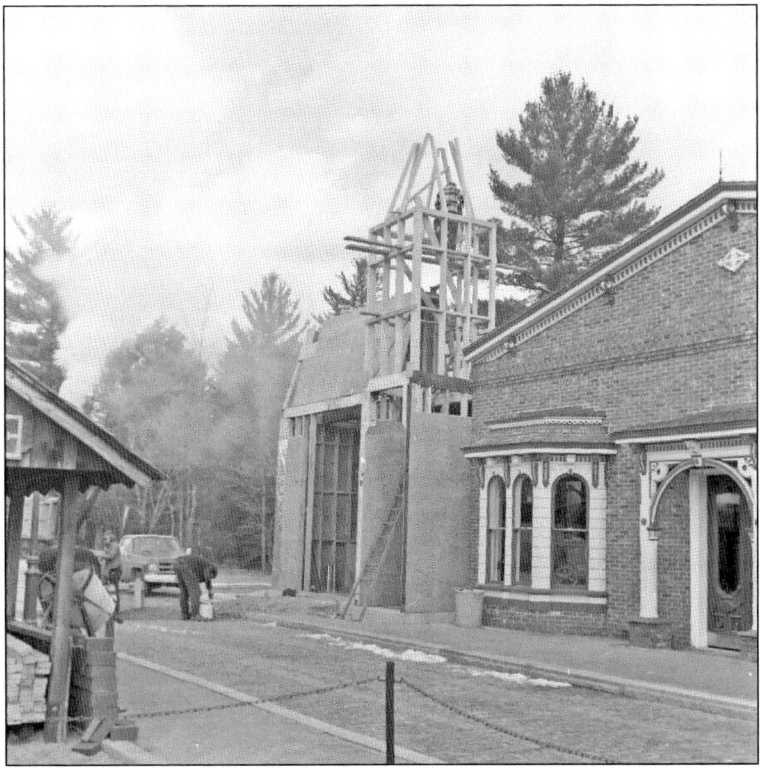

The Peppermint Saloon was a two-year building project that began in 1977. Ed had seen a small bank in Barre, Vermont, depicted on a *Saturday Evening Post* cover. That became the inspiration for the new structure. Here, David Clark is on the far left, and Eddie Clark is in the tower. (Photograph by Maureen S. Clark.)

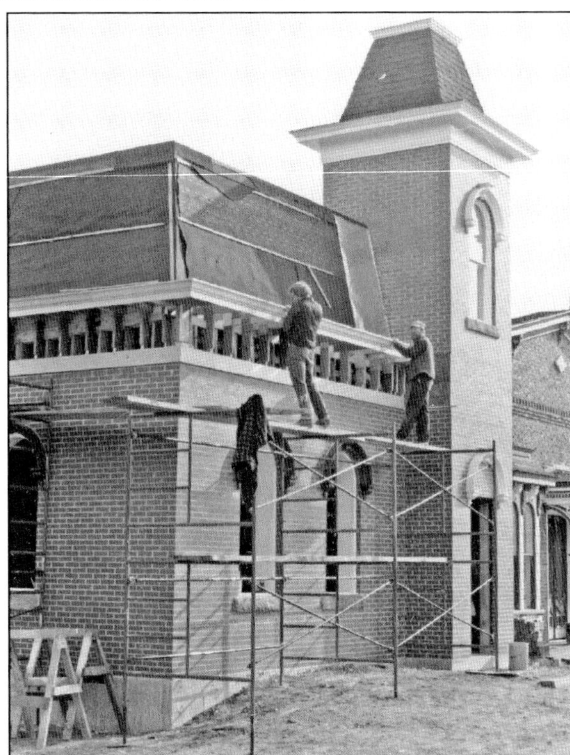

Jay Bartlett (left) and Don Showalter are framing up the mansard lip on the soon-to-be-completed Peppermint Saloon. (Photograph by Maureen S. Clark.)

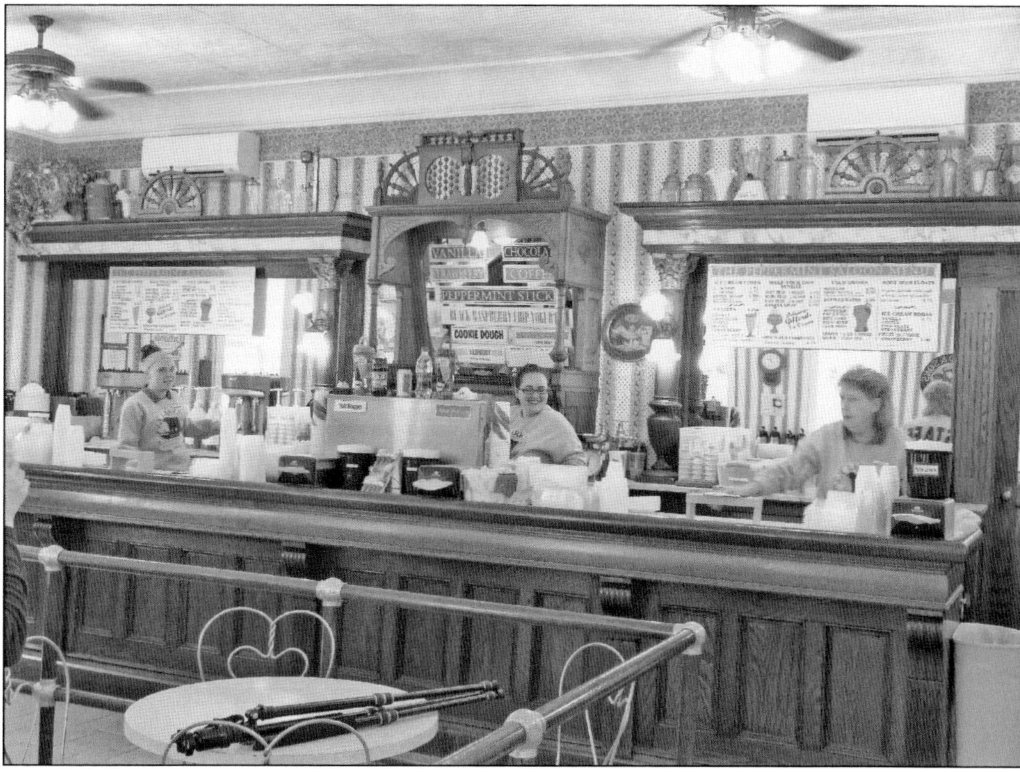

The Peppermint Saloon project gave the Clarks another opportunity to repurpose items they had salvaged. A section of famous prizefighter Jack Sharkey's bar was acquired from Pleasure Island in Wakefield, Massachusetts. It set the Victorian tone of the building and all of Main Street. From left to right are Brittney Libby, Paige Cloutier, and Barbara Craigie. Barbara has managed the saloon for over 15 years and mentored many a young employee. (Photograph by John K. Eisenhart.)

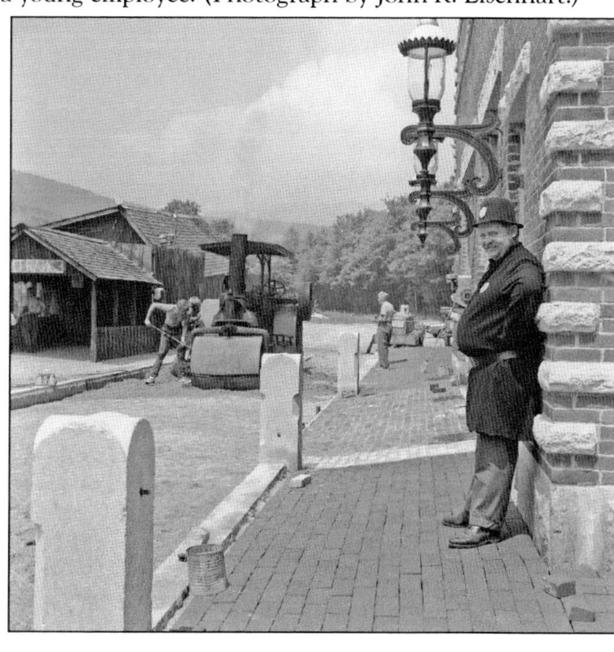

Sand is being leveled and steamrolled in 1972 prior to laying salvaged antique bricks to create Main Street. In the foreground, Bill Albrecht is dressed as a Keystone Kop. From left to right in the background, Leon Noel and David Clark are next to the steamroller, and Stanley Cook is on the right. (Photograph by W. Murray Clark.)

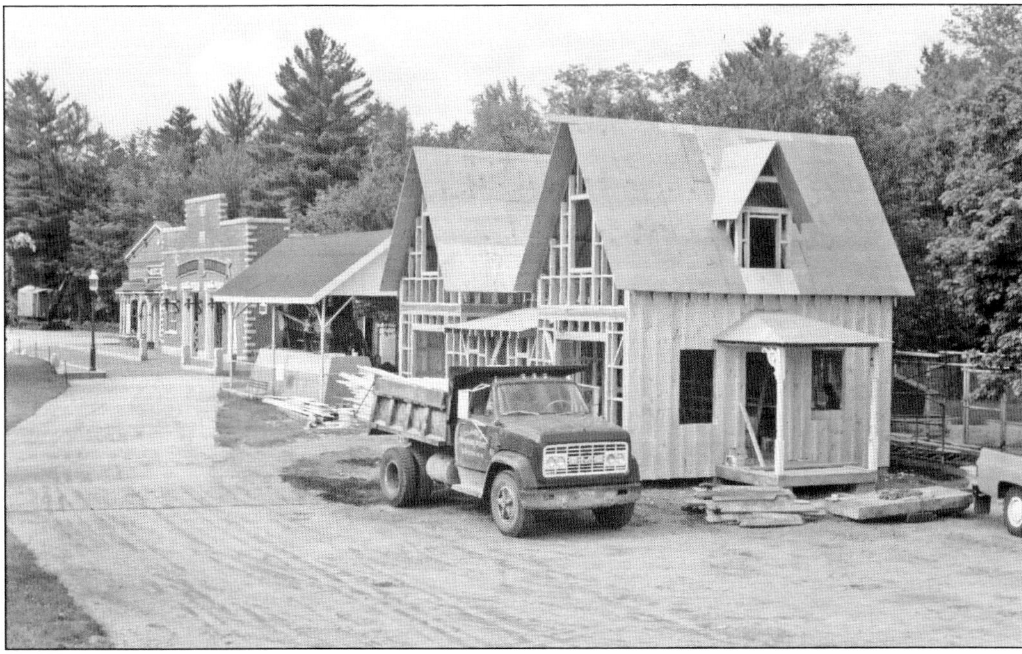

Kilburn's Photo Parlor was erected in two months during the summer of 1977. Murray did the sawing and finishing of all the wood in his sawmill across the street. On opening day, 38 pictures were taken and sold. Maureen Clark ran the photo parlor for 23 years, and Barbara Clark visited antique shops to buy vintage clothing for use in the photographs. (Photograph by Maureen S. Clark.)

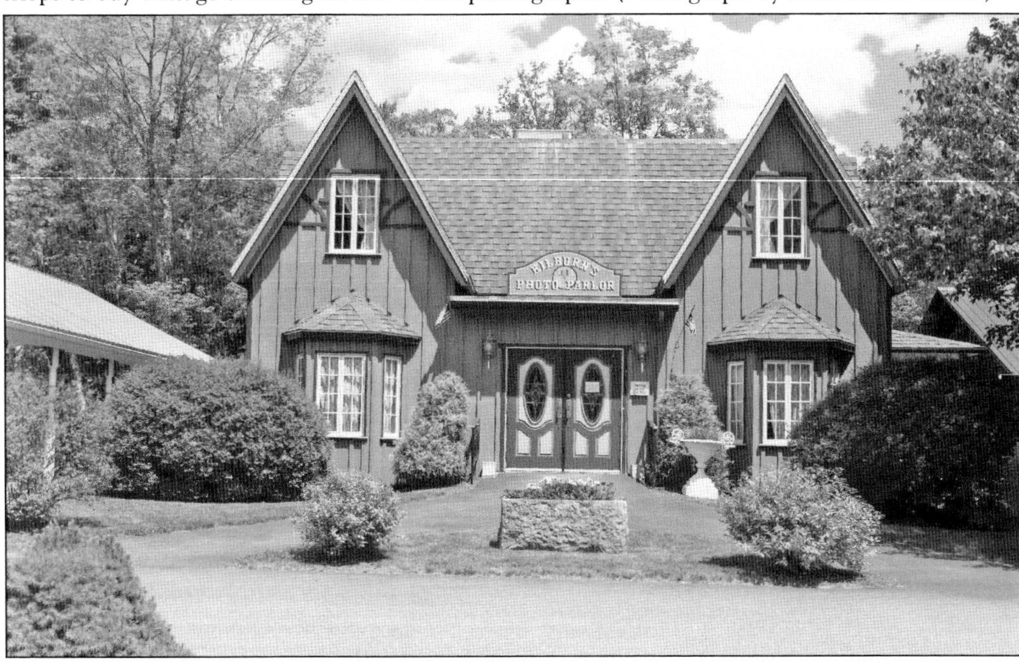

Later, Kilburn's Photo Parlor was moved back and placed on a foundation. All photographic equipment is now digital, and Andrew Clark has run the operation since 2000. "Vintage" photographs of families dressed in costume are a prized souvenir of a visit to the Trading Post. (Photograph by John K. Eisenhart.)

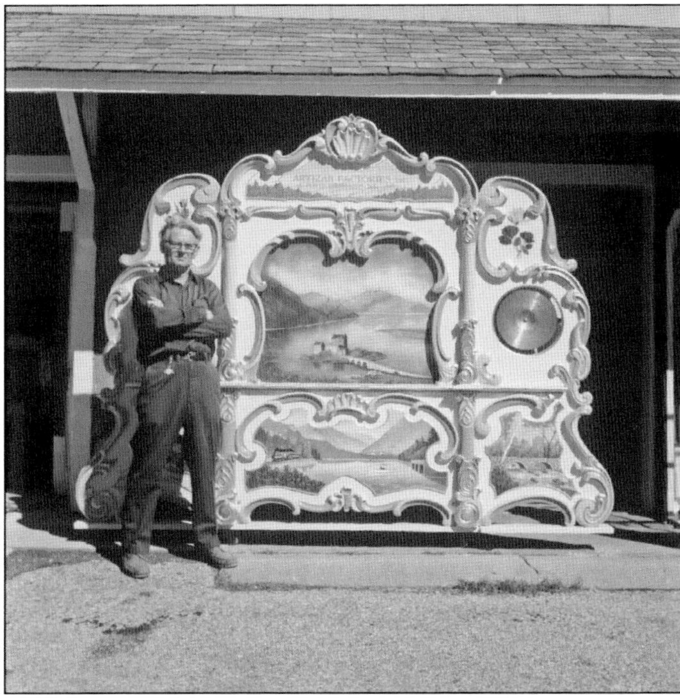

Murray Clark is seen in 1978 in front of the Artizan Band Organ he rebuilt, even making a new wooden front for it. George Thompson, a local sign painter, painted the beautiful scenes on the front. Ed used to say, "Clark's Trading Post: where you can hear the difference." He was referring to the vintage music played by the calliope and the other mechanical instruments he and Murray loved, collected, and restored. These instruments are scattered throughout the grounds and the gift shops and can still be played by guests. (Photograph by Maureen S. Clark.)

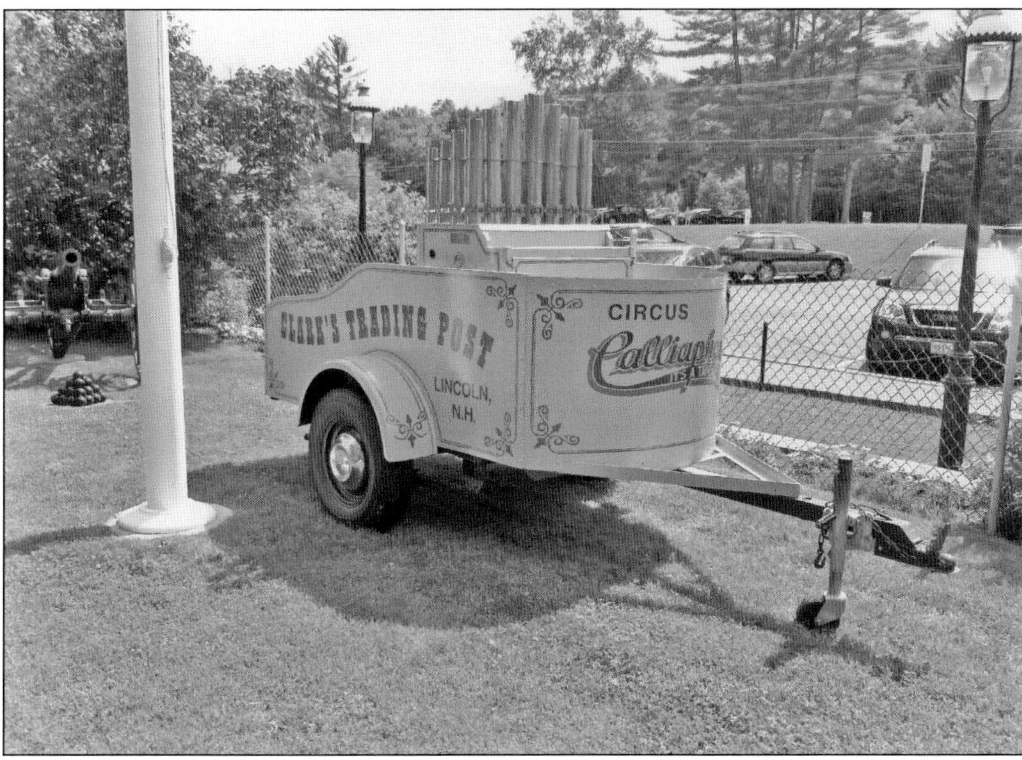

The calliope, which came originally from Coney Island, New York, resides at the train station. The music it produces is one of the best-loved sounds at the Trading Post, and people respond to the music with a spring in their step and a swing in their walk. (Photograph by John K. Eisenhart.)

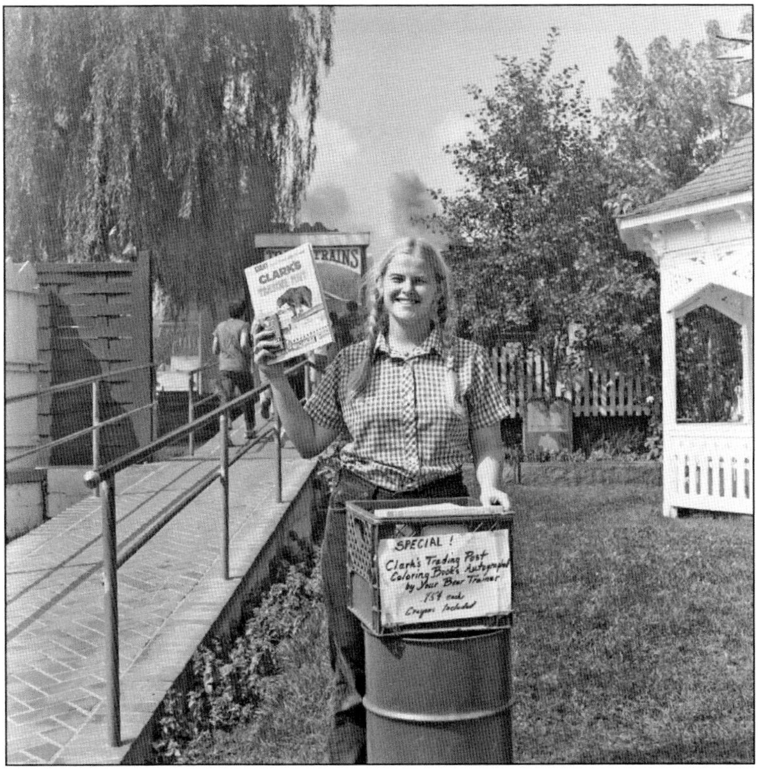

Anne Clark is seen here around 1975 selling coloring books autographed by Murray Clark, the bear trainer. Coloring books are still available at the Trading Post today. Anne was working full time during the summers giving tours in Tuttle's Rustic House by the time she was nine. (Photograph by Maureen S. Clark.)

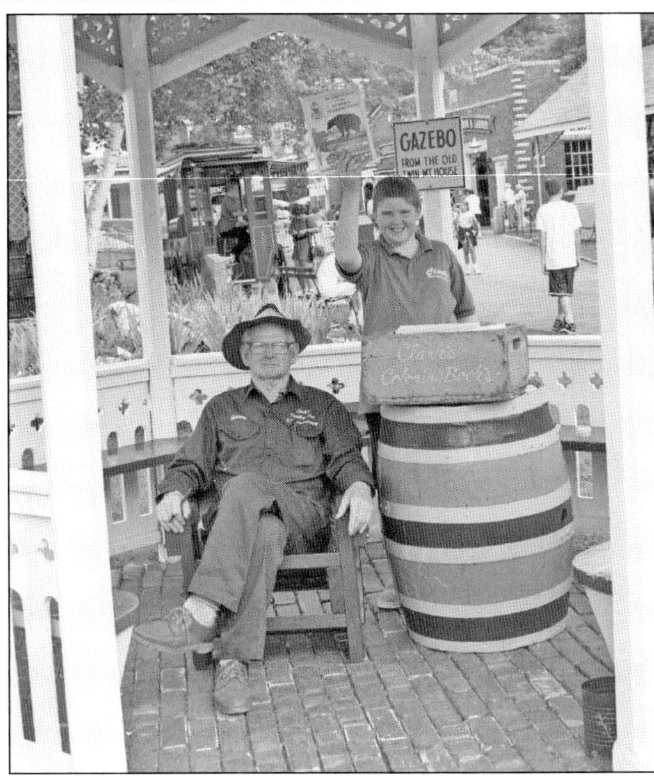

Murray (left) and grandson Iain Grant are selling coloring books in the gazebo in July 1998. Iain is the son of Nola and Callum Grant and is a fourth-generation Clark family member. Murray appears to be taking a short break from his bear show and bear training duties while making sure the younger generation stays on their toes.

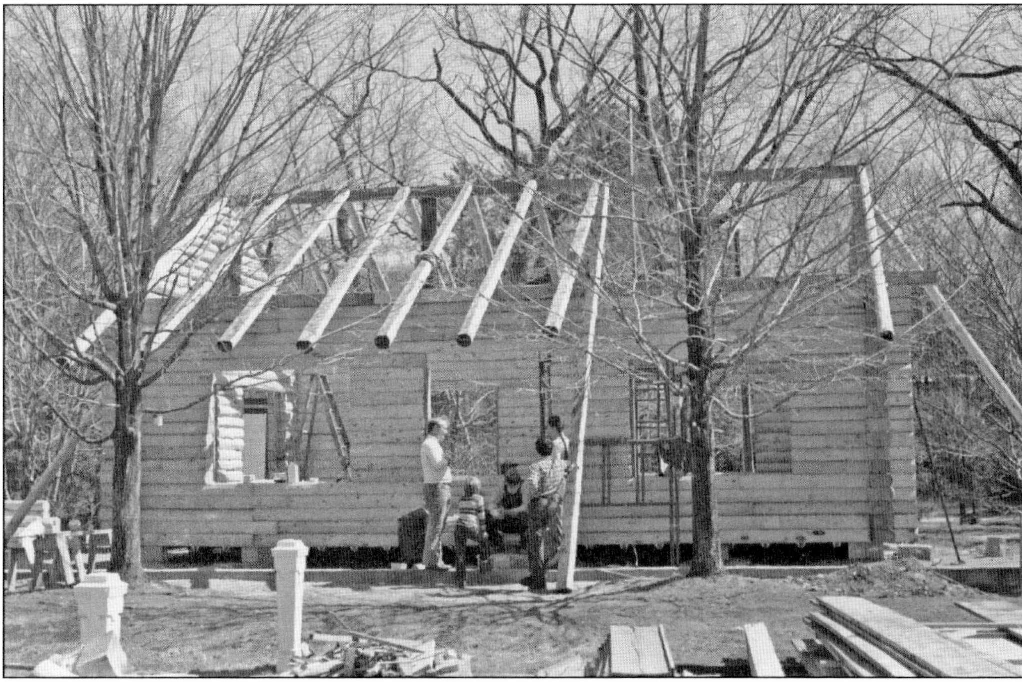

The Maple Cabin opened in July 1979. It was originally built to sell maple products including freshly made "sugar on snow" and maple candies. Before long, maple syrup became too expensive and the Maple Cabin was turned into a shop specializing in New England–made gifts. From left to right are Eddie Clark, Ben Clark, Don Showalter, Bob Henderson, and Elise Clark. (Photograph by Maureen S. Clark.)

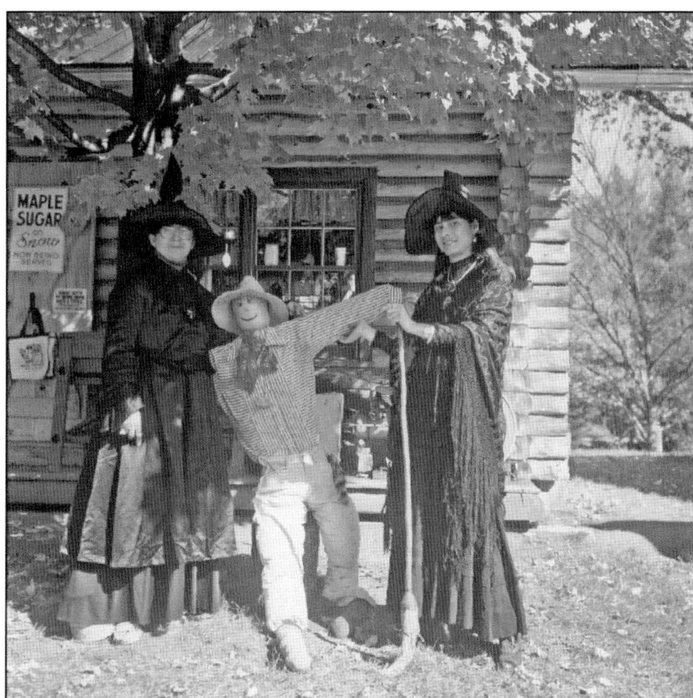

Annette Wiswall (left) and her sister Elise Clark are dressed as Halloween witches—likely to promote the sale of spiced cider kept hot on the woodstove inside the Maple Cabin. Elise Johnian married David Clark in 1975 and began her long and varied career at Clark's Trading Post. Always supportive of David's steam restoration projects, Elise has been a valuable and essential part of the success of retail operations at the Trading Post. (Photograph by Maureen S. Clark.)

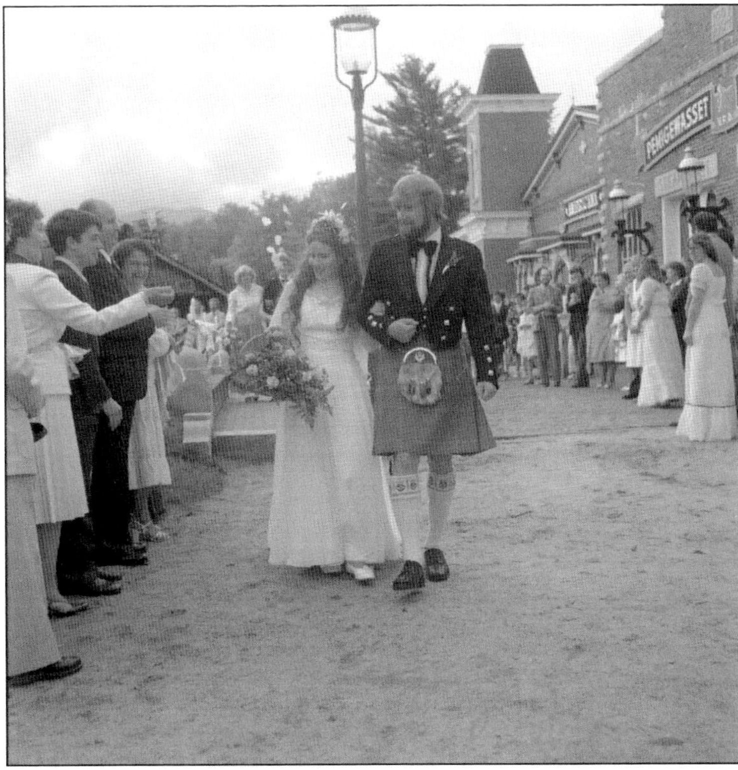

Nola Clark and Callum Grant are pictured here shortly after their wedding at the Trading Post in 1980. While they were the first couple to be married on the grounds of the Trading Post, other weddings have followed. In addition, several young couples who met while working at the Trading Post have gone on to marry, causing one Clark family member to muse, "I think we may be better at this than Match.com." (Photograph by John McIver.)

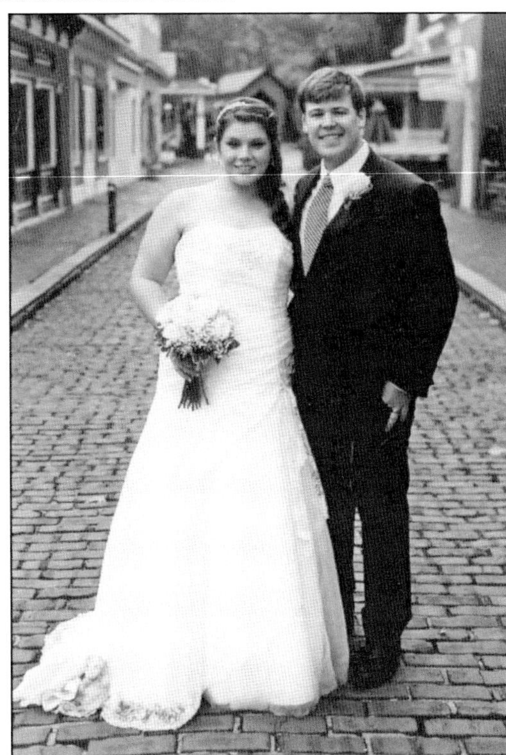

One of the more recent weddings was that of Kathryn Proulx and Christopher Englert in 2015. Guests were carried by train to the site of the wedding near the covered bridge, and Fred Englert, father of the groom, performed the ceremony. (Photograph by Mark Ducharme Photography Studio.)

Murray and Jasper are performing for a 1981 bear show. One of the most beloved tricks that Murray performed with his bears was "gargling." He would stand over the bear and drop ice cream into the bear's open mouth. No bear ever missed the ice cream. (Picture by Maureen S. Clark.)

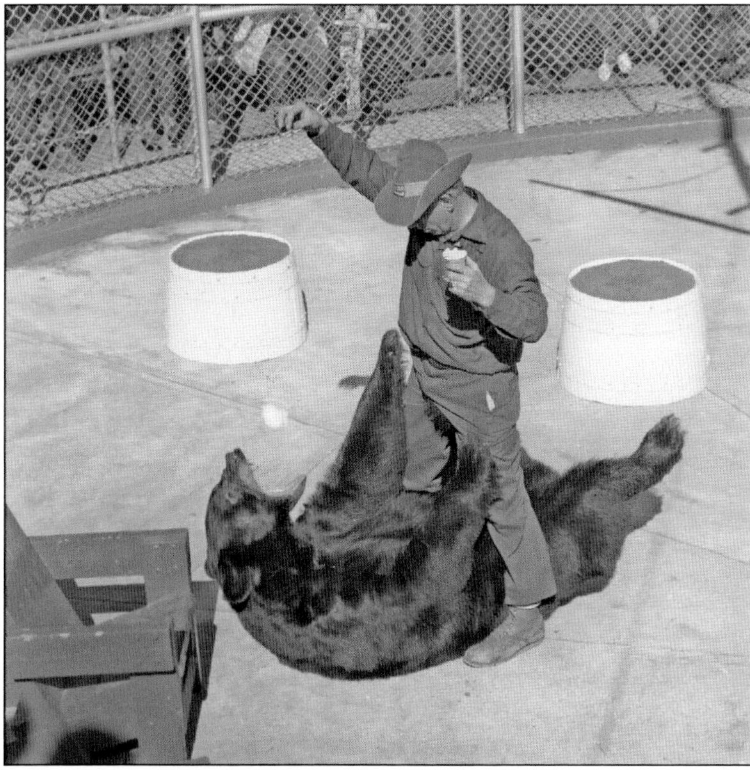

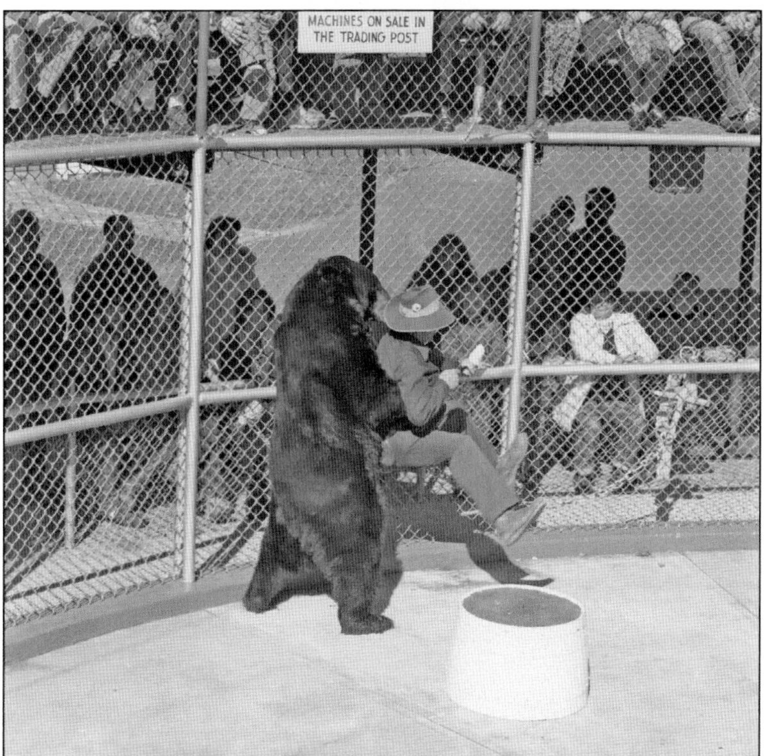

Jasper was one of the Clark family's finest show bears. There was a deep and loving bond between Murray and Jasper, with Jasper allowing Murray to sit on his tummy and tickle his feet. Jasper would respond by picking Murray up. In this 1981 photograph, Murray has likely just said, "I think I'll just go over here . . . " only to be picked up by Jasper and held in place. (Photograph by Maureen S. Clark.)

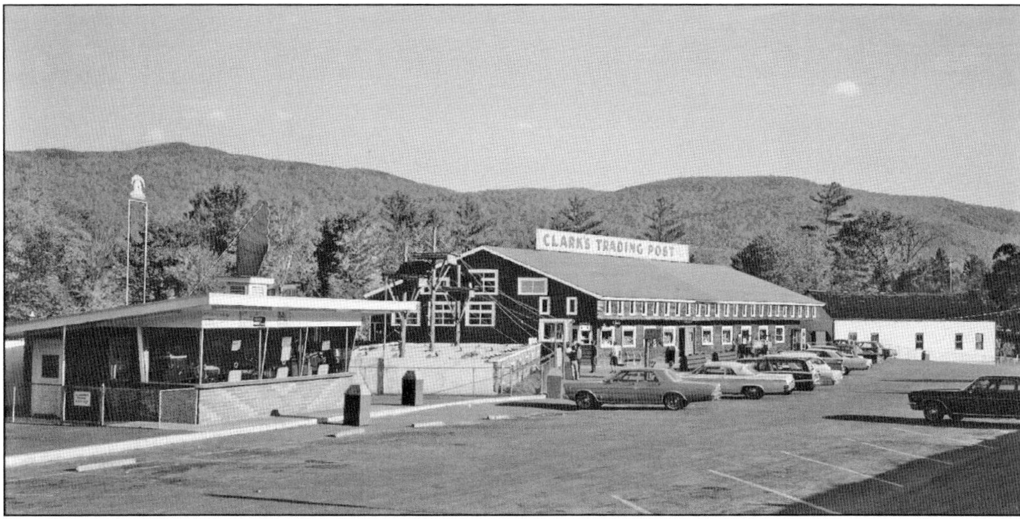

Seen here is the original Dairy Bar, built in 1962. In 1982, it was decided that a dramatic facelift was in order, one that would include raising the roof to gain more storage. (Photograph by Maureen S. Clark.)

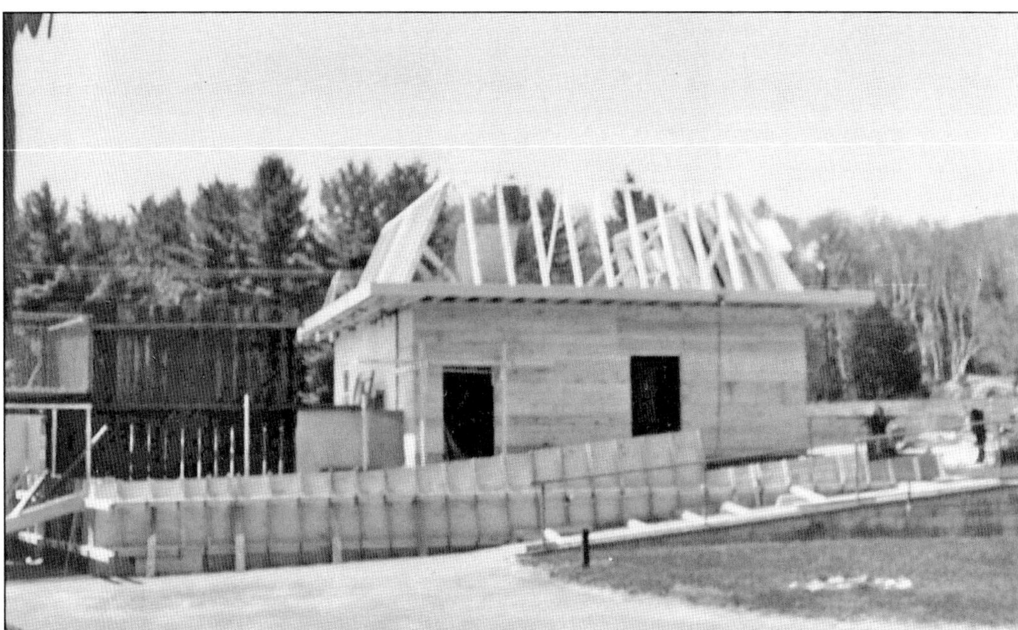

With the building stripped down and the new roof under construction, it is possible to see how much space is being added.

The work crew is taking a short break from the renovation of the Dairy Bar in June 1982. From left to right are Eddie Clark, Marcellin LaLiberte, and Fred Englert. (Photograph by Maureen S. Clark.)

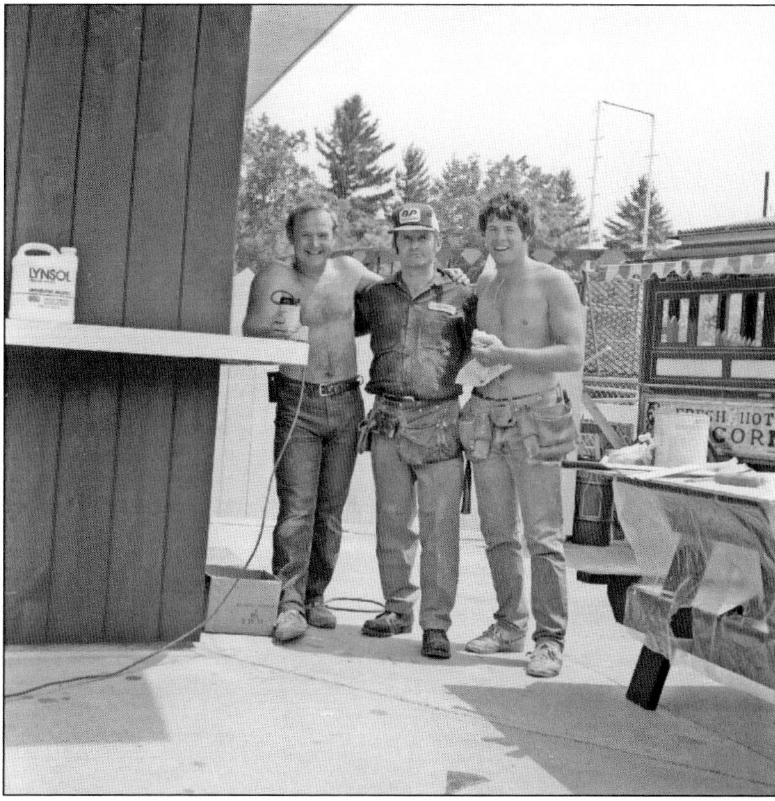

By July 7, 1982, the construction project was complete, and the renovated Dairy Bar, newly christened the Whistle Stop Snack Bar, was open for business. (Photograph by Maureen S. Clark.)

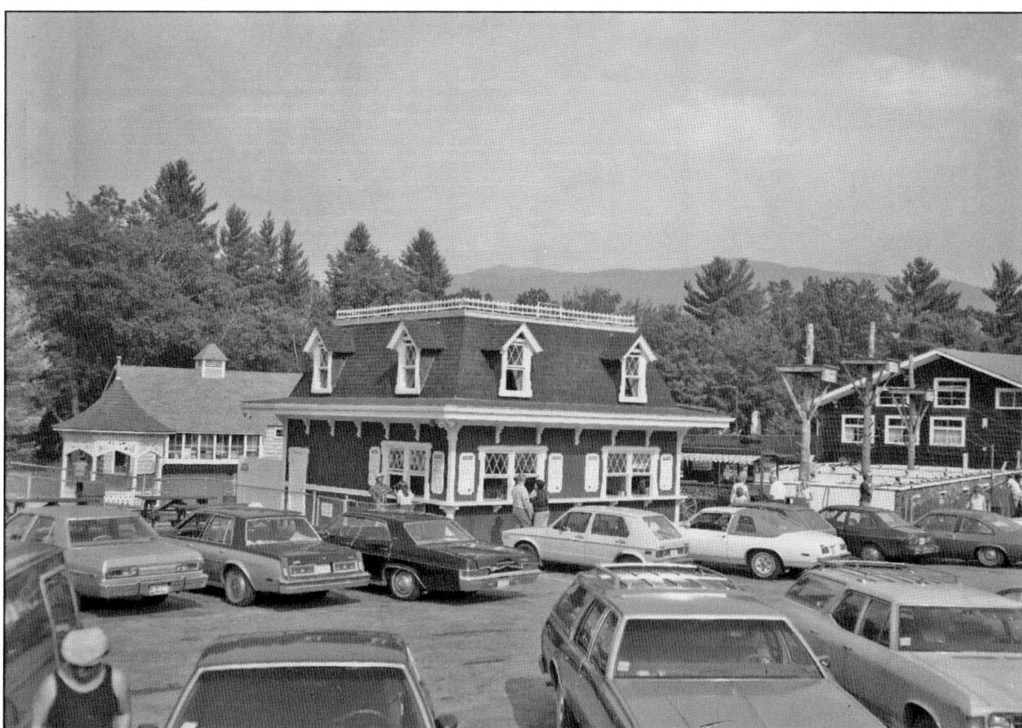

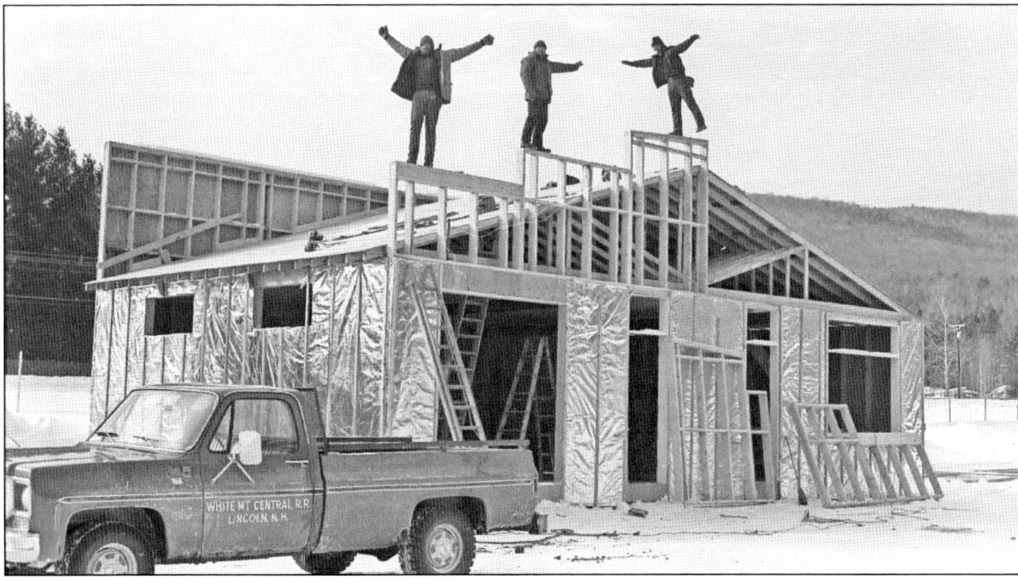

Construction of Avery's Garage began immediately after Thanksgiving 1980, and it opened the following year. It was named for Joyce and Barbara's father, Shirley Avery, who had been in the filling station business. From left to right are Leon Noel, Don Showalter, and David Clark. (Photograph by Jay Bartlett.)

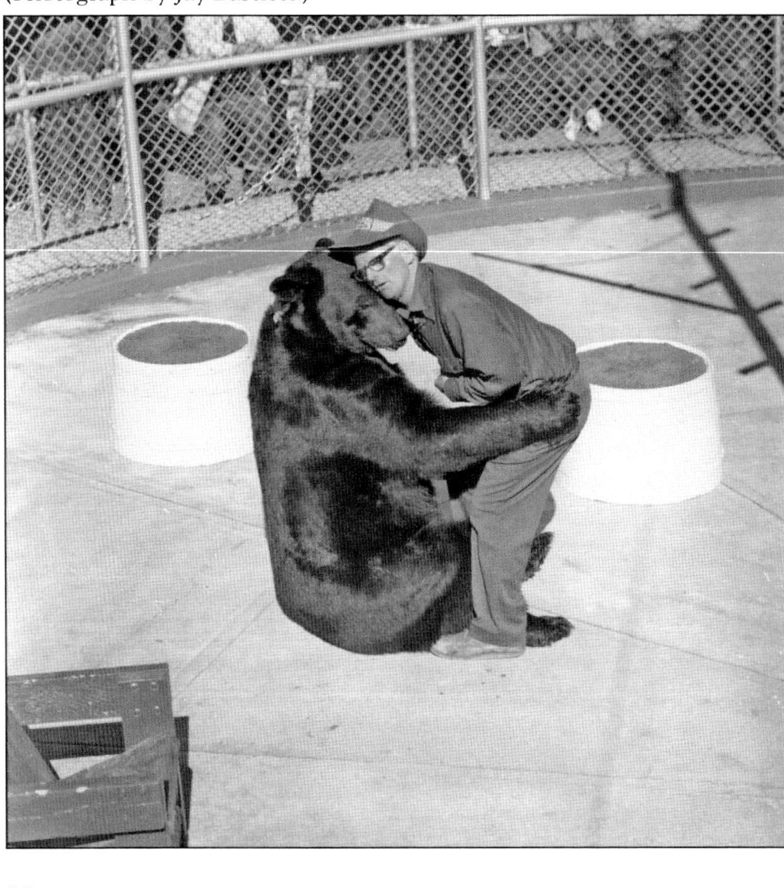

Jasper is holding Murray close for a cuddle. Murray ended many a show by asking the audience, "Well, ladies and gentlemen, what do you think of my friend Jasper? It's been my pleasure working with him all these years!" (Photograph by Maureen S. Clark.)

Andrew Clark (left) and Clark Govoni are outside the bear ring in August 1979. All the Clark family children began as bear helpers, and it was their responsibility to get an ice cream cone from the snack bar and have it ready for the bear trainer to use in the ring. Occasionally, they licked the cone "to keep it from melting." (Photograph by Maureen S. Clark.)

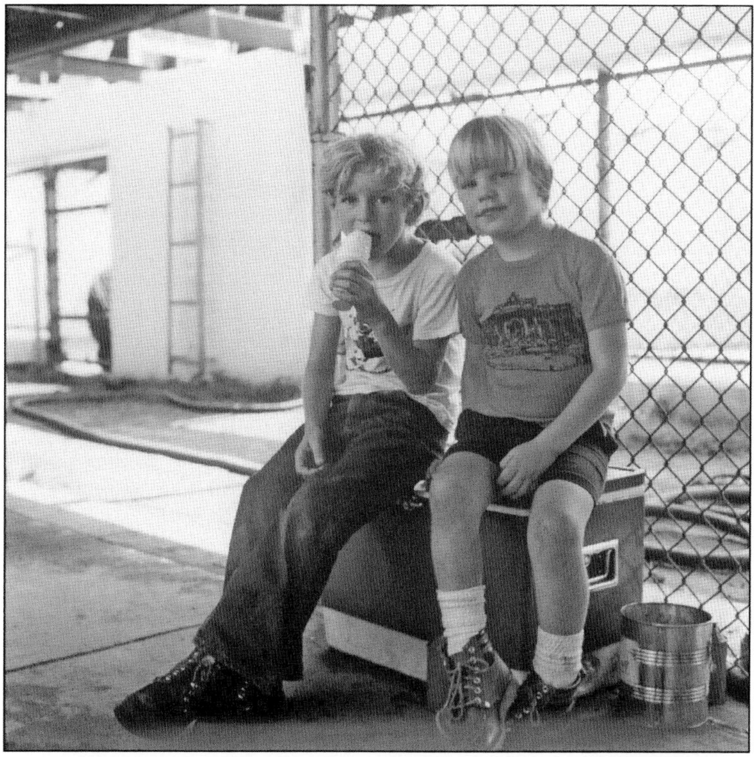

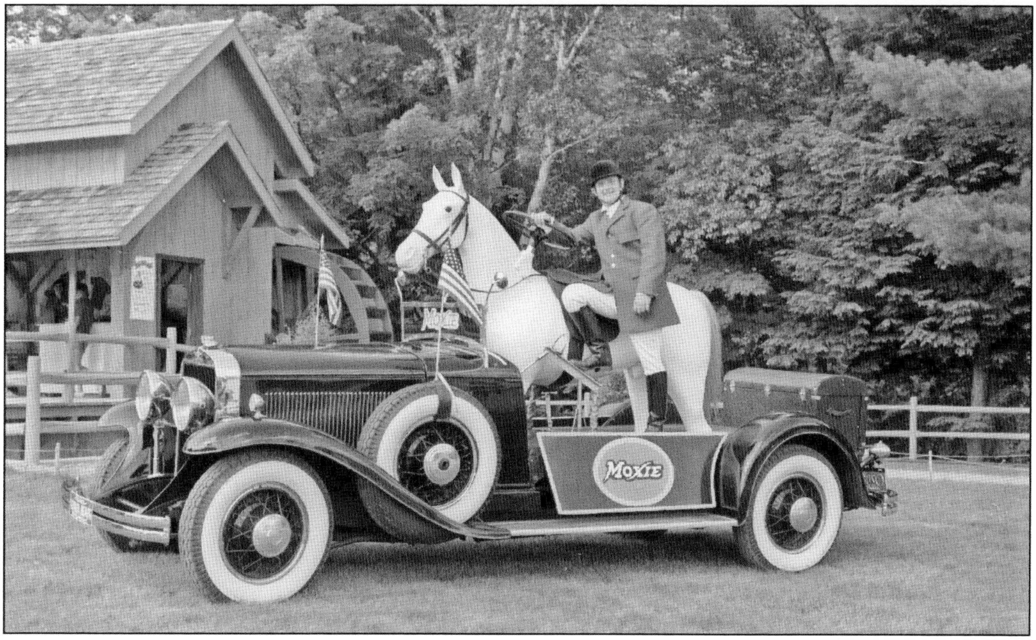

A unique advertising tool for the tonic Moxie was the Moxiemobile, a modified 1929 LaSalle automobile. The driver sat on a large model of a horse, and the vehicle was controlled by the rider with pedals where the stirrups were and a steering wheel connected through the horse. In this 1985 picture, Eddie Clark poses with the Moxiemobile, which can be seen on display in Avery's Garage. (Photograph by James W.S. Sykes.)

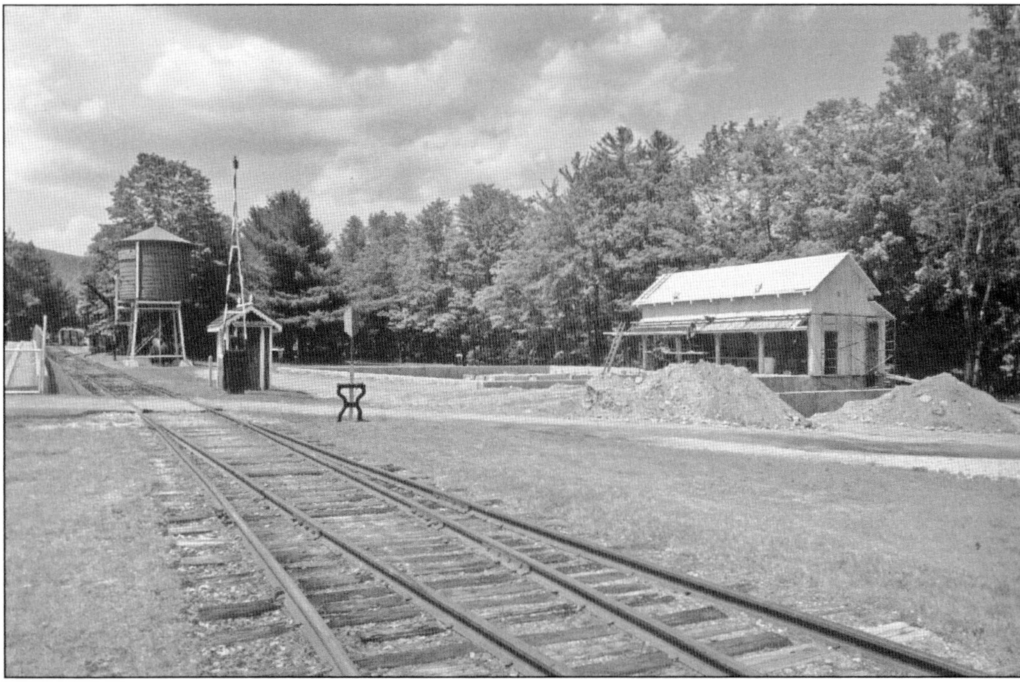

Construction of the Mill Pond Bumper Boat Ride was well underway by the spring of 1983. Originally the bumper boats were gas powered, but they have since been converted to battery power for easier maintenance. (Photograph by Maureen S. Clark.)

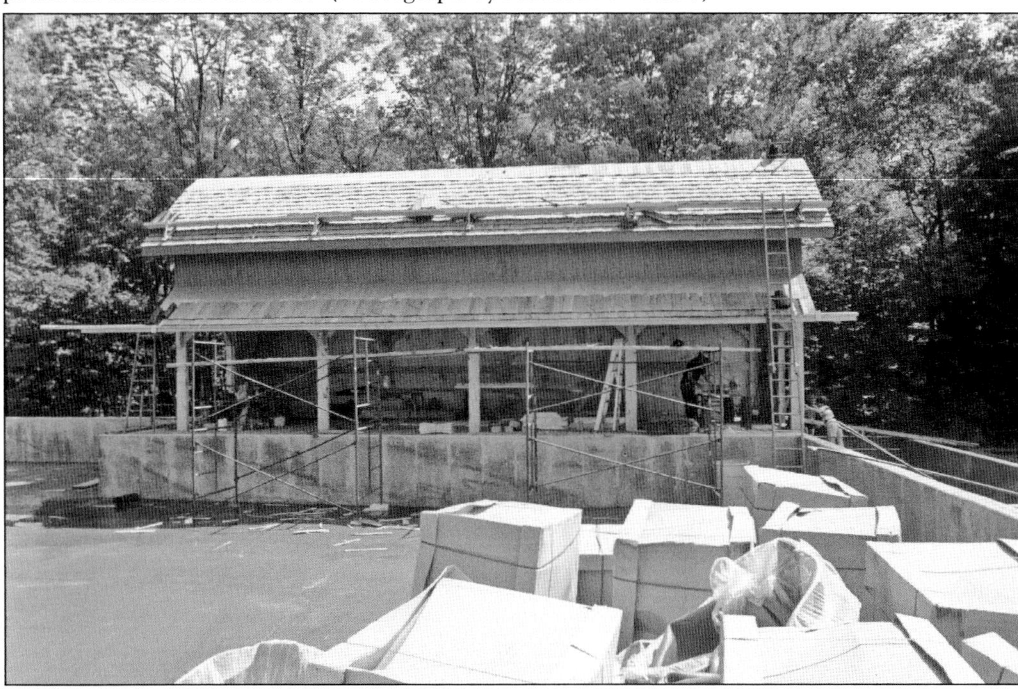

Guests are able to float around in small bumper boats on a shallow pond and spray each other with water. On a hot sunny day, the attraction provides an opportunity to cool off. (Photograph by Maureen S. Clark.)

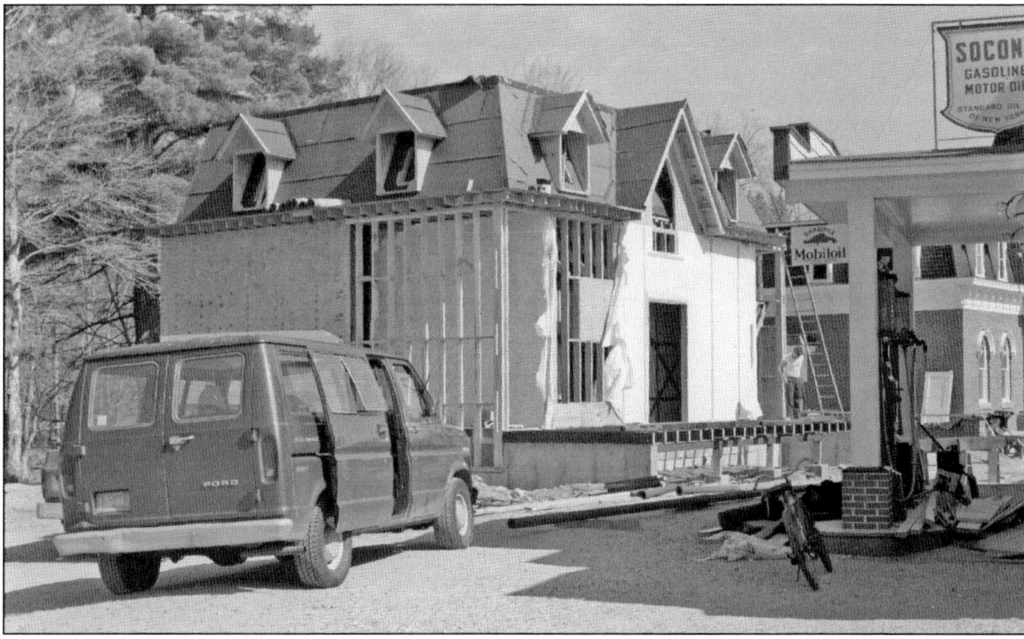

Merlin's Mystical Mansion, seen here under construction, opened in time for the 1986 season. Visitors are greeted on the porch and given the "history" of what they are about to experience. They are told that the building is constructed upon a unique "gravity point" on the Trading Post grounds and that they will meet Merlin's apprentice and witness magical powers firsthand. They are also warned that if they suffer from claustrophobia, motion sickness, or epilepsy, are afraid of the dark, or are just plain "scaredy cats," they should not enter. (Photograph by Maureen S. Clark.)

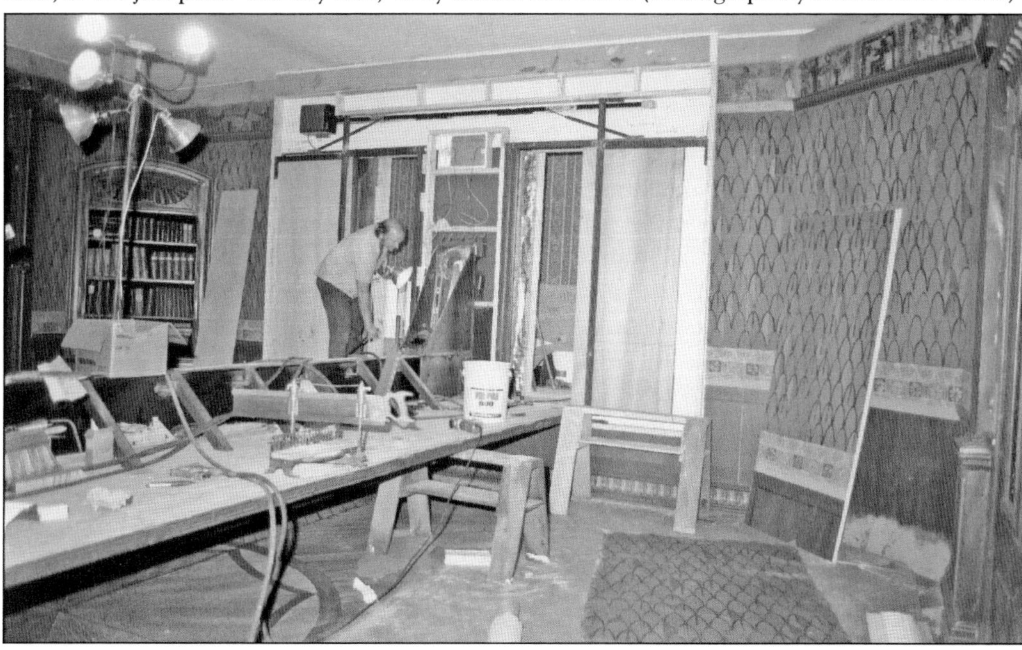

David Clark is working on the interior of Merlin's Mystical Mansion. Once inside, guests are seated in what appears to be a room in Merlin's house. A set designer from New York City was hired to help create this attraction. (Photograph by Maureen S. Clark.)

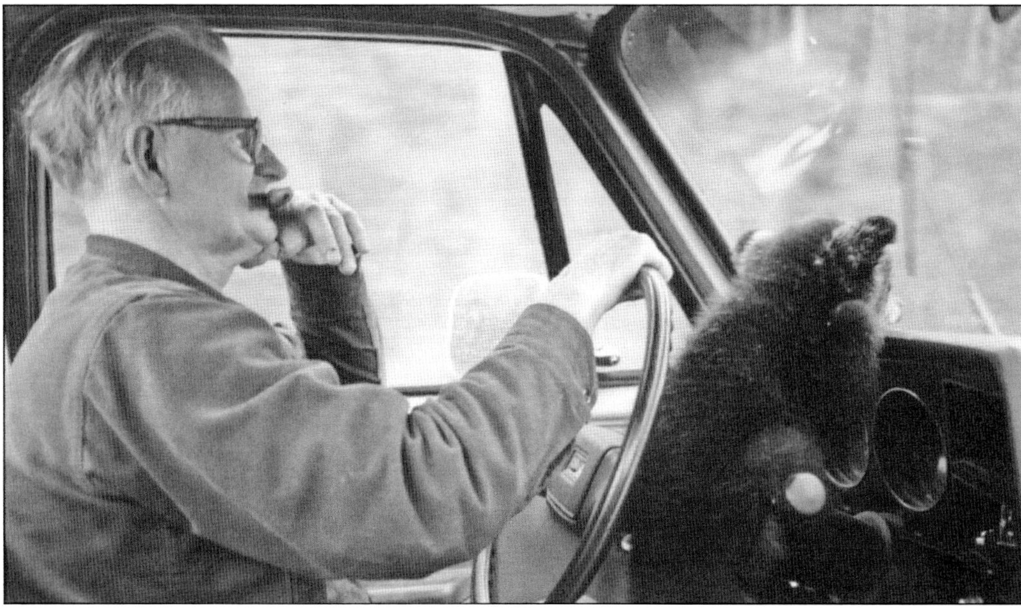

In 1985, a woman in northern Vermont asked if the Trading Post would adopt a bear cub that kept coming to her from the woods. The Clarks agreed, and Murray and Maureen Clark drove to Vermont to pick her up. Starving, she weighed only five pounds, even though she was approximately four months old. She had lungworms, pneumonia, and a birth defect of her mucus membrane, and it is likely that her mother had abandoned her. She is seen here on the trip home from Vermont. (Photograph by Maureen S. Clark.)

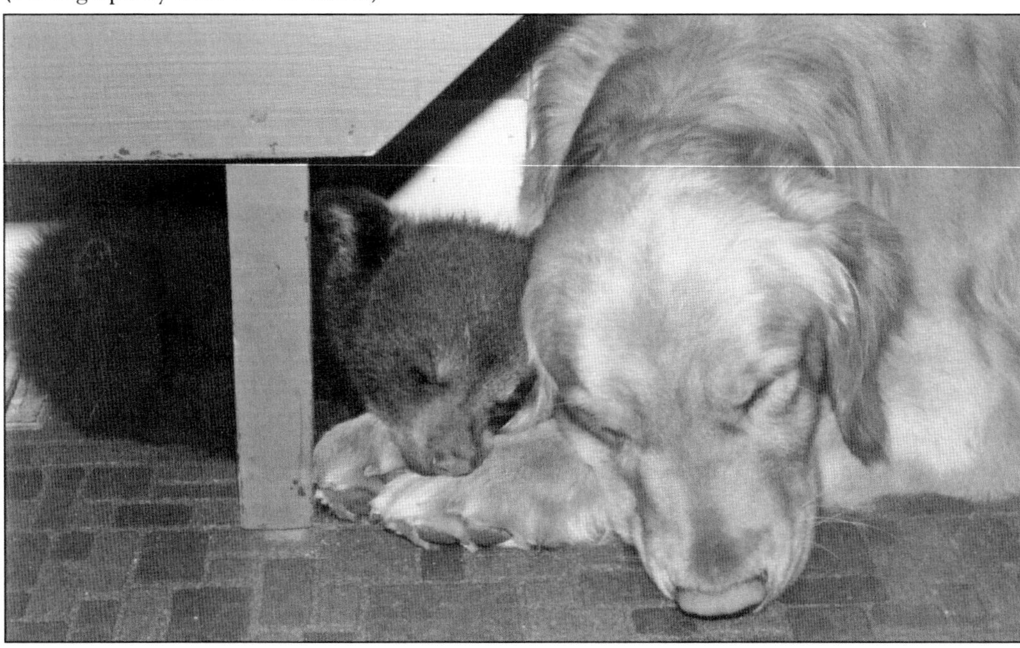

Naming the cub Moxie, the family took her into their home, and everyone took turns staying with her around the clock. Moxie needed to be with a bear, a human, or the dog at all times. Rhuardh (Rhua), a golden retriever belonging to Nola and Callum Grant, proved to be a wonderful cub sitter.

Moxie's veterinarian told the family not to get too attached to her, because it was likely she would not survive. Moxie was a finicky eater; helping her gain weight was difficult, and since the Clarks use food as a reward, training was a challenge. In this picture, Barbara Clark is feeding Moxie oatmeal at the kitchen table—a normal morning occurrence.

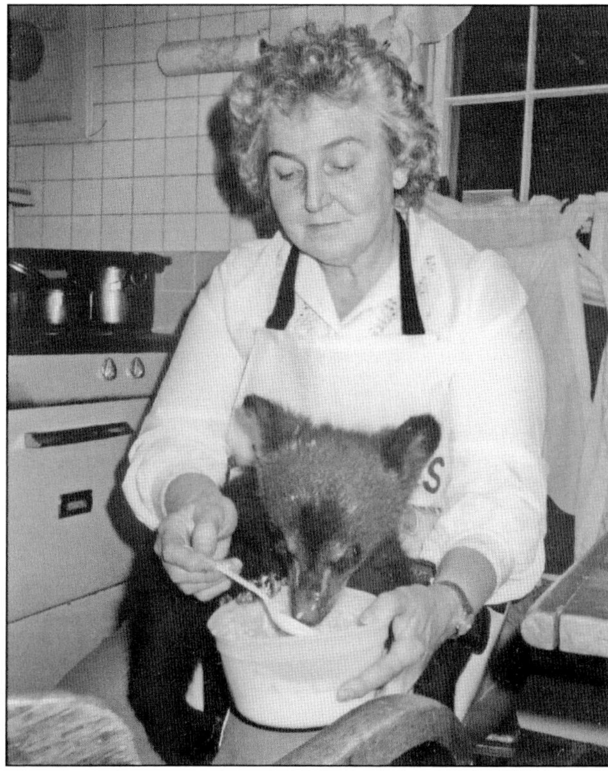

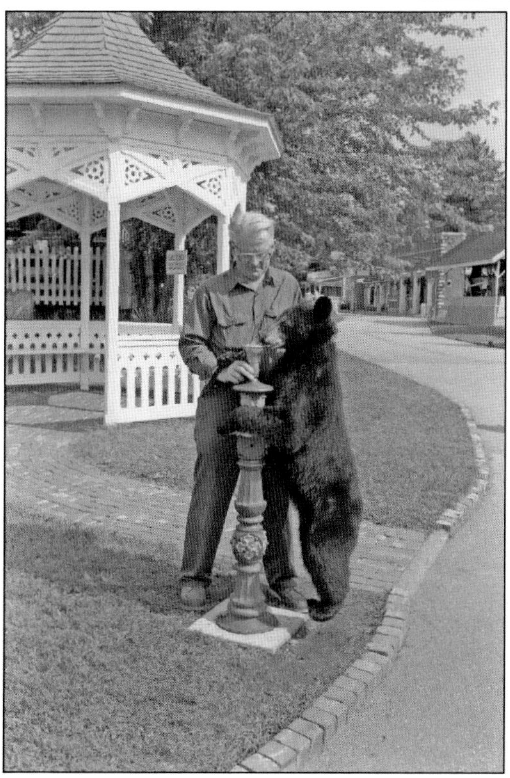

Under the Clarks' care, Moxie survived, thrived, and learned to perform in the ring as Maureen taught the cub a few simple tricks. Here she is seen with Murray at a water fountain near the gazebo. (Photograph by Maureen S. Clark.)

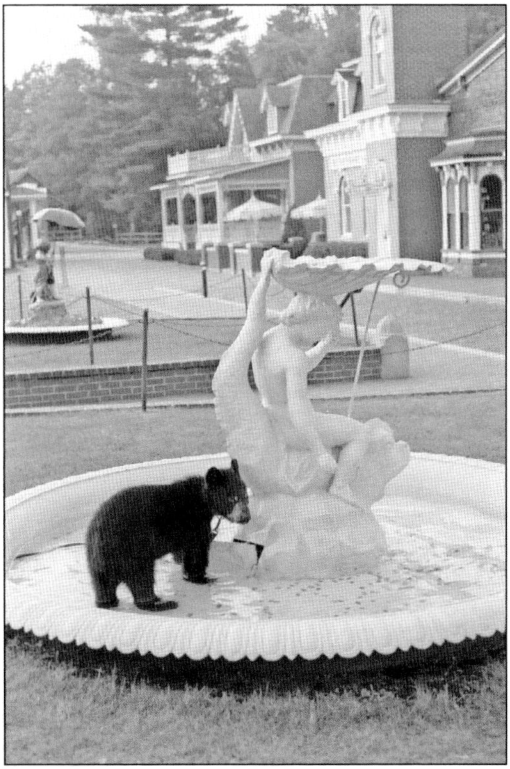

The bear cub in the fountain is Victoria. The dolphin fountain and the statue of Mercury (or Hermes) came from a 1971 auction of the New Hampshire estate of Denman Thompson, a notable actor and playwright in the late 1800s. The granite block on which Hermes now rests was a stagecoach stepping stone from the Profile House Hotel in Franconia, New Hampshire, one of the grand hotels in the White Mountains. The hotel burned to the ground in 1923, and a crack is visible in the granite block caused by the intense heat of the fire.

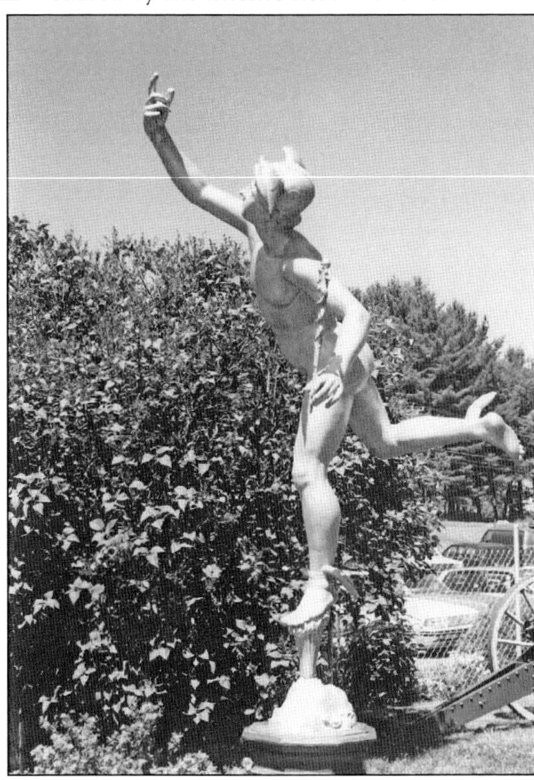

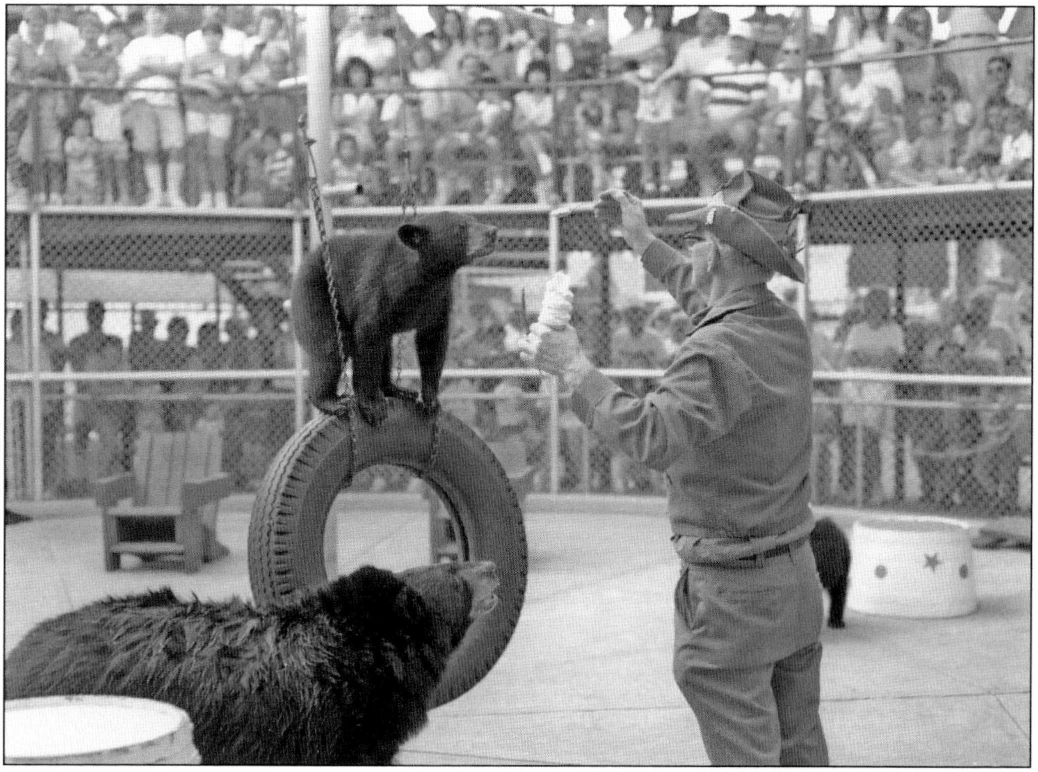

Murray appears in the ring in 1987 with Ursula on the tire swing. Pearl is looking on from the left, and Onyx is behind Murray to the right. Two years after Moxie arrived, Jasper and Pearl, after many years together, produced twins. The cubs, named Ursula and Onyx, were grandchildren of Ebony and represented the third generation of show bears performing at the Trading Post. Murray Clark used to say, "Bear cubs have little rounded ears, dark beady eyes, needle-sharp teeth and claws—and the shortest tempers on record." (Photograph by Maureen S. Clark.)

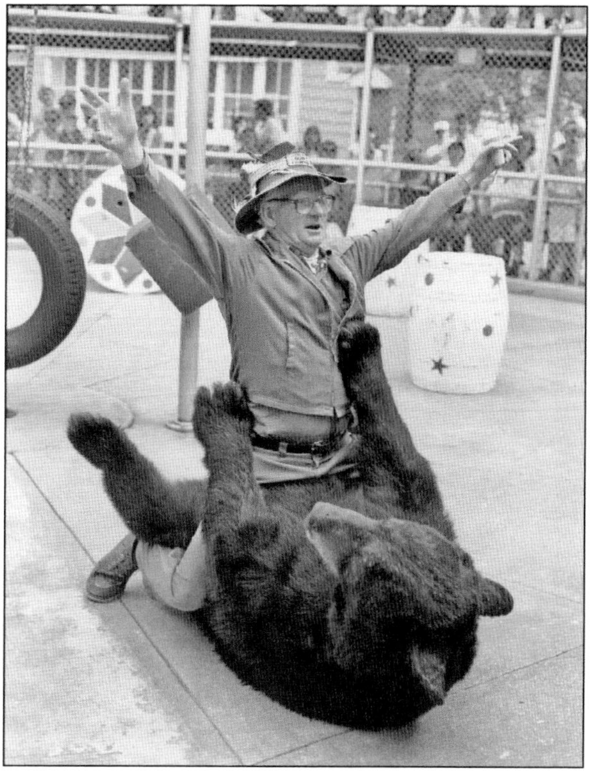

Murray is astride Jasper in this 1987 bear show. "I rub his chest and he becomes helpless . . . and makes a nice rocking chair" was a line he used in many a bear show. (Photograph by Maureen S. Clark.)

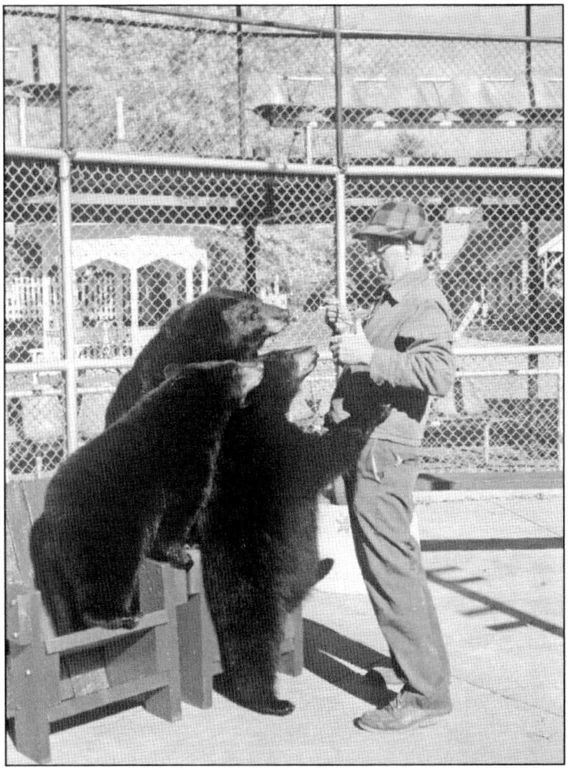

Murray Clark is seen here working with three bears simultaneously in a family portrait from 1987. On the left is Ursula; Pearl, her mother, is seated next to her; and Onyx, her brother, has his paw on Murray's coat. Pearl had been performing for years, and helped with training the cubs, straightening them out when needed.

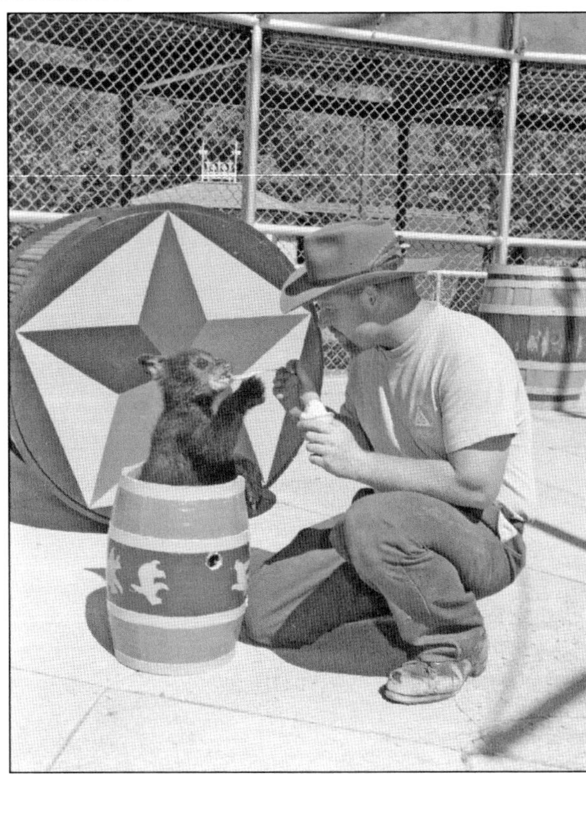

In this photograph, Murray Avery Clark is working with Nita, getting her accustomed to the bear ring and the props.

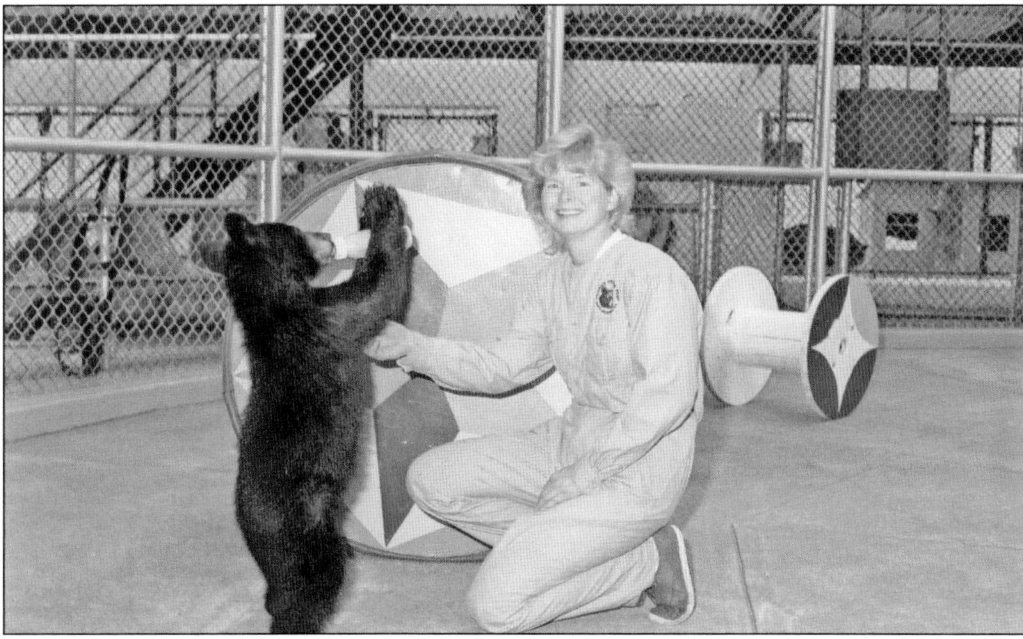

Victoria, the cub in this photograph with Maureen Clark, was a gift to Maureen from the famous bear trainer Albert Rix. While Maureen had been training the bears since the arrival of Moxie, she began doing bear shows in 1988, working with Ursula, Onyx, Pearl, and Saphire. (Photograph by James W.S. Sykes.)

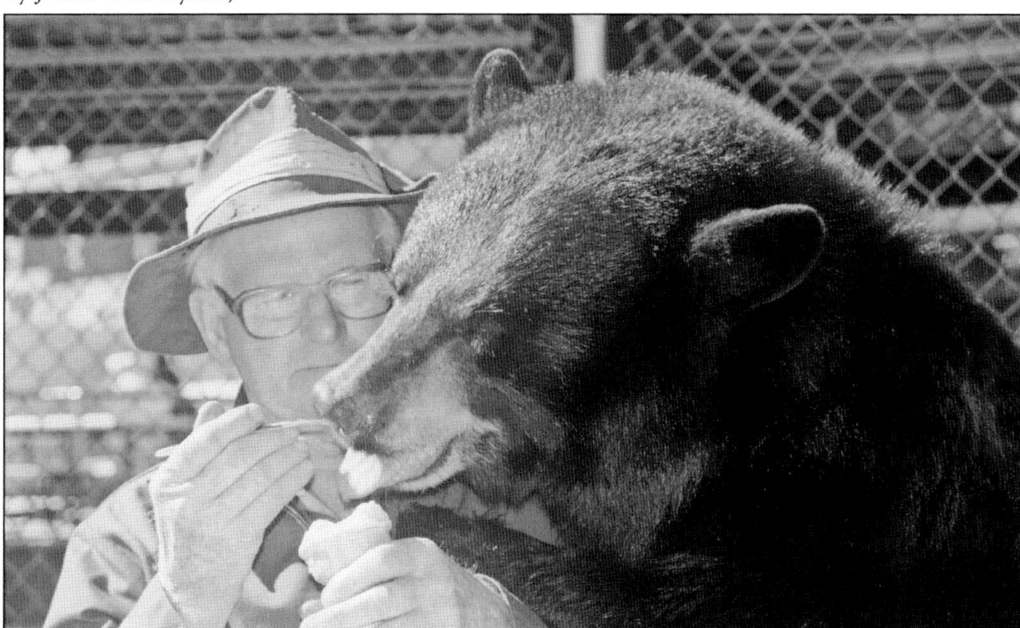

Murray is seen posing in the ring with a grown-up Victoria. Maureen's uncle Ed Clark said, "Maureen has made a breakthrough I never made. From the time they are cubs, they are with her all of the time, and they wouldn't think of harming her. Maureen is always there and spends hours with them. In my day, we were not with the bears all day. We had too many other things to do." (Photograph by Maureen S. Clark.)

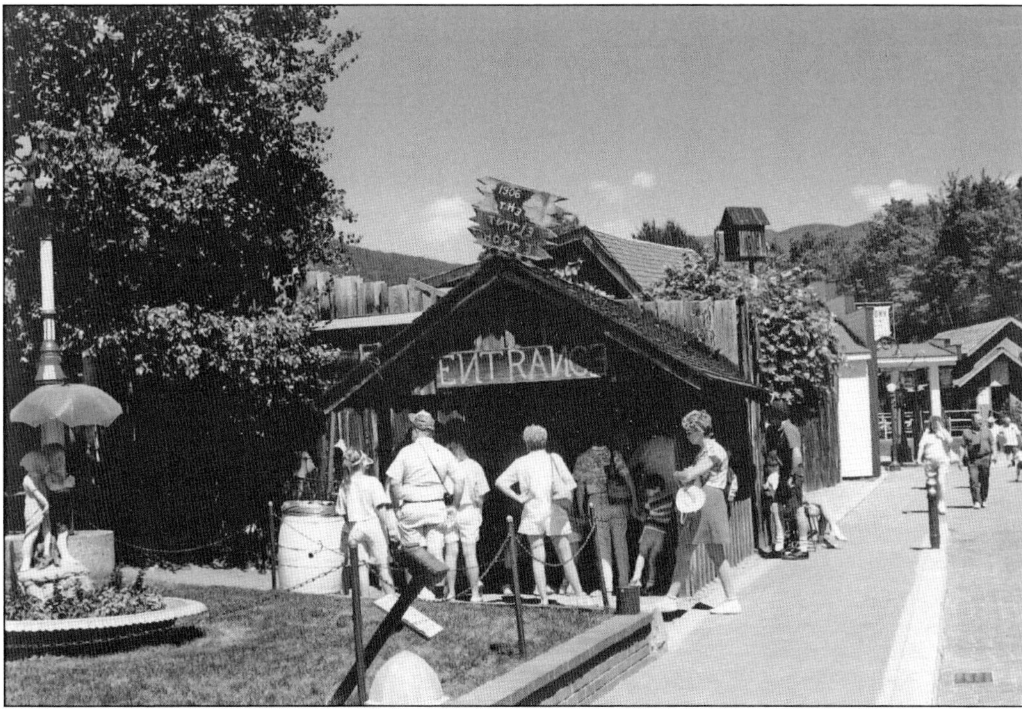

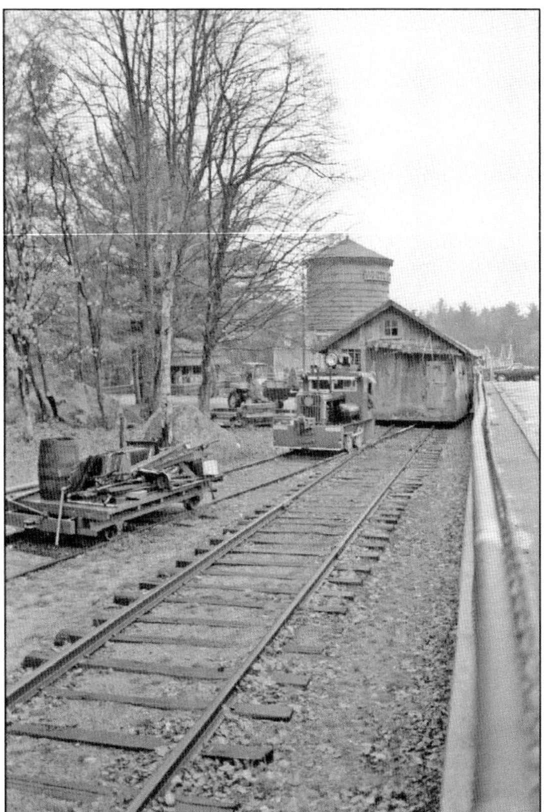

Tuttle's Rustic House opened to the public in 1970 and is seen here in its original location, where Pullman's Lunch is now located. The building was set on an angle and the floor was pitched in two directions, creating a gravity-defying experience. The name was a reference to the original owners of the property Florence and Edward Clark purchased when they settled in Lincoln.

In preparation for building the Pullman Block, it was necessary to move Tuttle's Rustic House. It was shifted onto the railroad tracks, which had been liberally greased, and pulled by the Vulcan to a new location north of the Mill Pond Bumper Boats. (Photograph by Maureen S. Clark.)

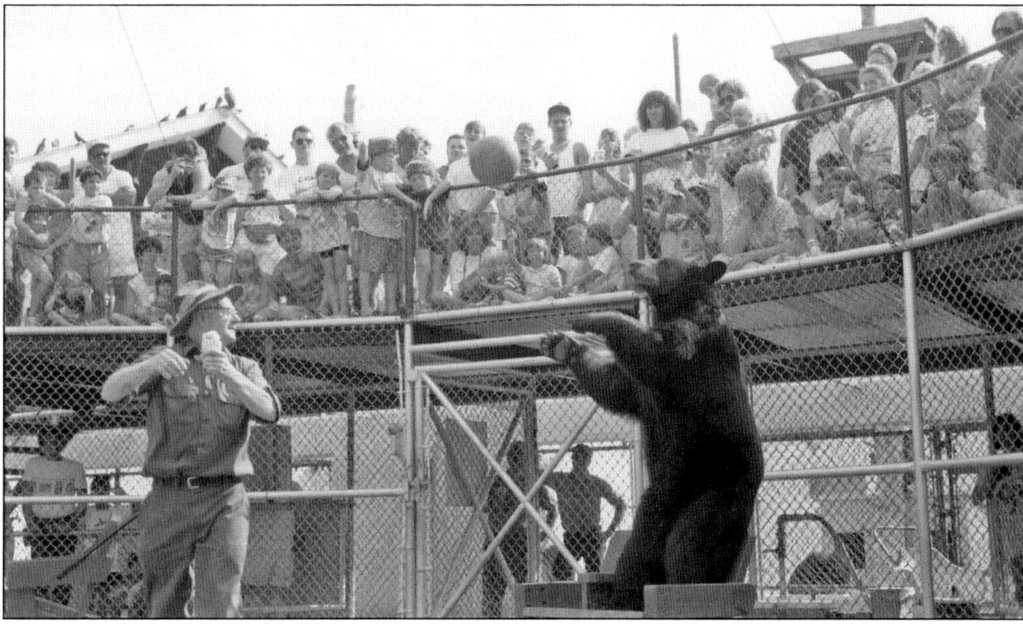

In this August 1992 photograph, Onyx prepares to catch the "bearsketball" thrown by his trainer, Murray. Onyx, like his father, Jasper, was an outstanding show bear. During every show, Murray would say, "We make you one promise: the bears are going to have a good time. We will see to it." And they did. It is something the family takes very seriously and is as true today as it was then. (Photograph by Maureen S. Clark.)

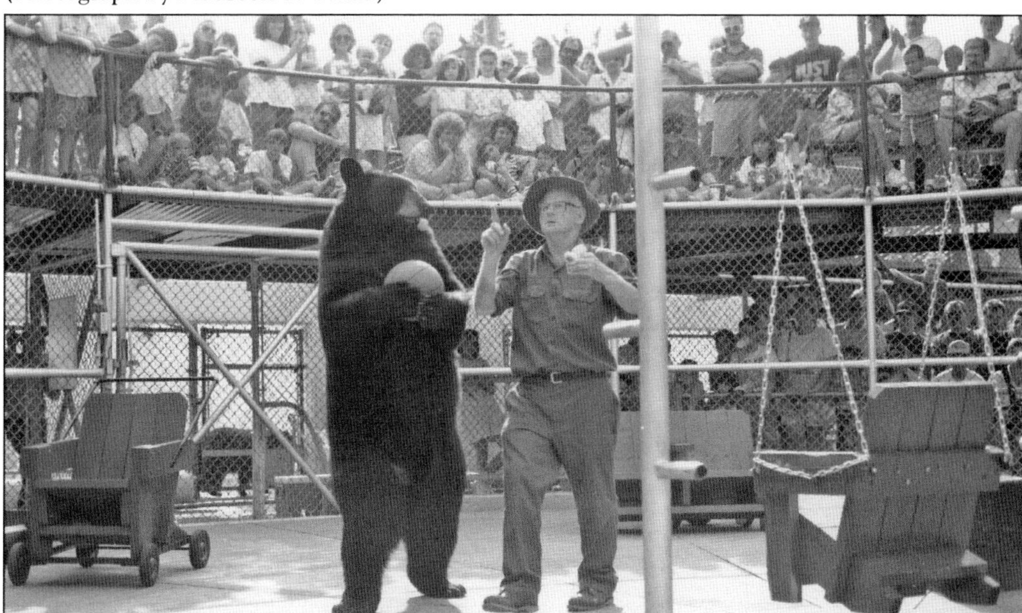

Every performance is a bit of an adventure; any number of things can affect the bears' performance—the audience, a sudden noise, "wedding season," even cooler weather signaling the approach of hibernation. The bear trainer must be alert to these factors and ready to change direction on the fly. In this photograph, Onyx holds his bearsketball and is ready to make a run for the bearsketball hoop when Murray tells him to go. (Photograph by Maureen S. Clark.)

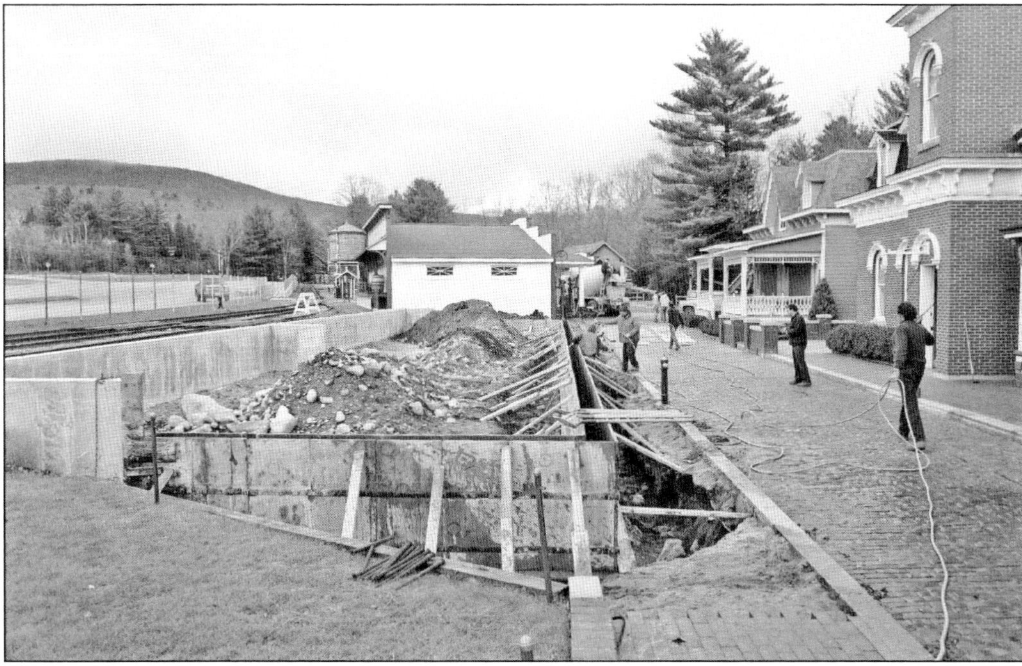

The footings were poured for the Pullman Block in 1990. Once Tuttle's Rustic House had been moved, construction began on Pullman's Lunch (named for Eleanor Pullman Clark, Edward P. Clark's mother), the You Name It Emporium, and the Candle Shop. (Photograph by Maureen S. Clark.)

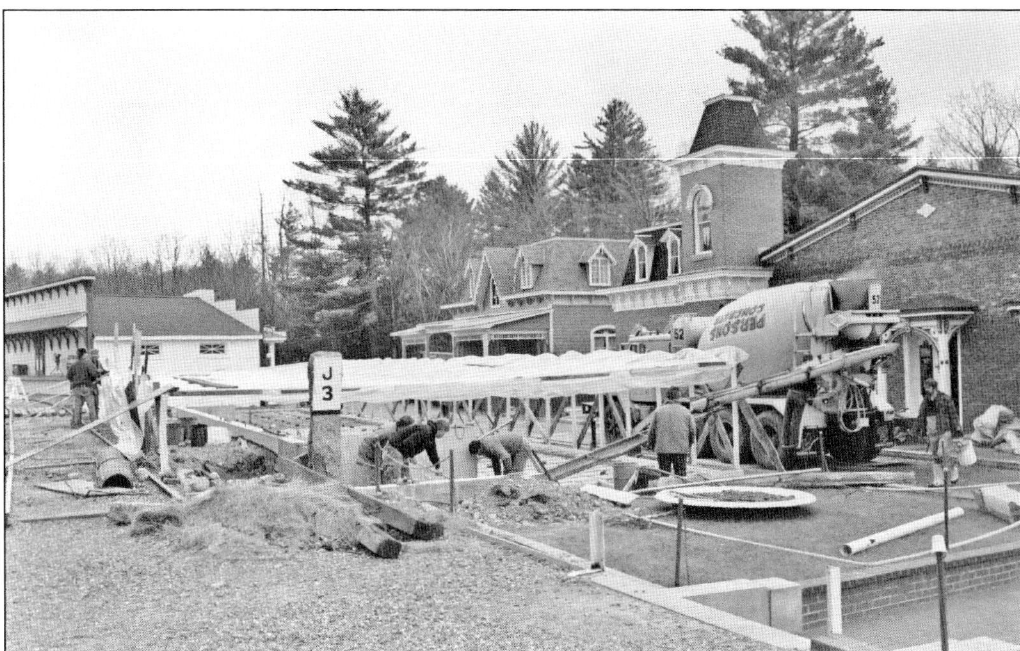

Here, the crew is preparing to pour the slab foundation for the Pullman Block. Avery's Garage can be seen at top left, and Merlin's Mystical Mansion, the Peppermint Saloon, and the Americana Museum are visible across Main Street. (Photograph by Maureen S. Clark.)

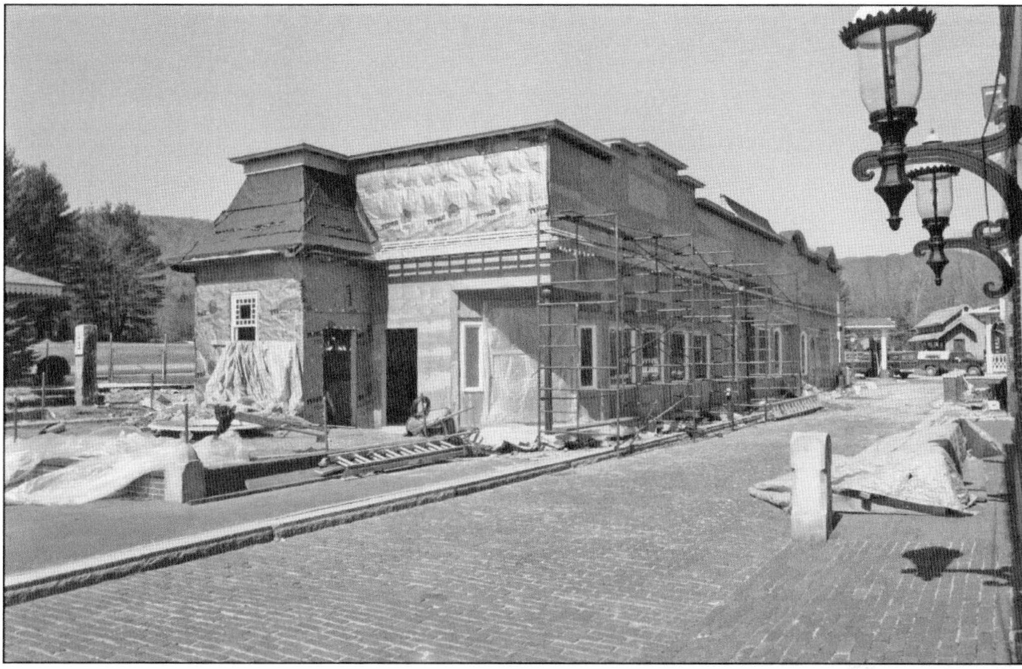

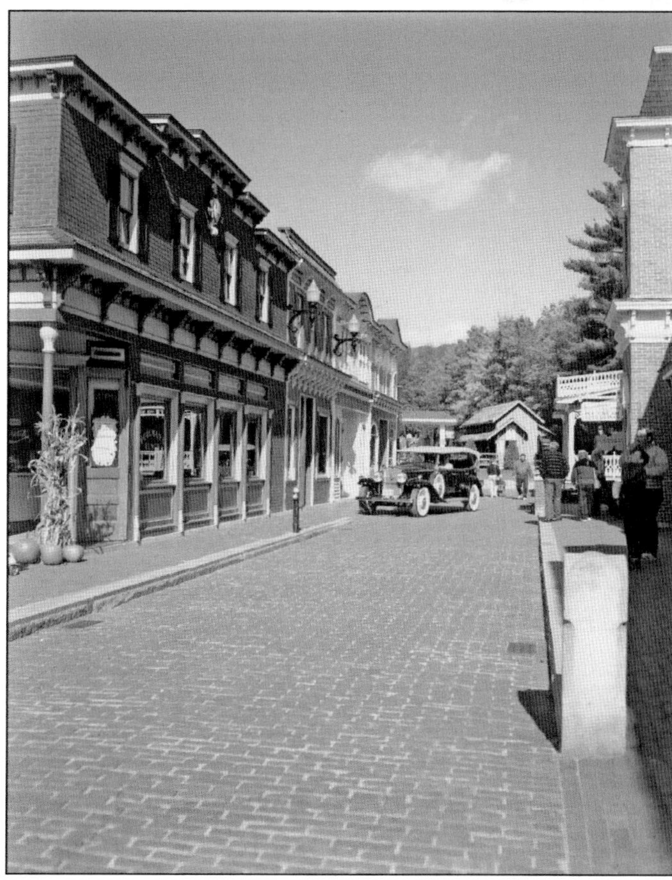

With increased attendance, a second food service facility was needed. This new construction, designed and overseen by Fred Englert, offered the chance to include new specialty shops. Fred took the opportunity to incorporate many architectural components previously salvaged by the family. (Photograph by Maureen S. Clark.)

Main Street is seen here with the completed Pullman Block on the left. The Clarks' LaSalle automobile is in the center of the street.

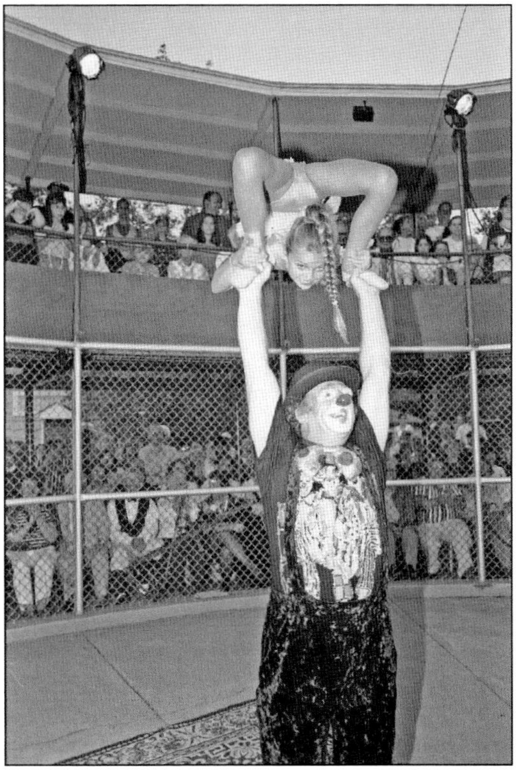

Eugene Shvartsman holds his daughter, Vicky, above his head as part of the original circus act. The circus acts began in 1998 as a special, two-week 70th anniversary celebration. The circus acts proved so popular that each year since, the Clarks have presented a show featuring accomplished circus artists from around the world.

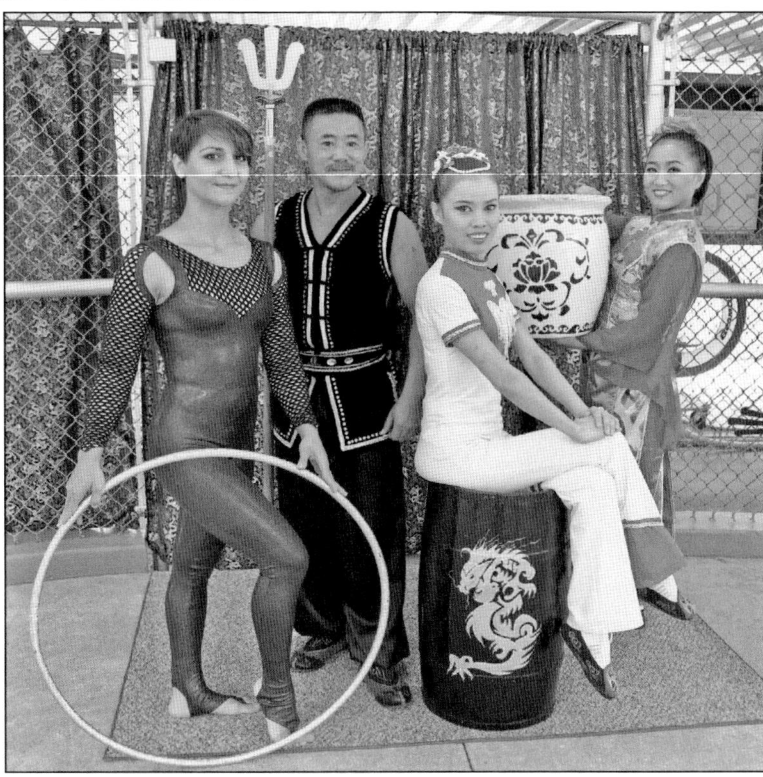

Over the years, the circus acts have been varied, but all have been popular and well received. A recent set of circus acts featured (from left to right) Arevik Seyranyan, seen here posing with her "Hurricane Hula Hoop," alongside the principals of the Yandong Chinese Acrobats: Yandong Wu (with trident), YaTing Li (perched on barrel), and Jingxia Xue (holding large pot).

When Onyx performed, he and Maureen Clark would walk into the ring together. It was an opportunity for the audience to see how tall he was. At maturity, Onyx towered over Maureen at a height of six feet, 10 inches. Onyx was a gentle giant beloved by audiences. As with the other show bears, he is buried at the Trading Post. His tombstone is inscribed "The Gentleman Bear." (Photograph by Bob Henderson.)

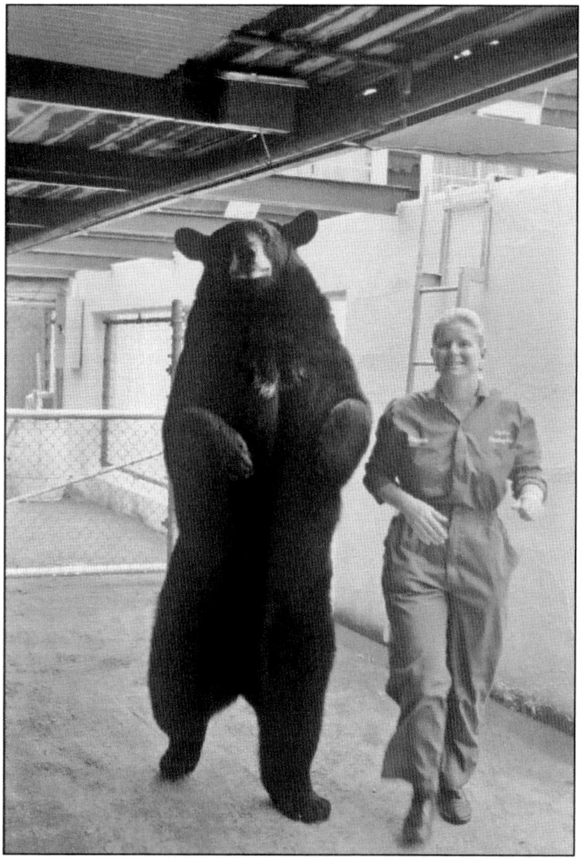

The 70th-anniversary celebration (1928–1998) provided an opportunity for a costume party. In this photograph, several Clark family members and employees show off their Roaring Twenties finery. From left to right, Annie Holtzman, Ellie Holtzman, Phebe Thurston, Katie Govoni, Ashley Clark, Emily Noel, and Sylvia Smith pose in front of Avery's Garage at the Trading Post. (Photograph by Jon P. Lasseigne.)

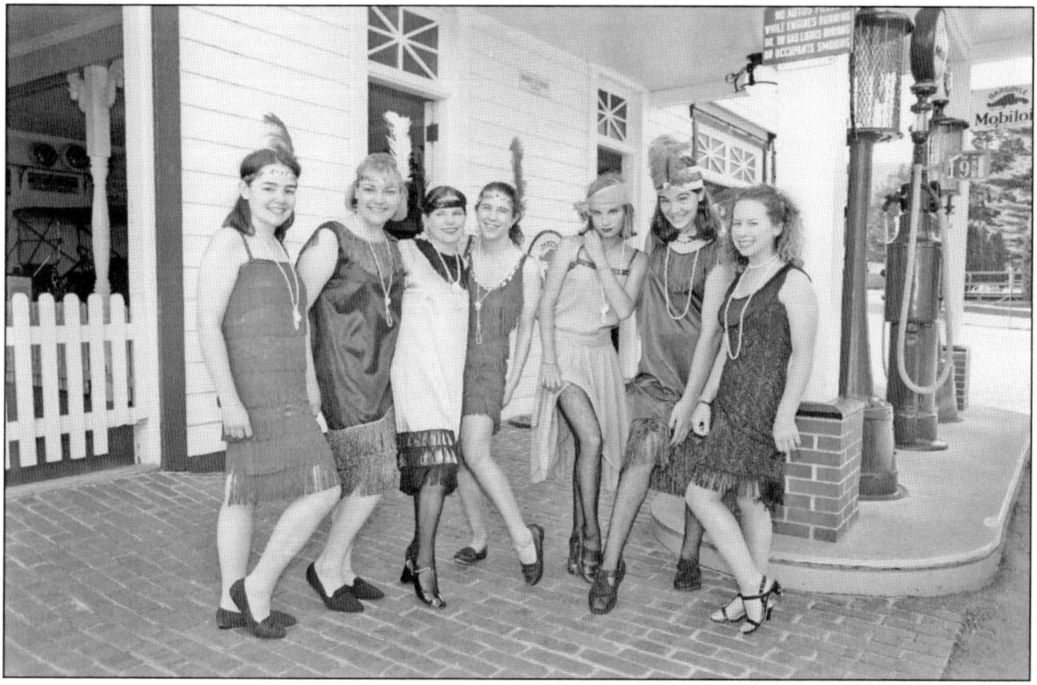

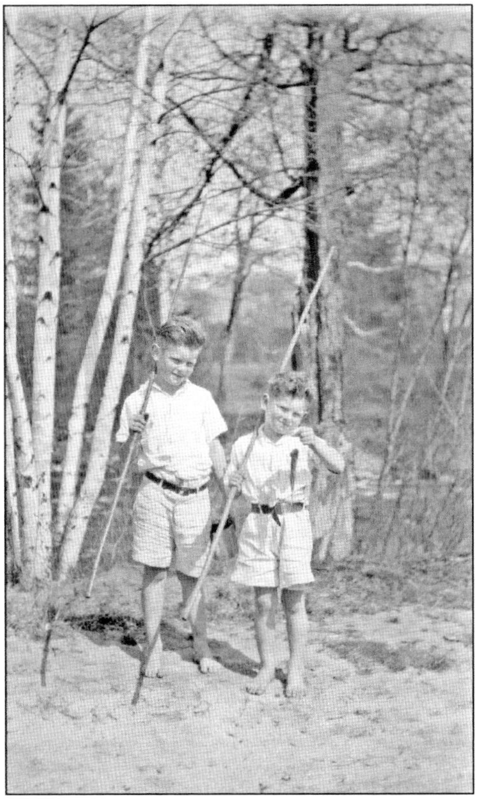

In 1932, young Ed (left) and Murray Clark pose on the bank of the Pemigewasset River with their fishing poles. Florence labeled this picture "Murray's First Catch."

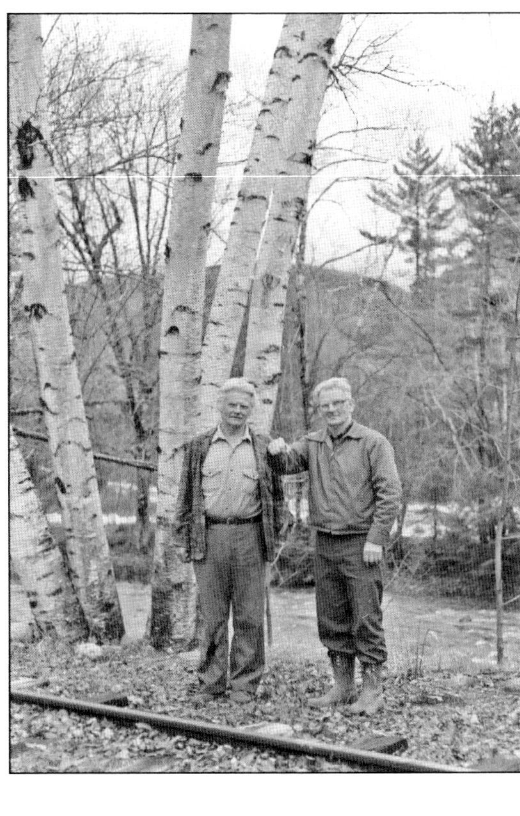

Fifty-four years later, in 1986, Ed (left) and Murray recreate the scene by the same stand of white birch trees. (Photograph by Maureen S. Clark.)

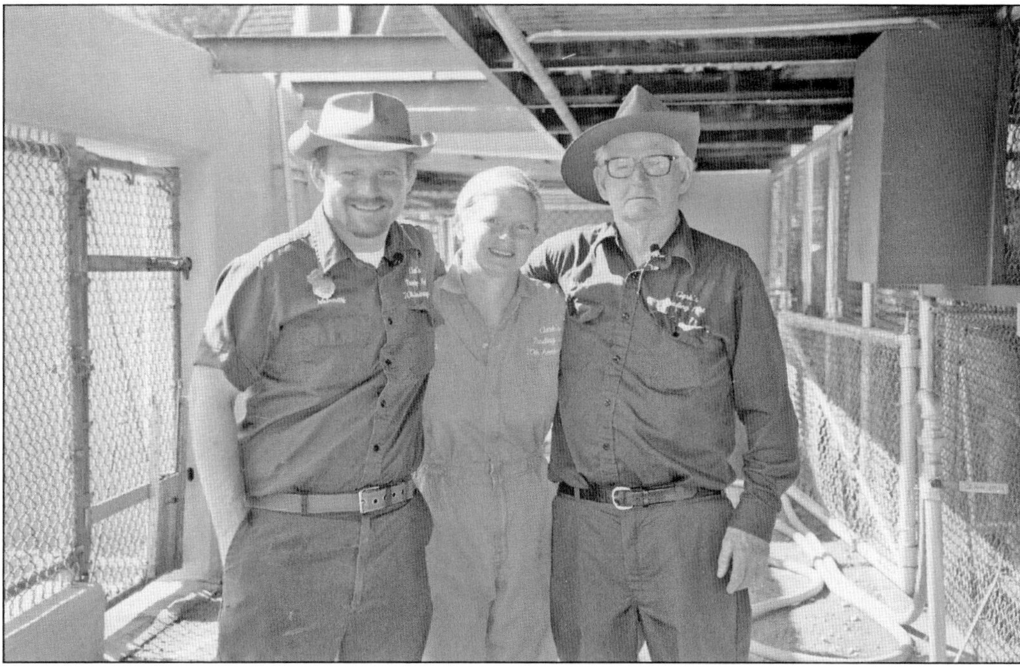

Clark's bear show has had only four trainers since 1948: Edward M. Clark, W. Murray Clark, Maureen S. Clark, and Murray A. Clark. Together, they represent thousands of hours working with and training bears. In all that time, the bears have always been treated with respect and love and the bond between trainers and bears is evident in every bear show. From left to right, Murray, Maureen, and W. Murray take a break from training to pose near the bear performance ring.

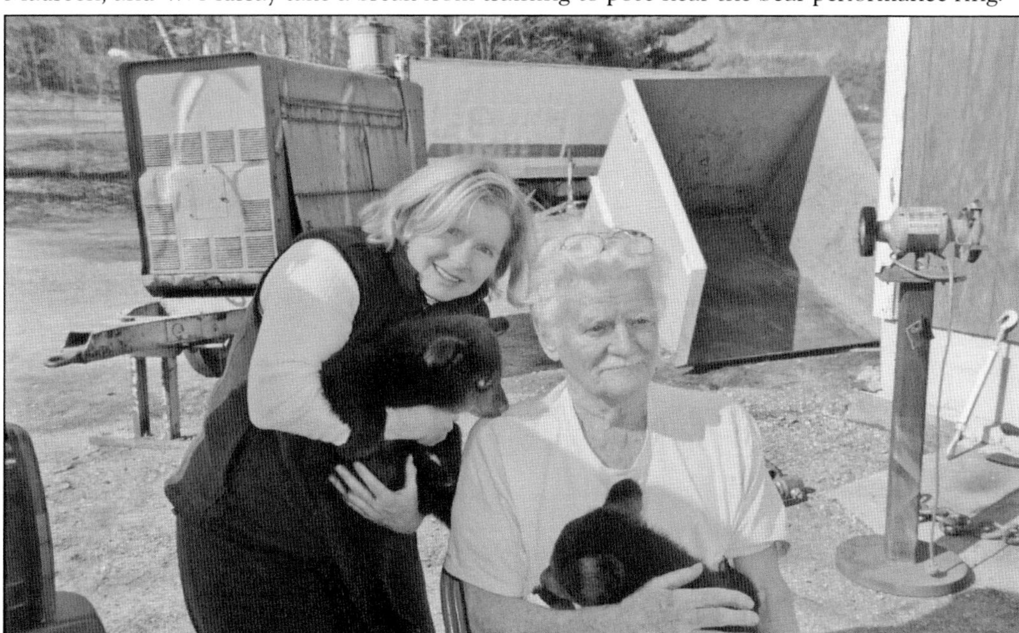

Maureen took Pemigewasset (Pemi) and Echo on a road trip in 2003 to meet Ed Clark, who was working at one of his hydroelectric facilities.

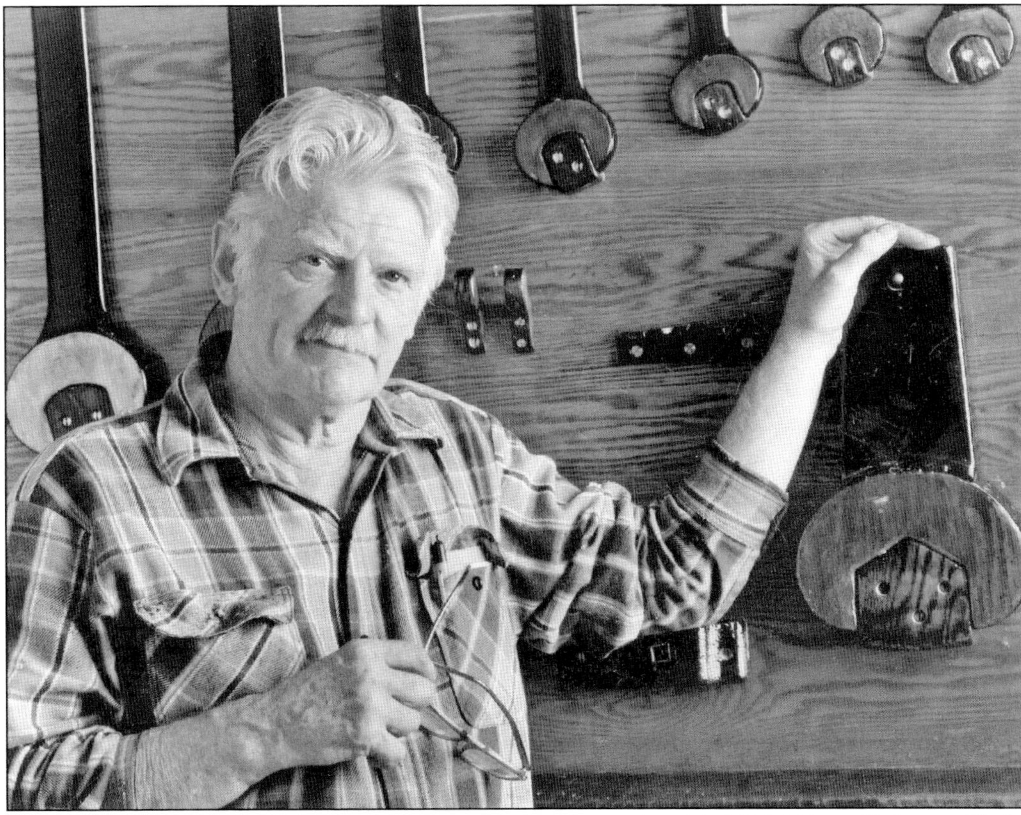

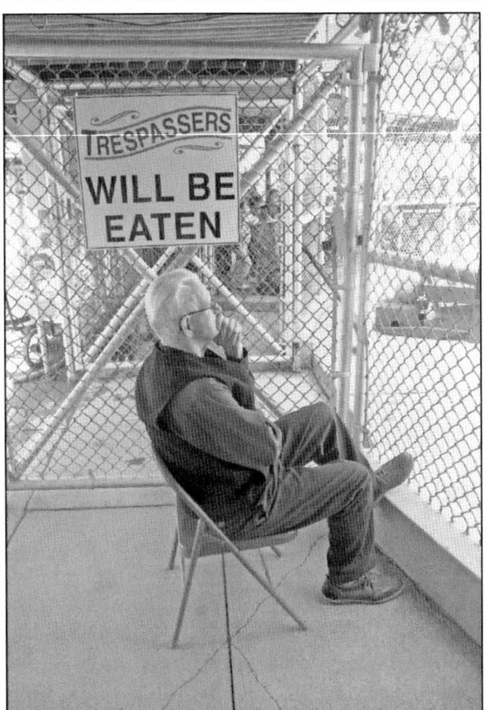

On September 24, 2009, Edward Murray Clark, seen above next to a display in one of the hydroelectric plants, passed away at the age of 85. He left behind a larger-than-life legacy at the Trading Post, in the White Mountains, and in New Hampshire. On January 7, 2010, W. Murray Clark, seen at left outside his beloved bear ring, died just shy of his 83rd birthday. He had performed with his cherished bears for an astounding 54 years. With their passing, the White Mountains lost two of its giants, a special breed of men who worked incredibly hard to forge a living while loving and promoting the area and preserving history for future generations. The deaths of the brothers within four months of each other was a huge emotional blow to the Clark family and to all who knew them. The lions of the White Mountains were gone, but their legacy and what they worked so hard to build continues. (Above, photograph by David Goodwin.)

Seven

Stepping Up to the Plate

With the deaths of Ed and Murray, leadership transferred to the third generation. While Ed was no longer actively involved in the business and Murray's involvement had slowed considerably, both were still guiding influences at the Trading Post. Dedication to the business and personal contact with guests were traditions to be carried on, but transition once again became the order of the day.

Computer systems were updated, advertising was stepped up, and a beautiful new sign (with a bear on top, of course!) was placed out front. Clark's Trading Post joined the social media scene with a website and a Facebook page.

The bears remain the most visible and famous feature of the Trading Post and they still function as "road stoppers." The love and respect with which they are treated shines through every interaction between bear and trainer, and guests respond to that. In return, the bears try very hard during each and every performance to entertain the audience—in spite of "wedding season," audience distractions, summer heat, and increasing sleepiness as hibernation approaches. Doing their part in the transition, they began learning additional tricks: Echo learned to ride a Segway and to play hockey, and Tula learned new, difficult, multi-step routines.

New attractions were carefully considered and resulted in the addition of Wolfie's Wheelin' Segway Park, a face painting station, River City Mining, the Anaconda Escape, and a conversion of Tuttle's Rustic House to Tuttle's Laser Shooting Gallery. Much-needed restrooms were added at the north end of the park.

What didn't change was the commitment to provide an outstanding, family-oriented experience for guests and to engage the upcoming generations in the business. Visitors are likely to find up to 20 family members working on the property on any given day. A strong sense of tradition and nostalgia is carefully nurtured. The feeling of familiar things staying the same, only better because of a few new additions, helps explain why Clark's Trading Post is thriving and going strong after nearly 100 years.

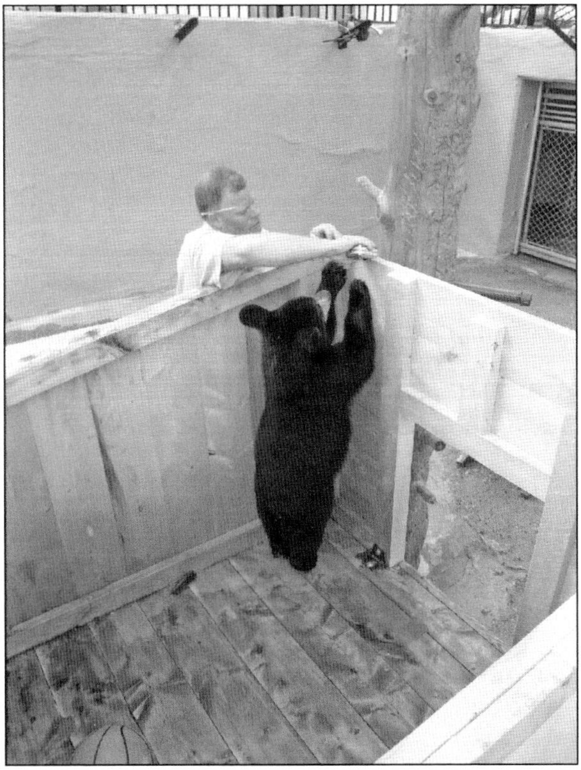

Tula and Mishka are assisting Fred Englert, making sure their new dens will be just right. The Trading Post welcomed these two new black bear cubs in 2010. The average lifespan of a North American black bear in the wild is less than eight years. With a good diet, love, and attentive care, the Clark bears can expect to do much better, usually living well into their 20s. When their performing days are over, they retire to their winter home, the bear habitat across the street. There, they continue to receive love, care, and human interaction, living out their lives contentedly and perhaps dreaming of their glory days in the ring. One bear, Victoria, has taken up paw painting in her senior years. Her paintings are sold in the gift shops. (Both photographs by Maureen S. Clark.)

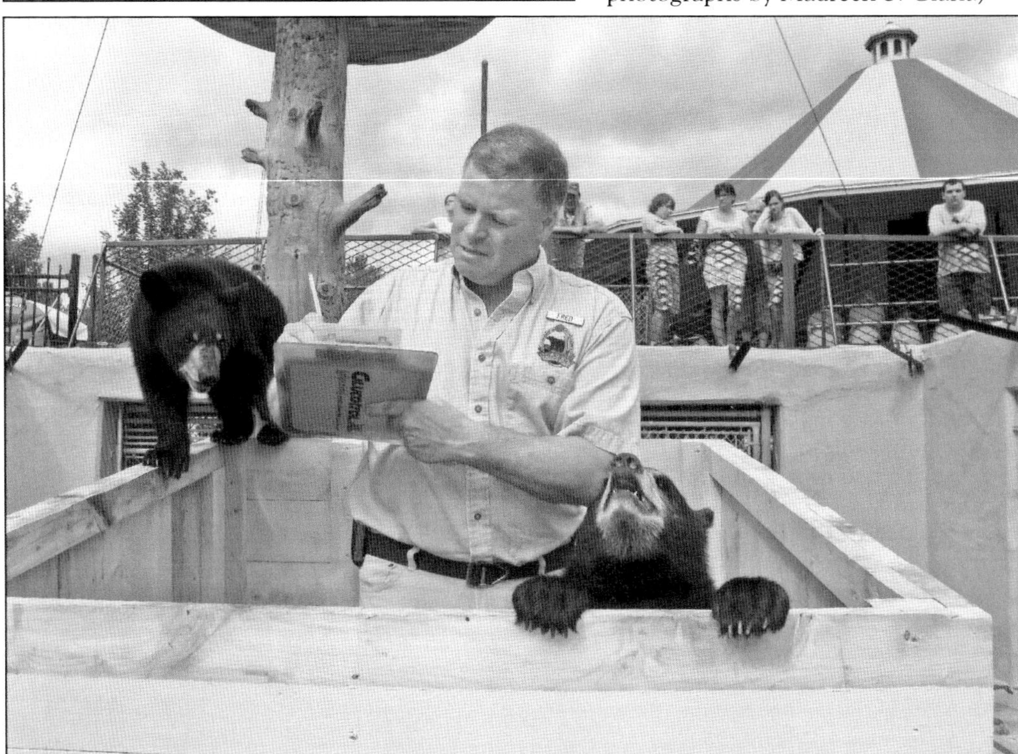

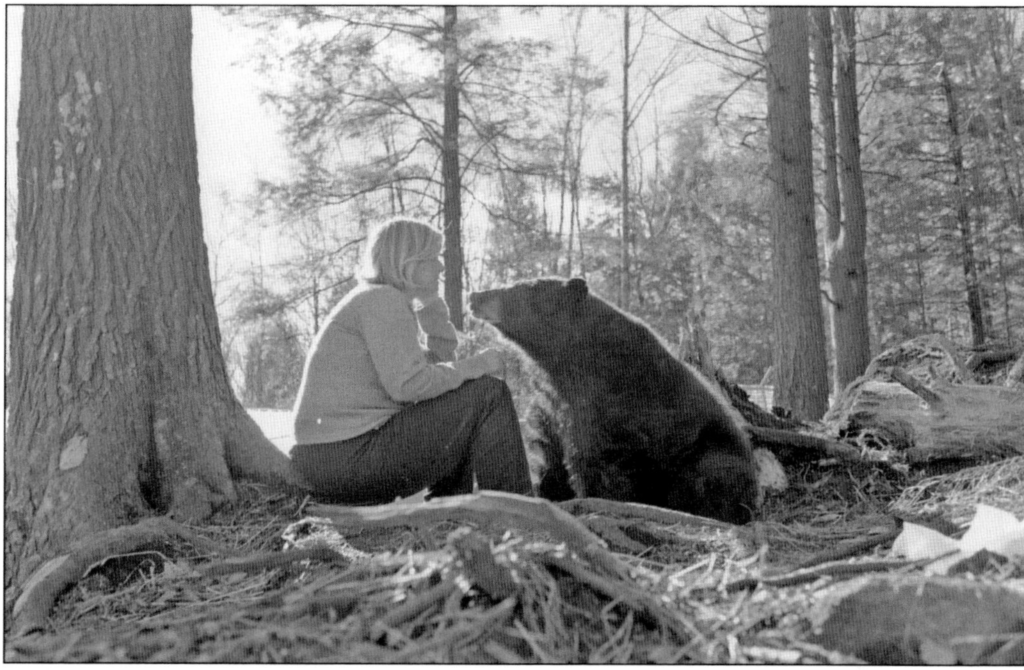

In this 2006 picture, Maureen and Moxie share a quiet moment in the bear habitat across the street from the Trading Post. Anyone who doubts the validity of interspecies communication has never seen Maureen with her bears. (Photograph by Lisa Marie MacKay.)

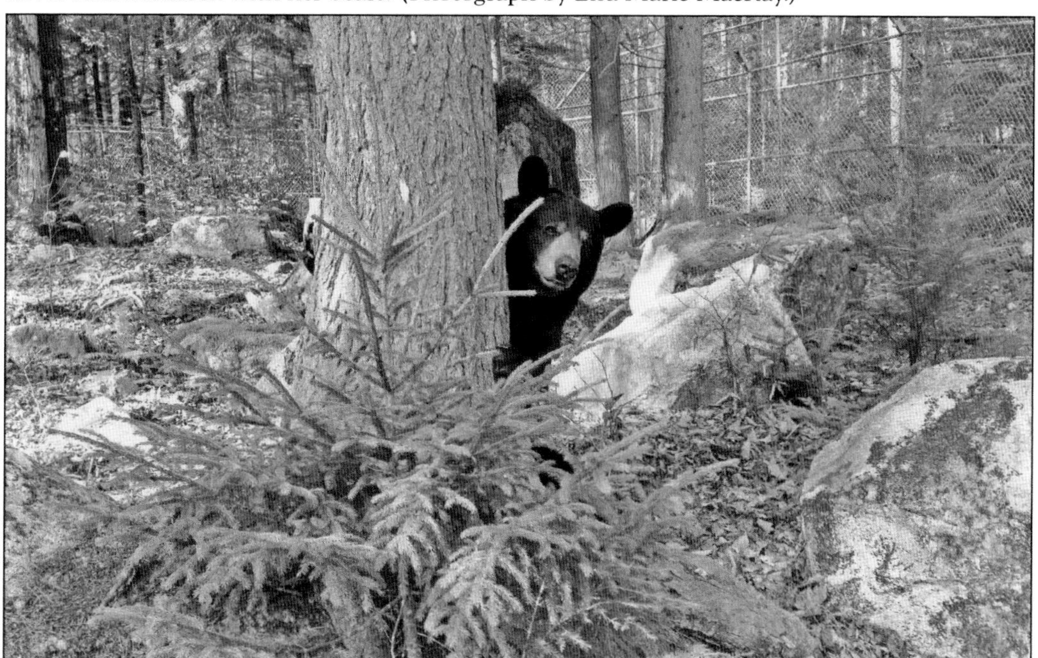

With trees to climb, rocks to play on, space to roam, and dens with lots of fresh straw for hibernation, life is good in the bear habitat. In this photograph, Pemigewasset peaks out from behind a tree. Note the peanut in the bark. Hunting for peanuts is just one of the many ways the Clarks engage the bears to keep their minds agile. (Photograph by Maureen S. Clark.)

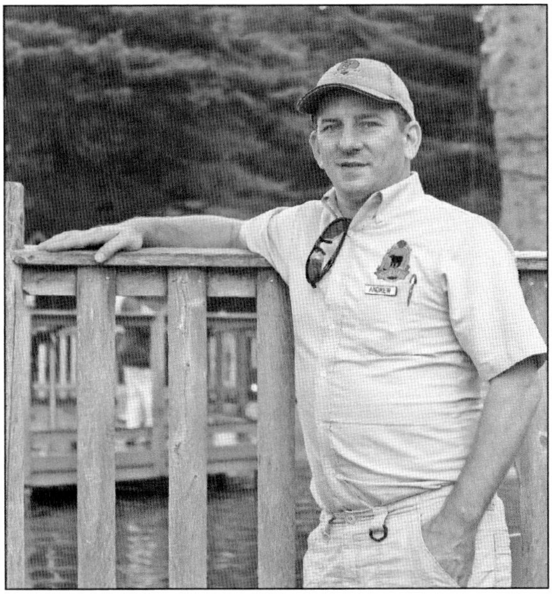

The fact that the Trading Post is not overwhelmingly large, and one is almost certain to interact with family members at some point during a visit, creates a bond of familiarity and intimacy for guests that cannot be duplicated at a large amusement park. Andrew Clark is vice president of Clark's Trading Post, runs Kilburn's Photo Parlor, and is the resident IT guru who oversees the technologically advanced attractions such as Tuttle's Laser Shooting Gallery. (Photograph by Carolyn Grant.)

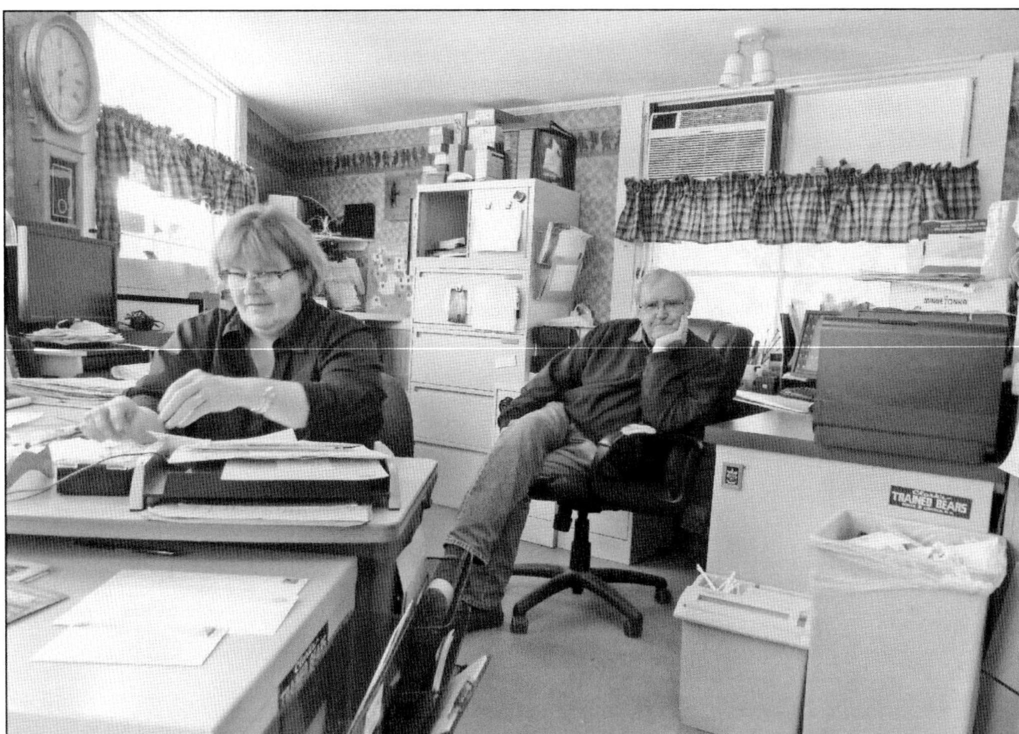

The family work ethic is strong and stretches across the generations. The intention is for the Trading Post to remain a family enterprise where responsibility and capability are bedrock values. Callum Grant is president of the White Mountain Central Railroad. He and his wife, Nola, run the front office, handling all day-to-day business affairs for the Trading Post. Nola, an accomplished artist, handles graphics, and Callum, an experienced emergency medic, is on call should the need arise. (Photograph by John K. Eisenhart.)

As president of Clark's Trading Post, Carol Govoni understands that the responsibility for maintaining the Trading Post's success lies on the shoulders of her generation. Like all the Clark children, she has been involved with the operation of the business from a young age. She can, and has, worked at everything from short order cook to running the locomotive. (Photograph by John K. Eisenhart.)

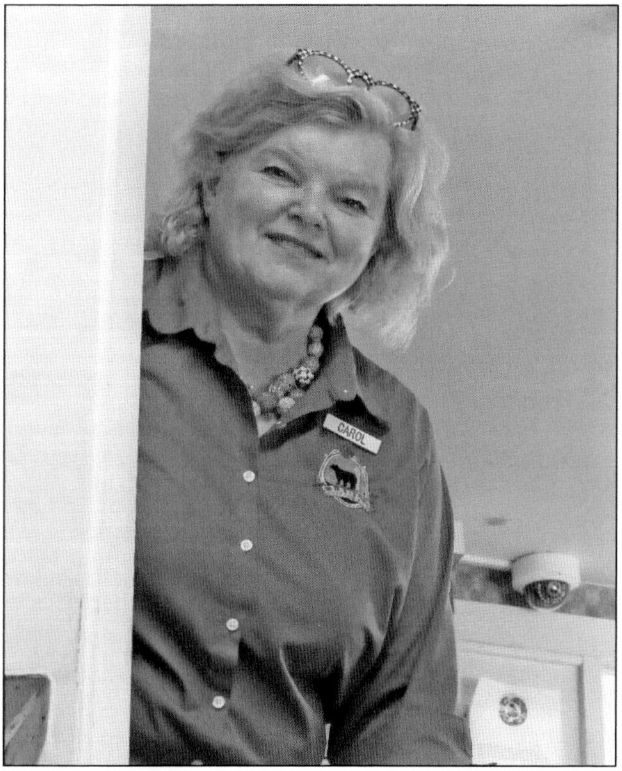

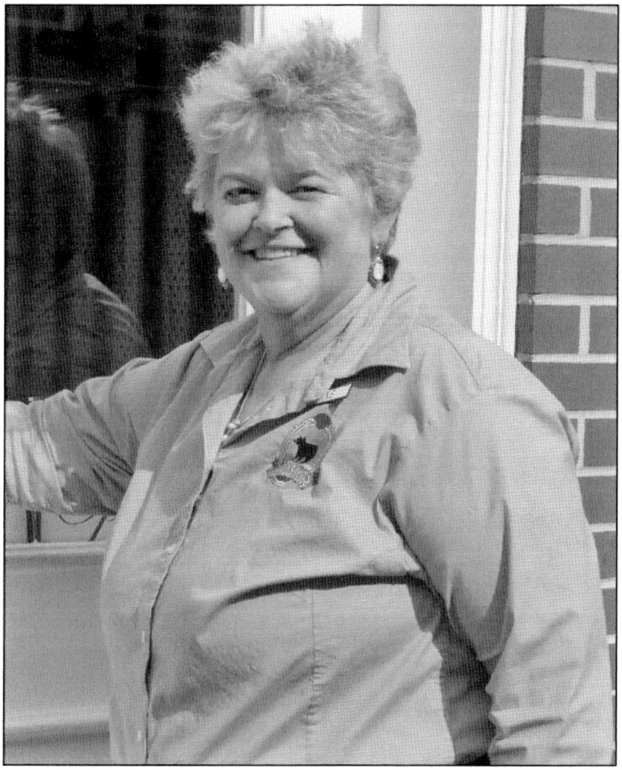

As a child, Anne Englert had a typical Clark family childhood—starting early and working hard. With a business degree from New Hampshire Technical Institute, she worked at Disney World in Florida, returning home with new ideas to try at the Trading Post. She is secretary of the Trading Post Corporation, in charge of group sales, and handles human resources, where she is responsible for staffing and scheduling. (Photograph by John K. Eisenhart.)

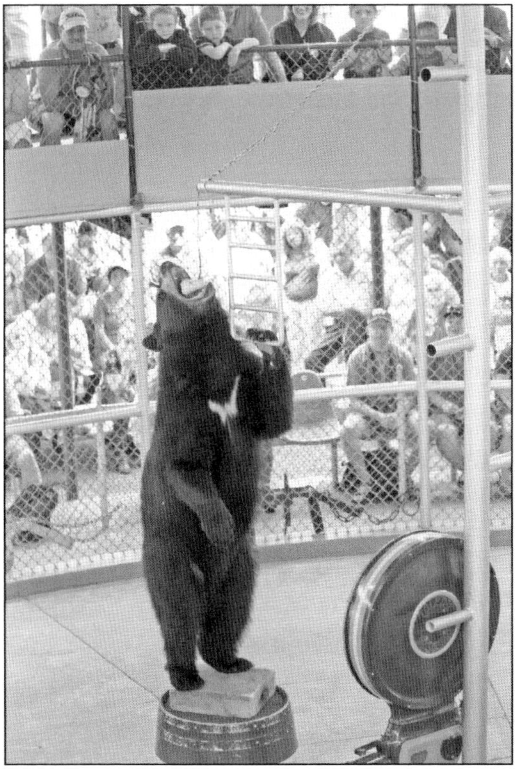

Tula performs muti-stage tricks in the performance ring. She knows how to open a cabinet mounted on the fence of the ring, extract a bottle, and later return it. In this photograph, she placed the wooden box on top of the barrel, climbed on, and then reached up to secure her reward. (Photograph by Carolyn Grant.)

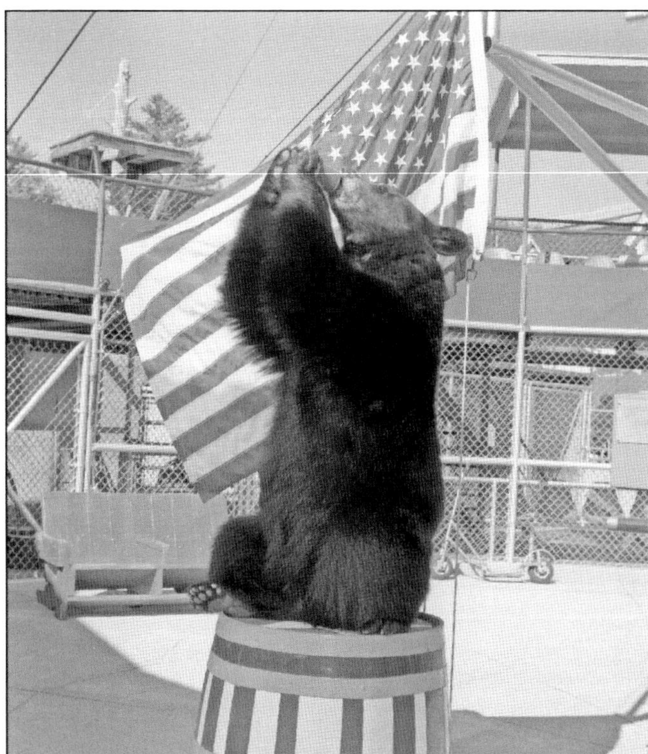

Patriotic displays have always been a part of the Trading Post. Nita raised the flag whenever she performed in the ring. Sitting on a barrel and enjoying a tasty reward was just a plus.

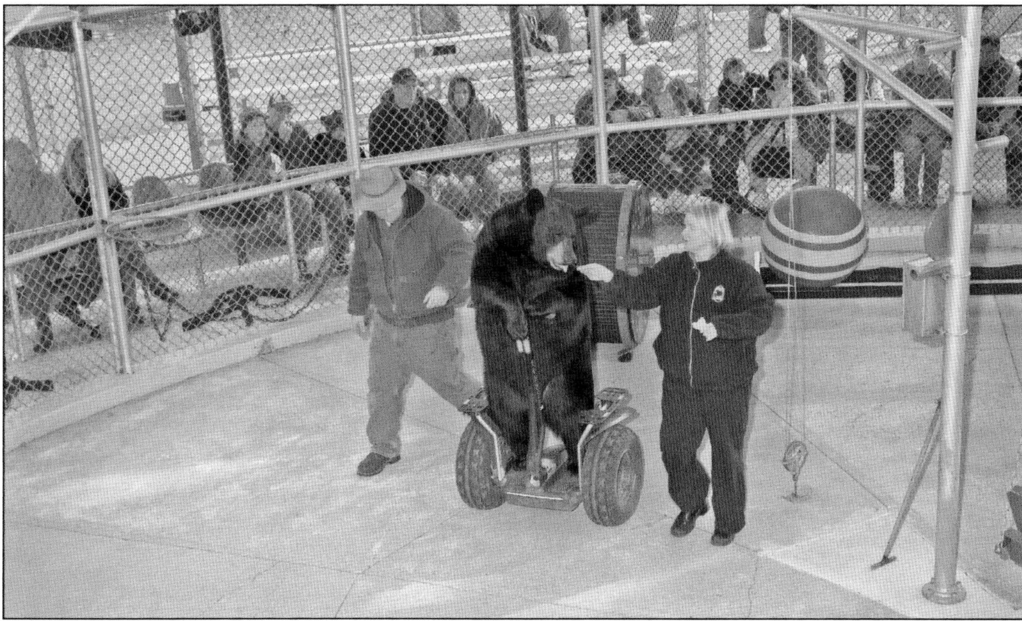

When Segways were introduced in 2009, Nola Grant wondered if a bear could ride one. Bear trainers Murray A. Clark (left) and Maureen Clark set to work teaching Echo to ride a specially modified Segway—and she loved it! Soon, the saying around Wolfie's Wheelin' Segway Park was, "It's so easy even a bear can do it." This, while true, does not take into account how many hours it took to teach her.

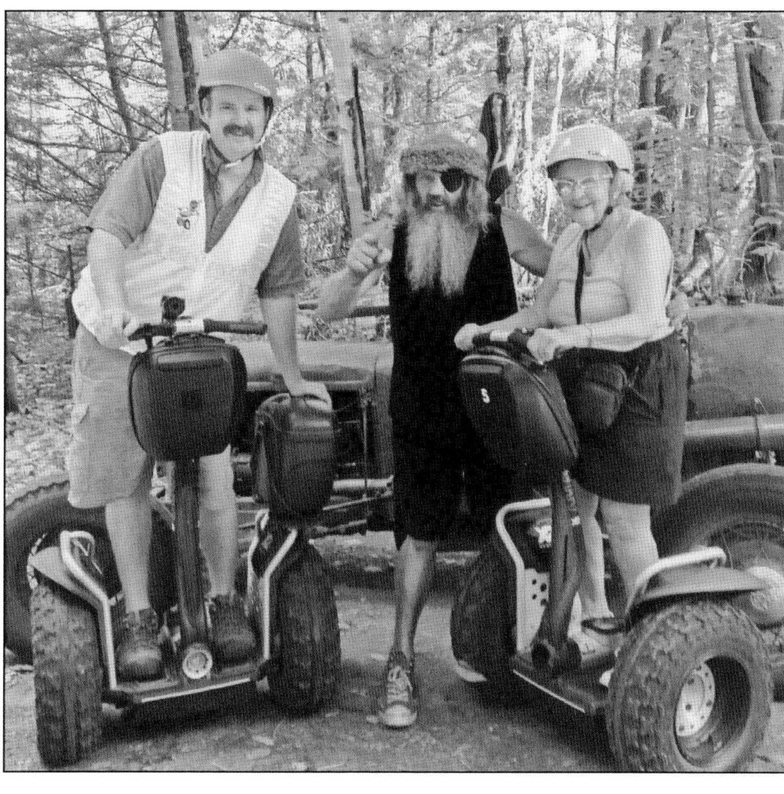

Wolfie's Wheelin' Segway Park is included with Trading Post admission. For the more adventurous, a guided tour in Wolfman's Territory can be scheduled. In this picture, 91-year-old Audrey Maloon (right) of Plymouth, New Hampshire, joins Wolfman and Iain Grant for her fifth consecutive year enjoying the Segway Safari.

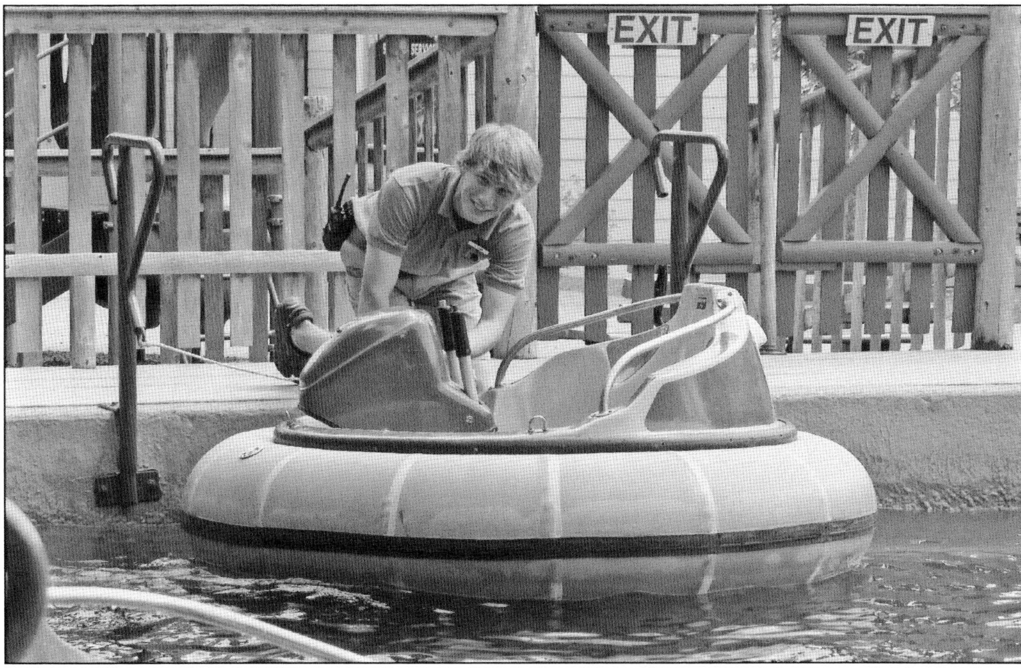

Liam Clark is seen checking on the motor of one of the Mill Pond Bumper Boats. A guest is just as likely to encounter him working on the Anaconda Escape or teaching someone how to ride a Segway. Liam is a fourth-generation family member who pitches in wherever he is needed. (Photograph by John K. Eisenhart.)

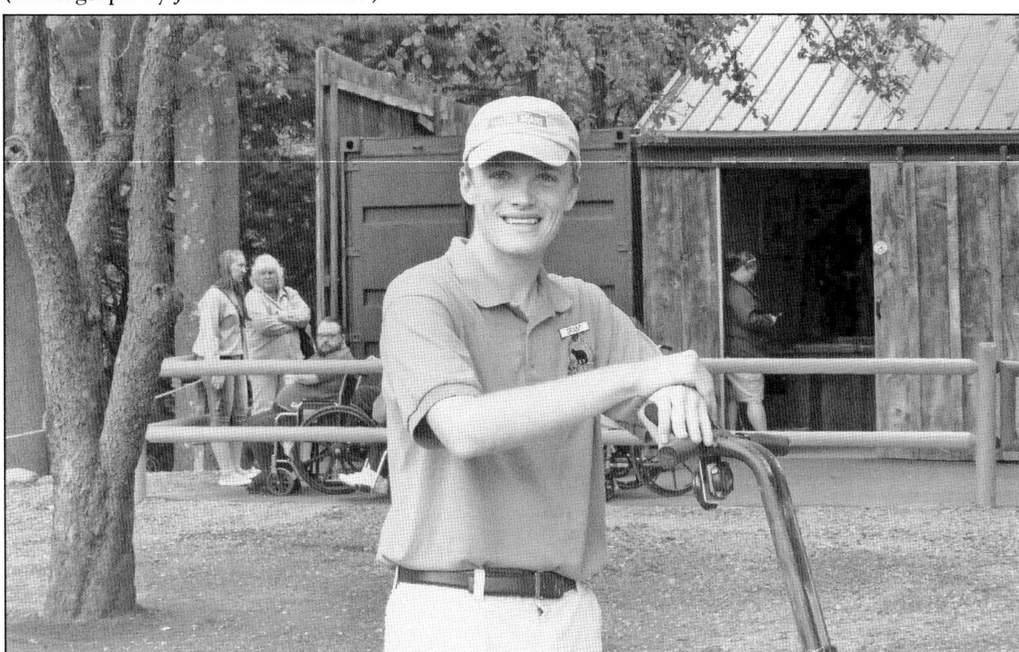
Grant Clark, Liam's older brother, also works summers at the Trading Post. He has seen duty at the hand stamping station and at River City Mining, helping out in park services, or, as in this picture, working with the Segways. (Photograph by John K. Eisenhart.)

Mackenna Mack is a fifth-generation family member, and while one of the youngest, she has enjoyed helping out for several years. She can often be found scooping ice cream in the Peppermint Saloon. (Photograph by John K. Eisenhart.)

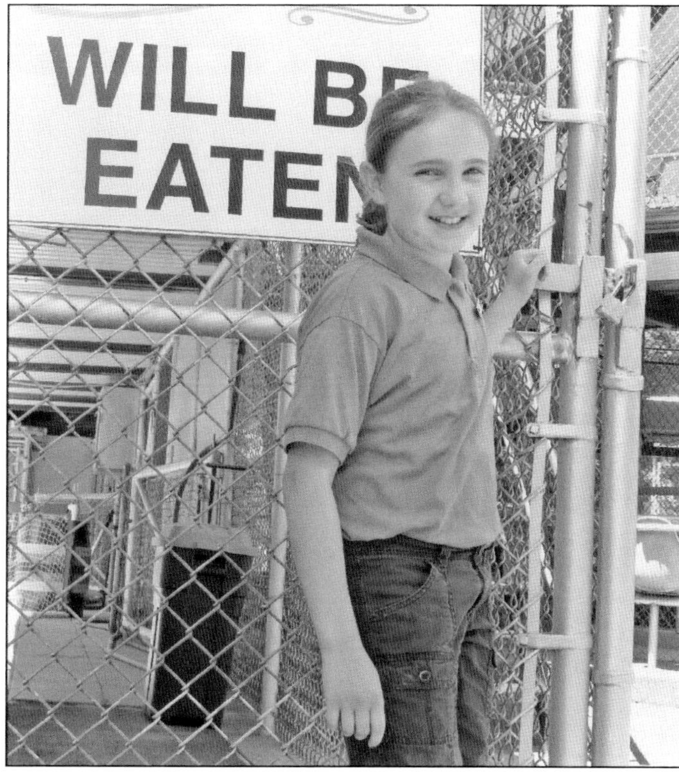

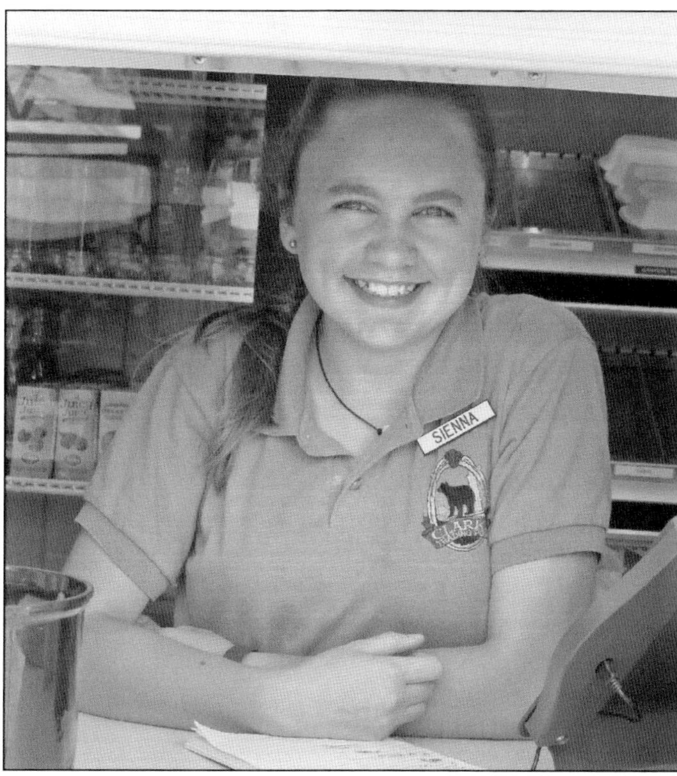

When Sienna Mack, Mackenna's older sister, is not busy behind the window of the Whistle Stop Snack Bar, she is usually found in the Popcorn Wagon. (Photograph by John K. Eisenhart.)

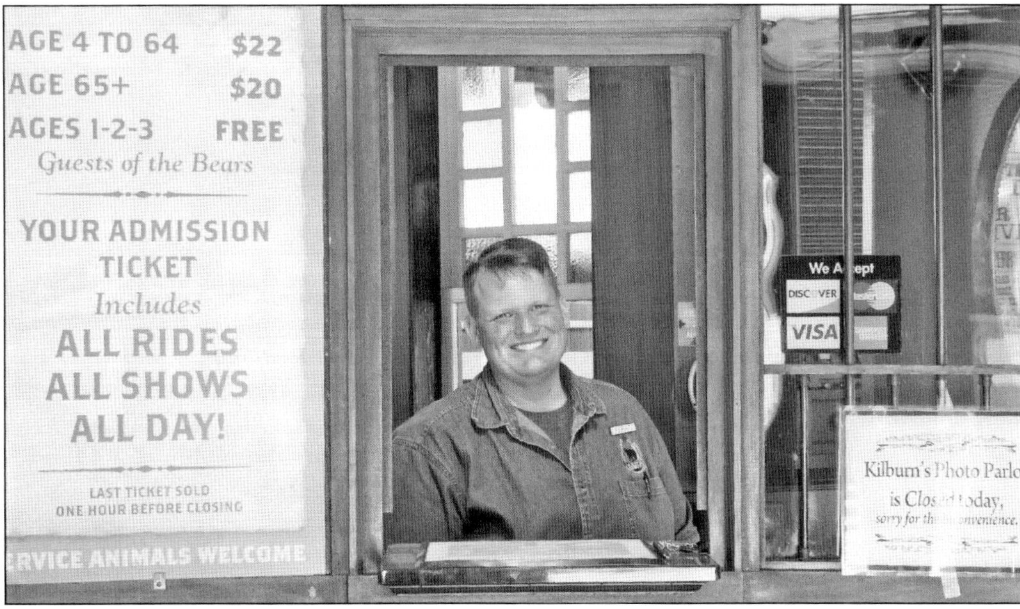

Robert Wetherell's smile is often the first one to greet guests at the main entrance. There are really three families at the Trading Post: the Clark family, the bear family, and the employee family. The latter is in large part responsible for the experience of a guest on any given day. One of the most-asked questions for employees is, "Are you one of the family?" The answer is usually, "No, and yes." "No," not an actual family member, but "yes," because the Clarks treat their employees as family and expect them to maintain the same high standards. (Photograph by John K. Eisenhart.)

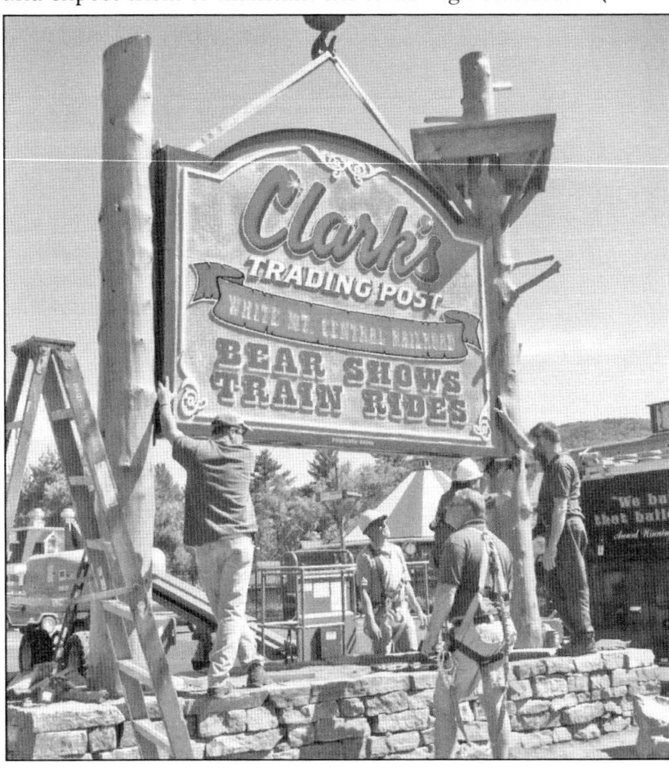

In June 2011, a new sign, which includes a bear on a platform, was erected in front of the gift shop. A second, similar sign appeared on the main street in Lincoln. The main support logs came from trees felled on Clark property in the spring, when logs debark most easily. Branches were snubbed off and the poles sealed. The same process is used for supports in the bears' pens.

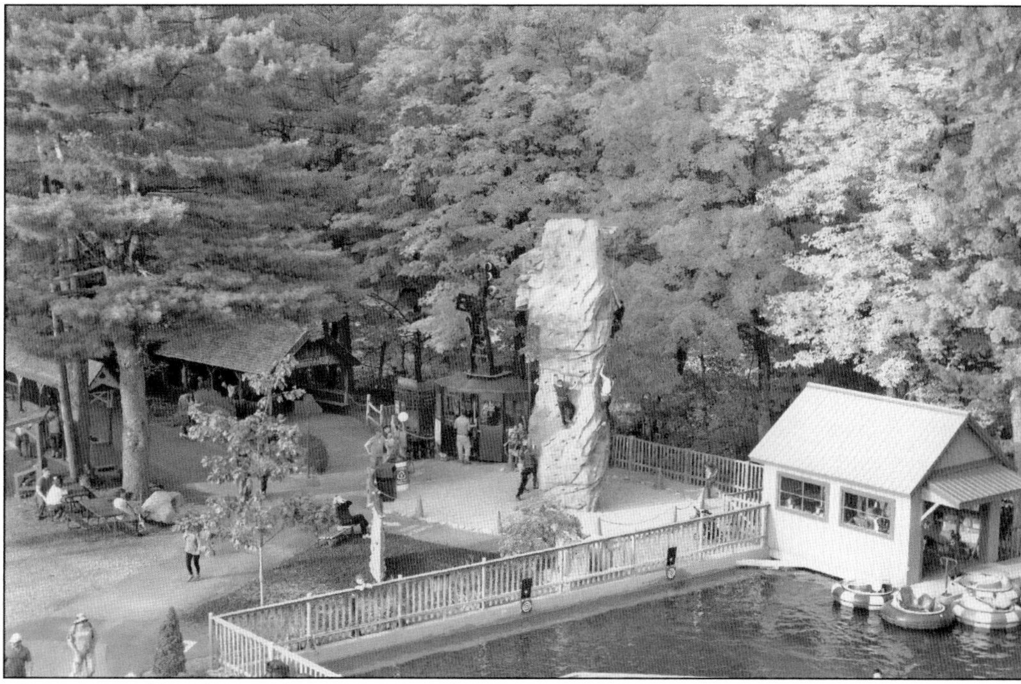

Plans were well underway for a quarter-scale replica of the Old Man of the Mountain as a climbing tower when the original Old Man crumbled and fell to the valley floor in Franconia Notch in 2003. This 30-foot copy attracts a great many guests each year as they try their skill at rock climbing. At the base of the tower is one of the original Cannon Mountain tramcars, which is now used for storing climbing equipment. (Photograph by Maureen S. Clark.)

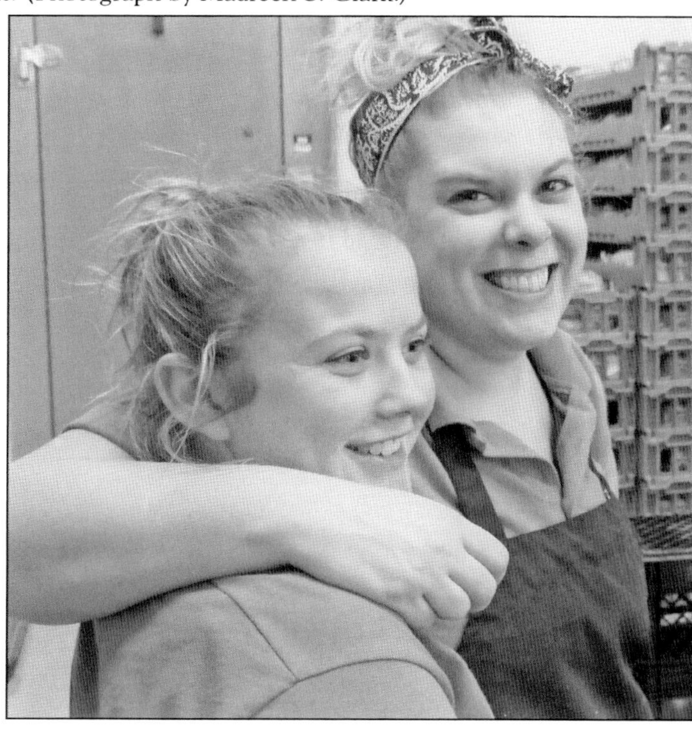

Libbie Hilliard (left) and Cassie Campbell are typical of the loyalty engendered in Trading Post employees. Libbie has worked at the Trading Post since she was barely 14. (She was still 13 when she interviewed.) She has worked in Food Services all through high school and college. Cassie started in 2004 at the age of 15. She, too, worked through high school and college and now, as a high school math teacher, still returns each summer to work in Food Services. (Photograph by John K. Eisenhart.)

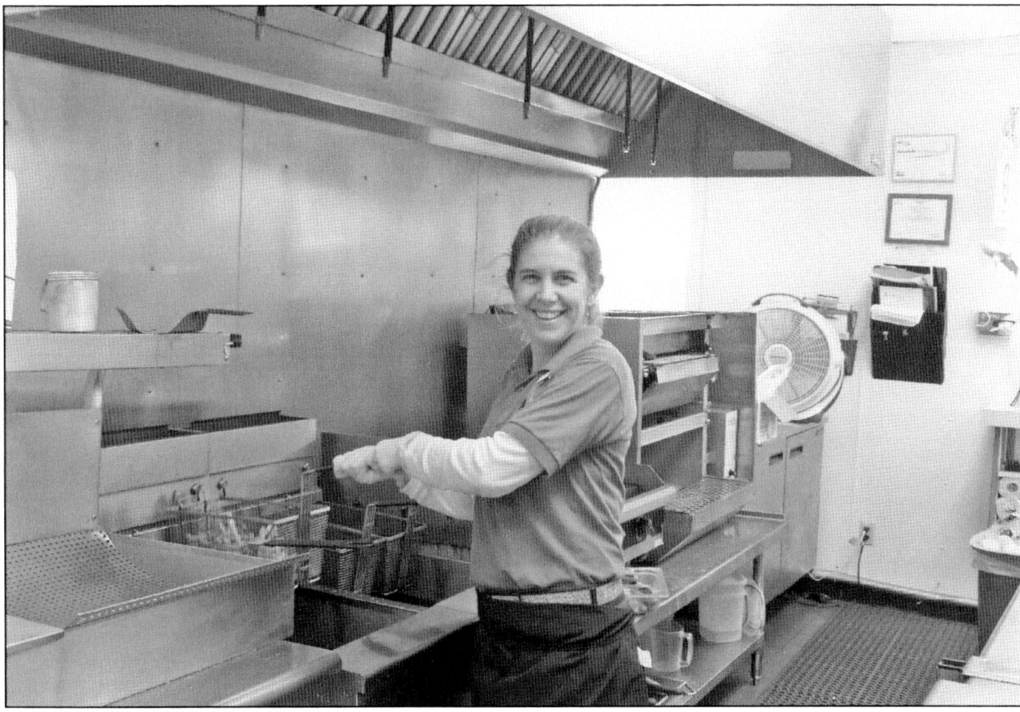

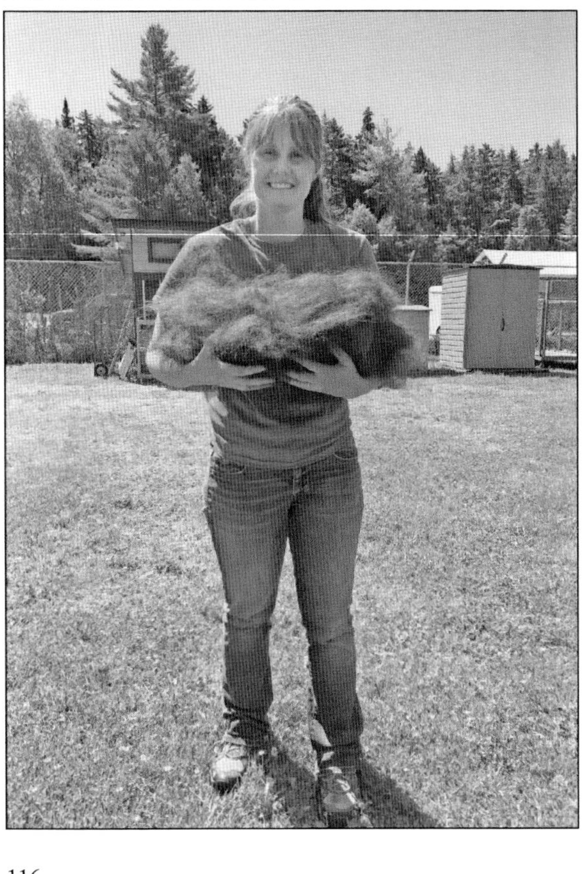

Katie Mack is a fourth generation family member in charge of Food Services. A great favorite with her young crew members, she can usually be found in the Whistle Stop Snack Bar or in Pullman's Lunch taking a hands-on approach to maintaining a high standard of quality and employee morale. Katie took over Food Services when her mother, Carol Govoni, assumed responsibility in the gift shop so her mother, Joyce Clark, could retire. (Photograph by John K. Eisenhart.)

Lisa MacKay is holding an armful of bear hair combed from a bear during a grooming session. The hair is washed, spun into yarn, and knit into mittens, small teddy bears, and sweaters. These have been given to individuals who have done extraordinary things for the bears. Lisa has worked with the bears for many years and the bears know and trust her almost as much as they do their trainers. (Photograph by Maureen S. Clark.)

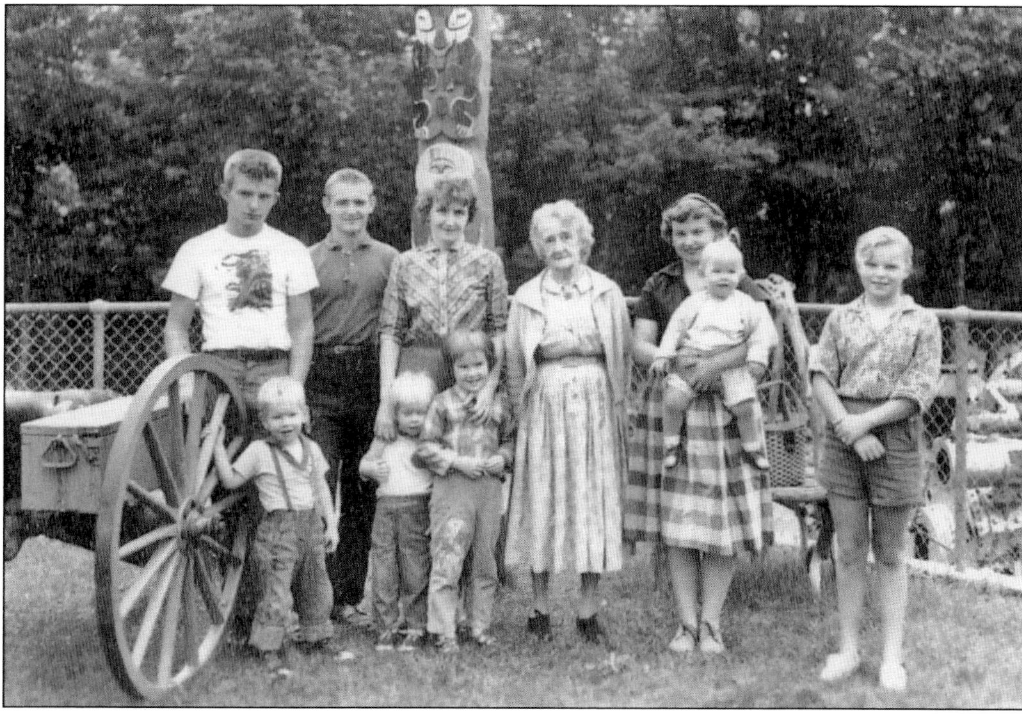

During a 1962 visit from Emma Jane Stillman Murray (Florence's mother), several members of the younger generation can be seen. From left to right are (first row) Tom Clark, Maureen Clark, and Nola Clark; (second row) David Clark, Eddie Clark, Barbara Clark, Grandma Murray, Joyce Clark (holding Anne Clark), and Carol Clark.

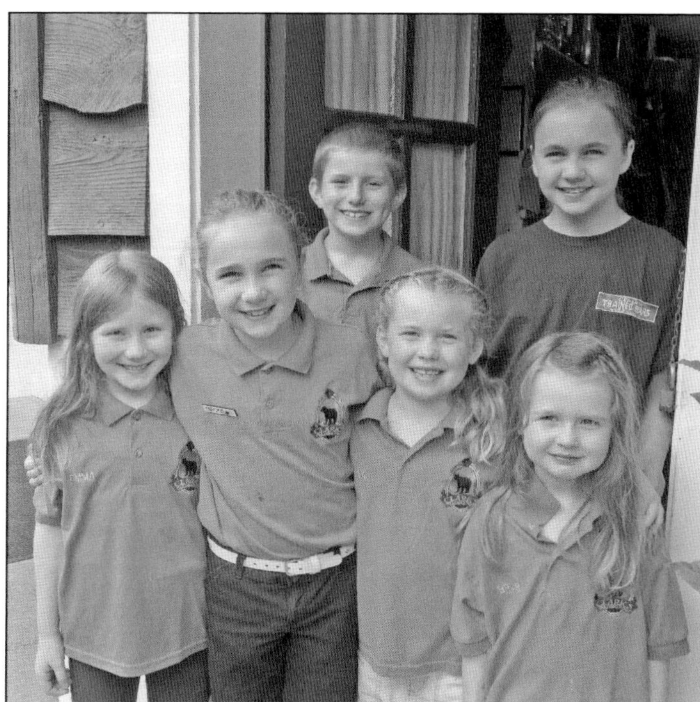

Members of another upcoming generation are shown in this more recent photograph. From left to right are (first row) Emma Clark, Mackenna Mack, Willa Clark, and Briar Clark; (second row) Mason Clark and Sienna Mack. (Photograph by Maureen S. Clark.)

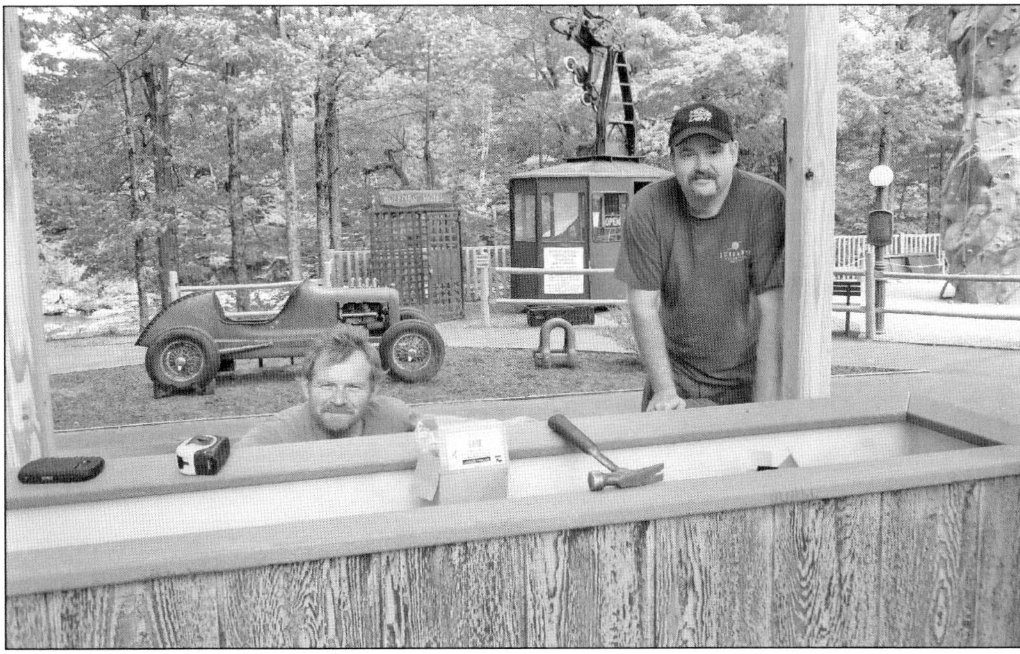

Murray Avery Clark (left) and Iain Grant are constructing the sluice for River City Mining, which opened in 2012. The name comes from *The Music Man*, one of Ed Clark's favorite plays. Bags of mining rough filled with sand, gravel, gemstones, and fossils are sold from a building purchased during the salvage expedition to the bankrupt Freedomland, USA. (Photograph by Maureen S. Clark.)

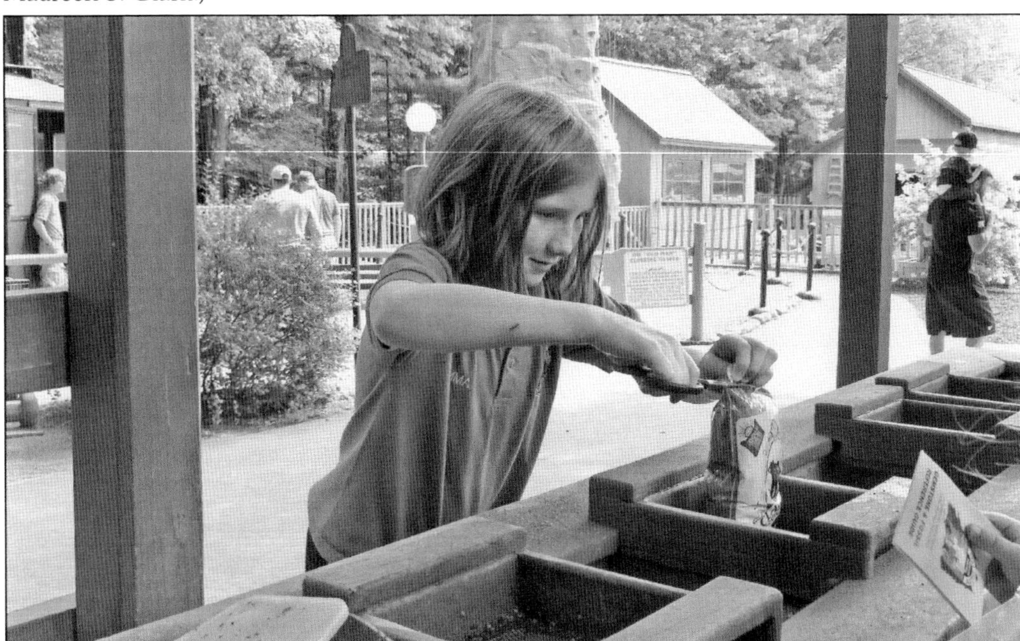

Once the mining rough is purchased, it is taken to the mining sluice where the "miner" on duty assists in panning for gemstones. Emma Clark is seen assisting a guest in opening a bag of mining rough prior to placing it in the mining sieve. (Photograph by John K. Eisenhart.)

In this photograph, Pemigewasset, one of the Clarks' most beloved bears, is walking with Maureen Clark. Pemi is carrying a barrel bank. In the early years, Murray Clark, working mostly alone, built a steam mill to help make ends meet. In later years he produced barrel banks and billy clubs for sale in the gift shop.

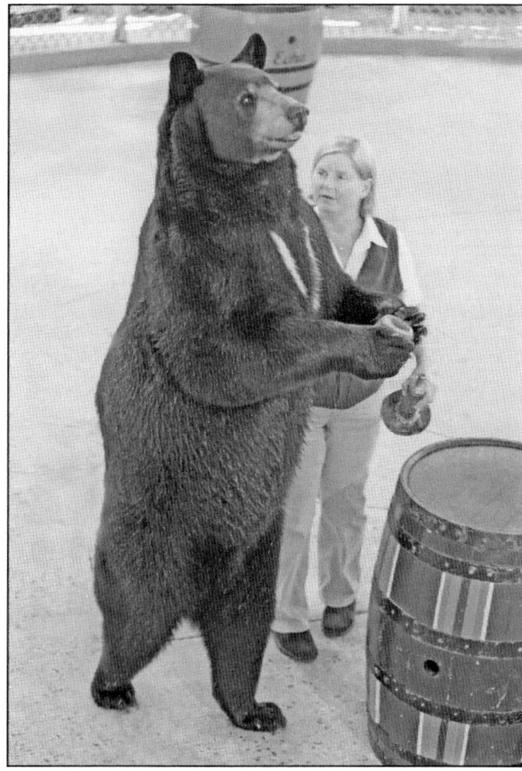

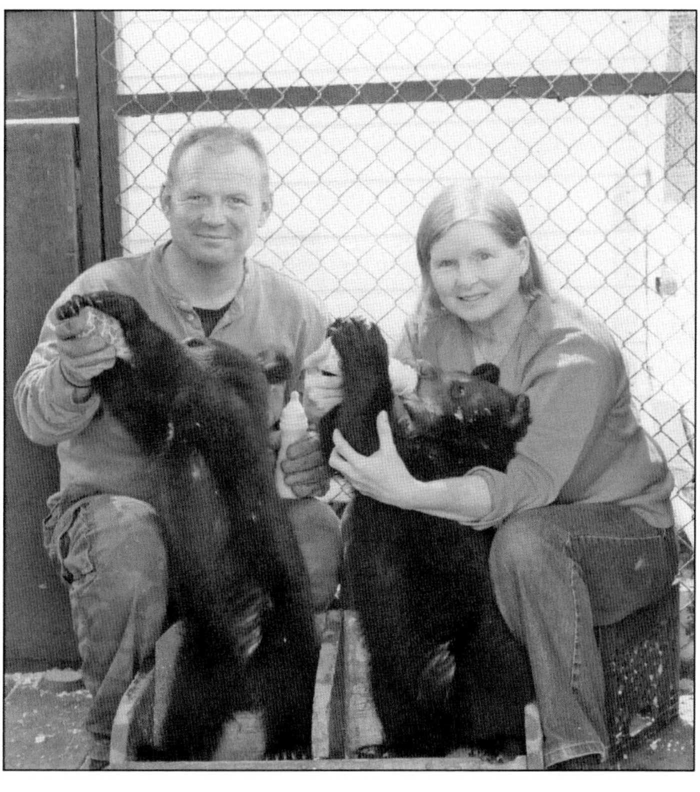

In this 2010 picture, young Murray (left) and Maureen are holding the new cubs, Tula and Mishka. The cubs come to associate their trainers with love and tasty things.

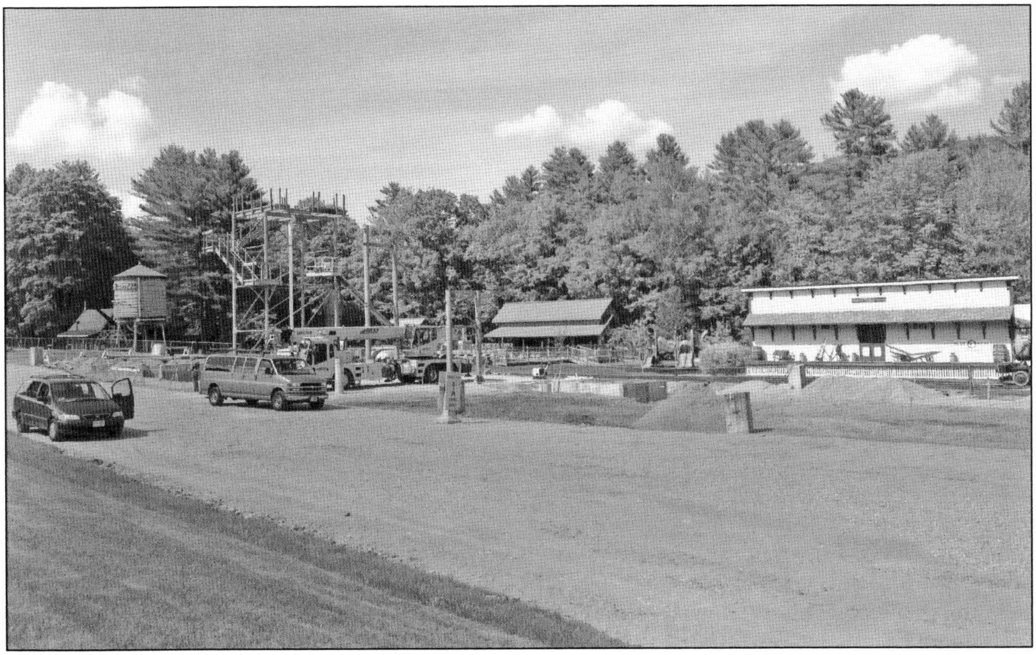

In 2015, the largest of the new attractions at the Trading Post was introduced: a water raft ride that was christened the Anaconda Escape. Following family tradition, the ride was repurposed from a New Hampshire theme park and given a new twist with the addition of a huge snake's head and a snakeskin paint job. (Photograph by Maureen S. Clark.)

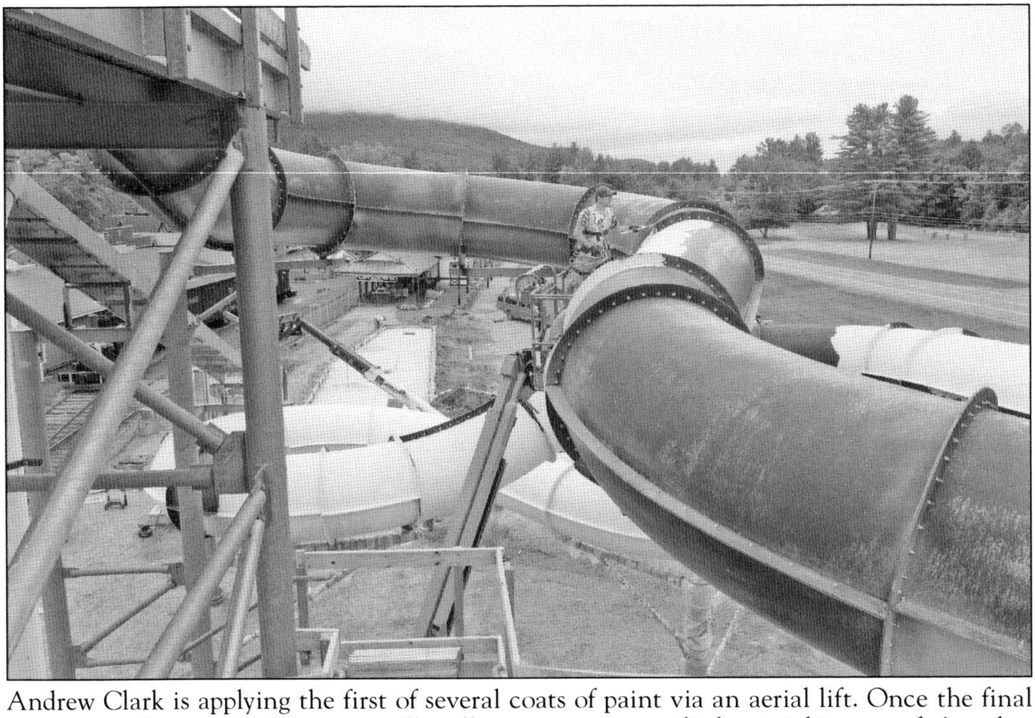

Andrew Clark is applying the first of several coats of paint via an aerial lift. Once the final green coat of paint was dry, an overall scallop pattern was applied, mimicking a snake's scales. (Photograph by Maureen S. Clark.)

Andrew Clark, who was in charge of the Anaconda Escape theme and worked with the sculptor and the painter on the head, is seen standing next to it. The head was built in Massachusetts by Joseph Pesce of Pygmalion Elements and Sculpture. The Anaconda Escape had to be located on a portion of the parking lot north of the railroad station, due to its size. This required significant changes to maintain the safety of guests and the integrity of Trading Post grounds.

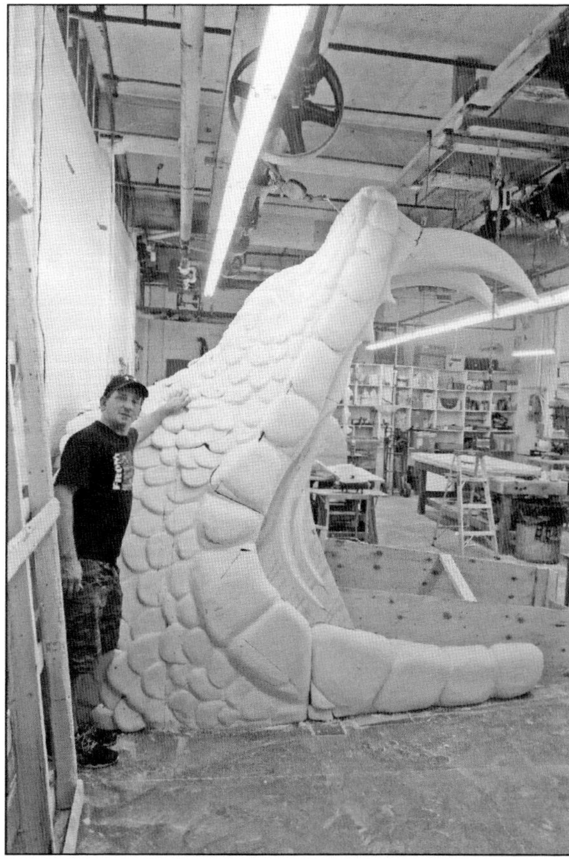

A crew of Clark's employees is attaching the head to the body of the anaconda in this photograph. The pattern of the scales has not yet been applied. (Photograph by Maureen S. Clark.)

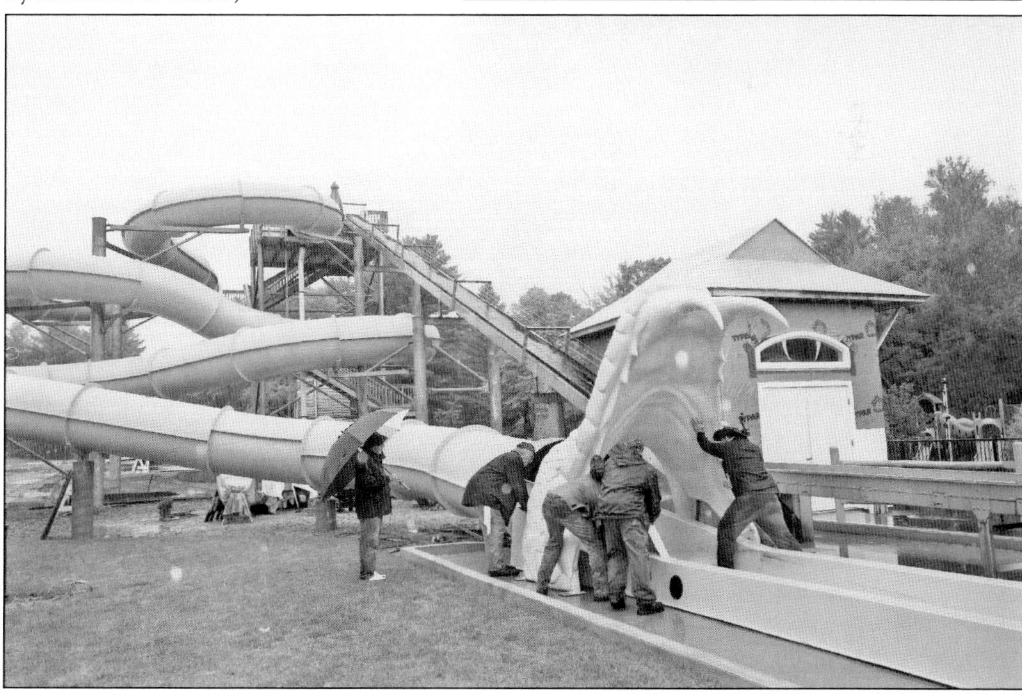

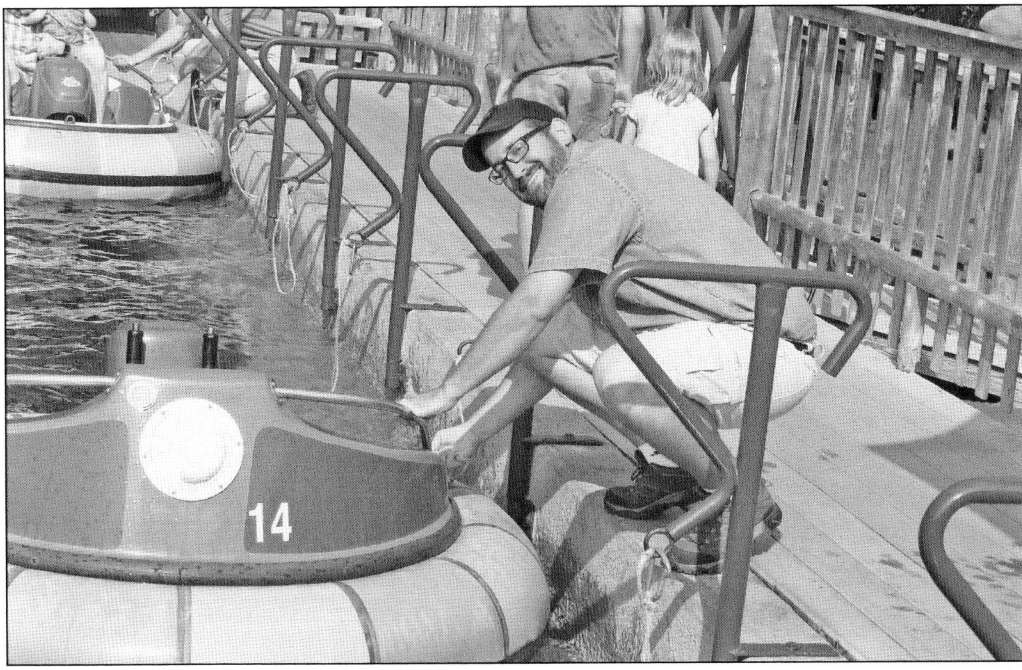

Matt Hunt began working in park services at the age of 16. He eventually moved to the rides department, where he has mastered the operations and behind-the-scenes organization and now mentors other young employees. Many youngsters find their first job at the Trading Post, and the Clarks take the time to mentor and train them, instilling a work ethic and good habits that will benefit them throughout their lives. (Photograph by John K. Eisenhart.)

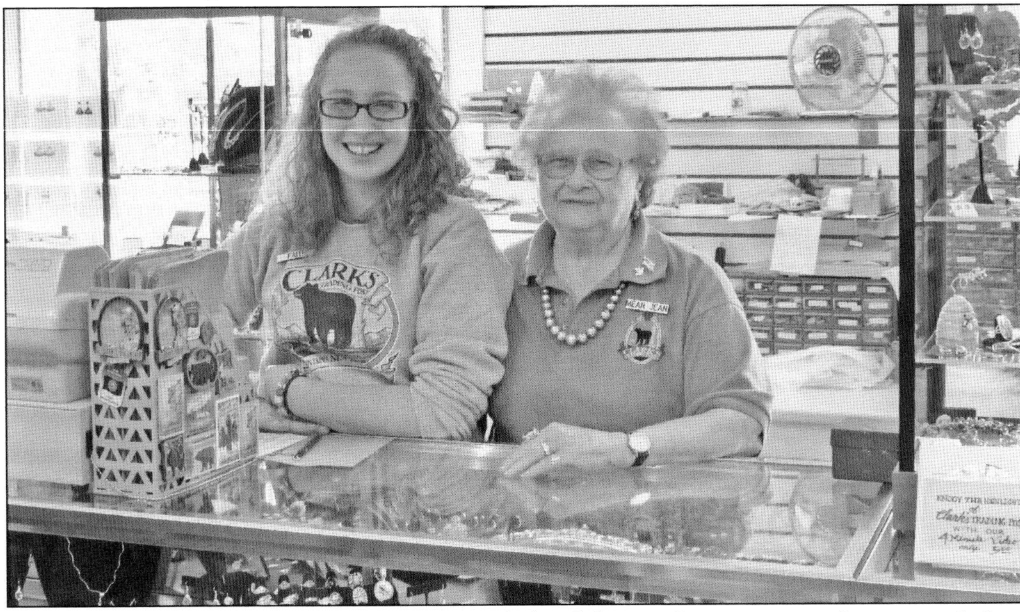

Faith Englert (left) and Jean Brosseau are seen behind the jewelry counter in the main gift shop. Jean has been working at the Trading Post since 1978, and returning guests often stop by to say hello to "Mean Jean," as her nametag reads. She is part of the feeling of tradition guests have come to expect at the Trading Post. (Photograph by John K. Eisenhart.)

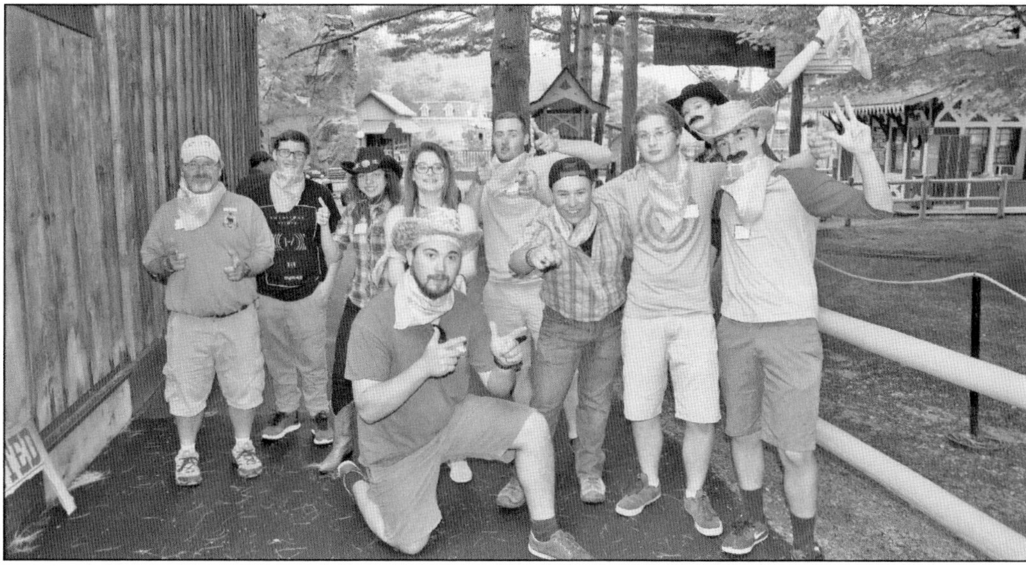

In addition to mentoring their young employees, the Clarks make sure they have fun. A "Getting to Know You Party" is held in June; a talent show (during which employees showcase their talents in the bear ring) is held in August, and an end-of-year staff party is held in late October or November. This photograph was taken during the 2017 Getting to Know You Party. From left to right are (first row) Billy Carbino; (second row) Chris Peck, Chad Neilson, Sage Walsh, Kayla Noonan, Nate Englert, Joey Mitchell, Noah Englert, and Sam Martin; (third row) Samantha Young. (Photograph by Maureen S. Clark.)

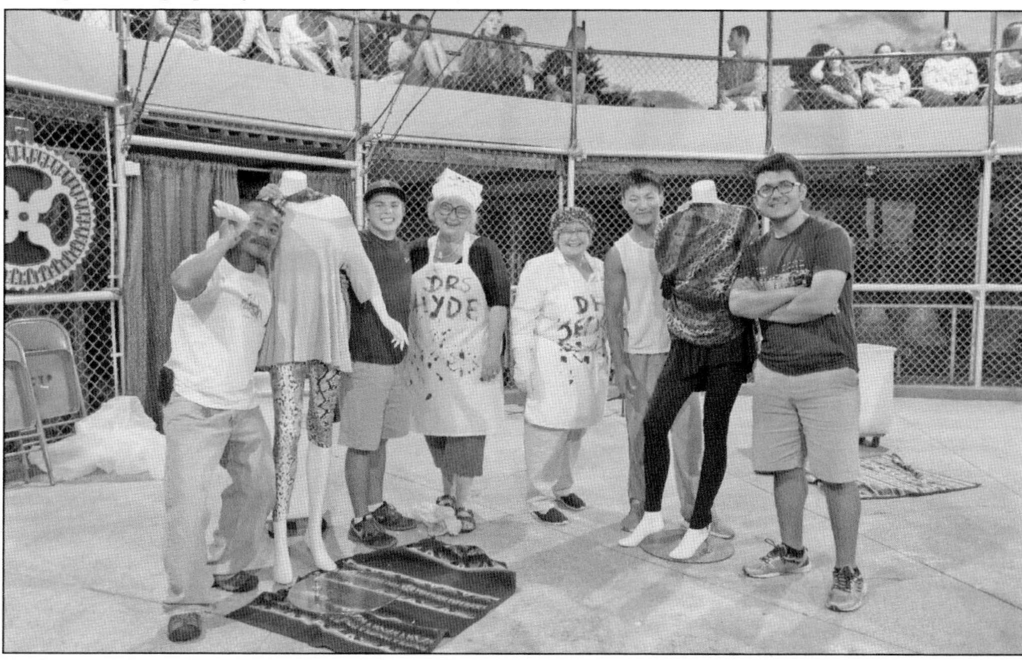

A skit spoofing *The Strange Case of Dr. Jekyll and Mr. Hyde*, by Robert Louis Stevenson, was the basis for this 2015 talent show photograph. From left to right are Yandong Wu, Joey Casey, Carol Govoni as Mrs. Hyde, Nola Grant as Dr. Jekyll, Yuan Peng Zhang, and Ahmet Oktay. (Photograph by Maureen S. Clark.)

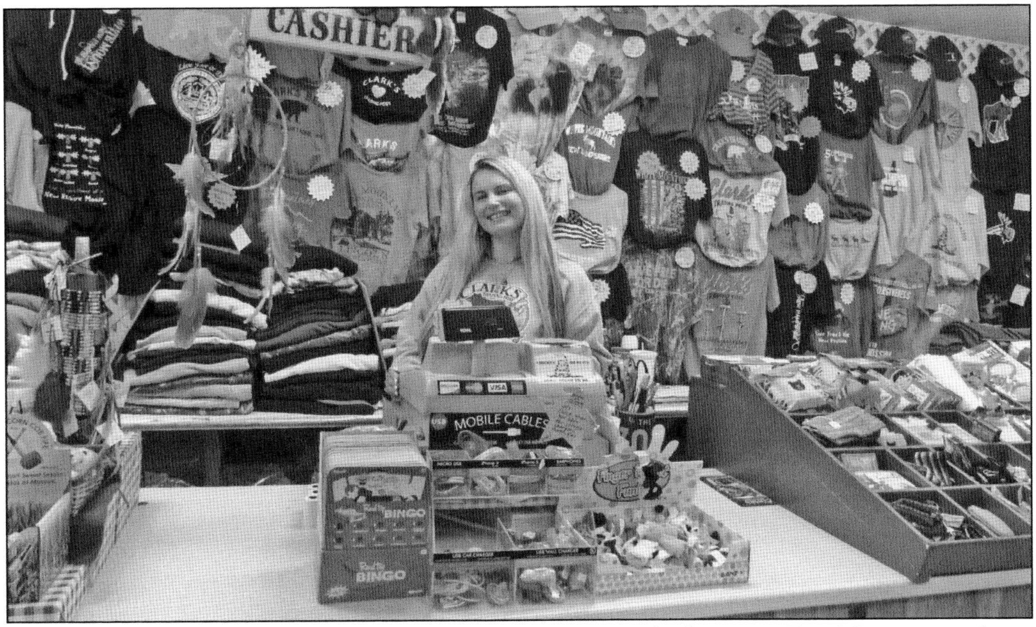

Ashley Clark is another member of the fourth generation. She began in Food Services and can now often be found behind the T-shirt/sweatshirt counter helping guests find the perfect souvenir. (Photograph by John K. Eisenhart.)

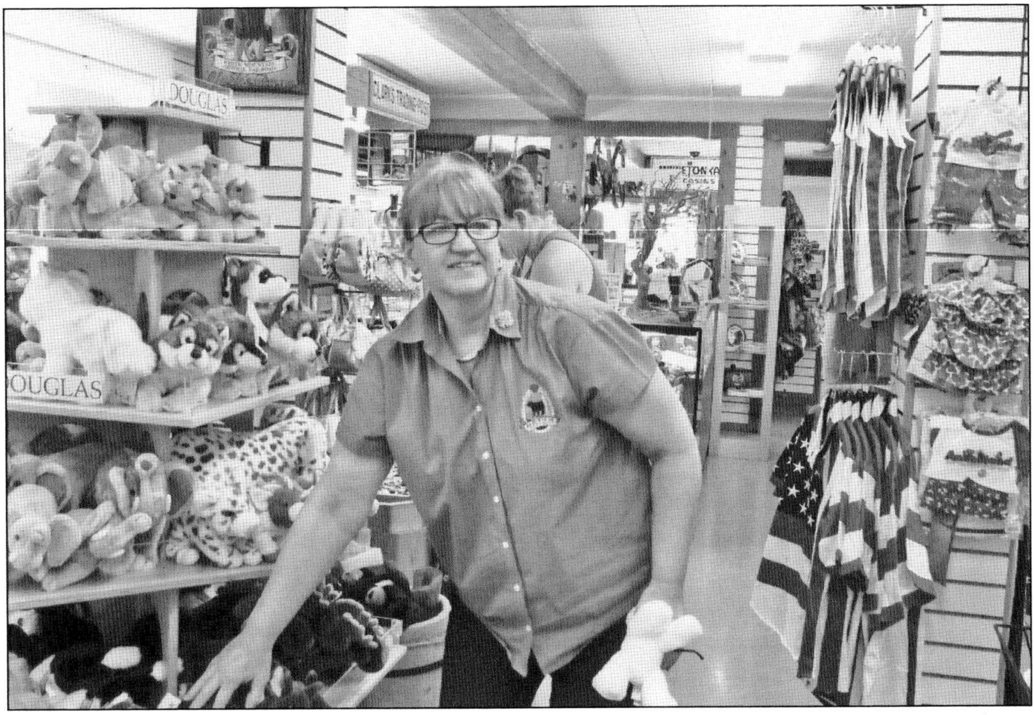

Diane Clark is seen here preparing for another busy day in the main gift shop. Clark women have traditionally managed the gift shops, handling the buying, staffing, and sales and providing a valuable and reliable source of income throughout the history of the Trading Post. (Photograph by John K. Eisenhart.)

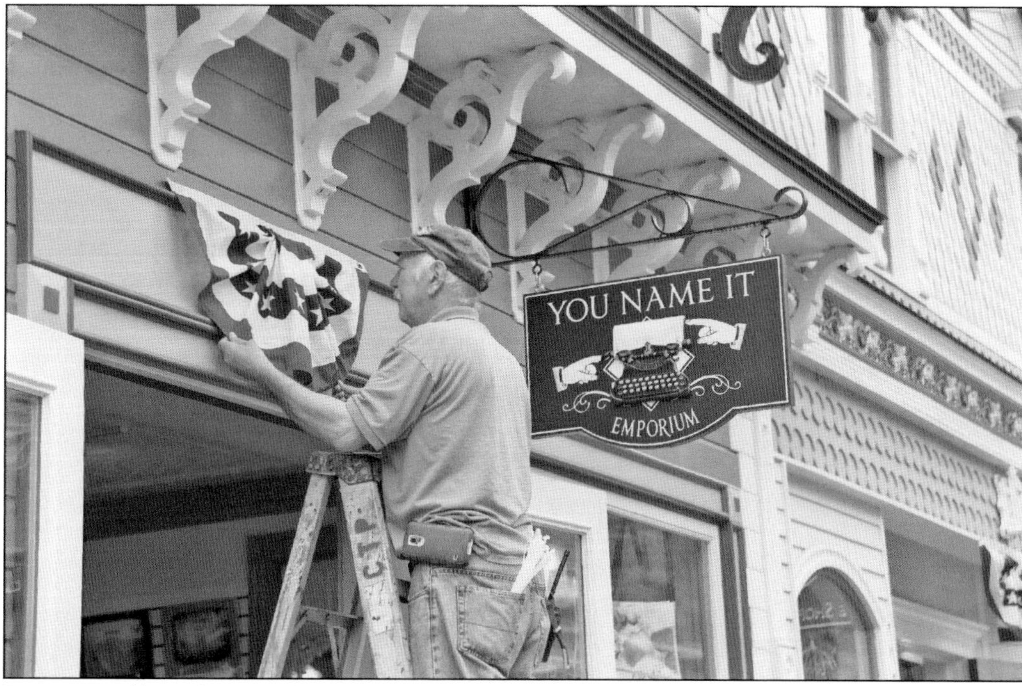

Dave Merrill is adjusting the bunting above the You Name It shop. Patriotic pride is another tradition at Clark's Trading Post. Holidays such as Memorial Day, Fourth of July, and Labor Day find the park decked out in red, white, and blue bunting and employees sporting patriotic clothing and jewelry. (Photograph by Maureen S. Clark.)

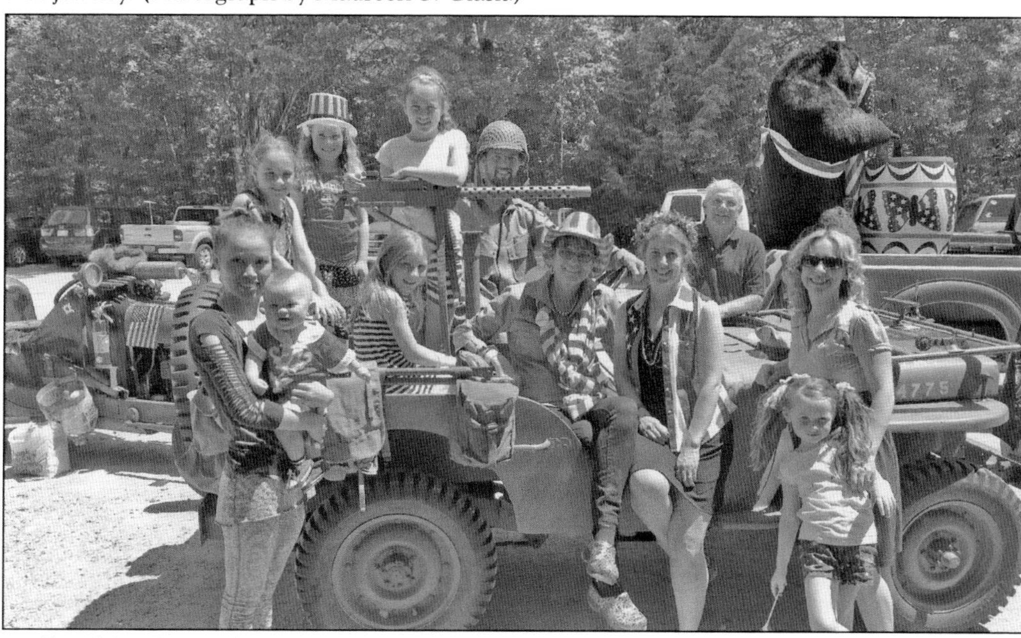

Staff and family members are preparing for the 2016 Fourth of July Parade. From left to right are (standing in front of the Jeep) Ya Ting holding Albert Wu and Sylvia Clark with her hand on Briar Clark; (seated in the Jeep) Mackenna Mack, Emma Clark, Elise Clark, and Katie Mack; (back) Willa Clark, Sienna Mack, Mark Evans, and David Hiltz. (Photograph by Maureen S. Clark.)

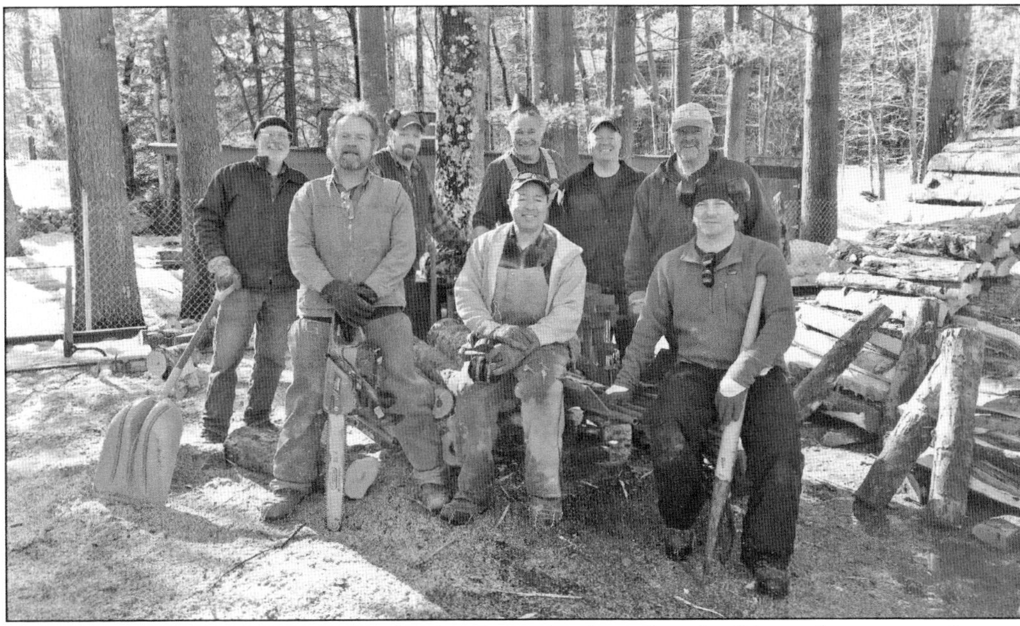

The Trading Post burns approximately 45 to 50 cords of wood in the Climax locomotive during a season. Once logged, the wood is cut into 36-inch lengths, stacked, and dried for use the following season. From left to right are (first row) Murray Avery Clark, Bob Henderson, and Andrew Clark; (second row) Dave Merrill, Iain Grant, Leon Noel (with funnel on his head), Fred Englert, and Brad Ruggles. (Photograph by Maureen S. Clark.)

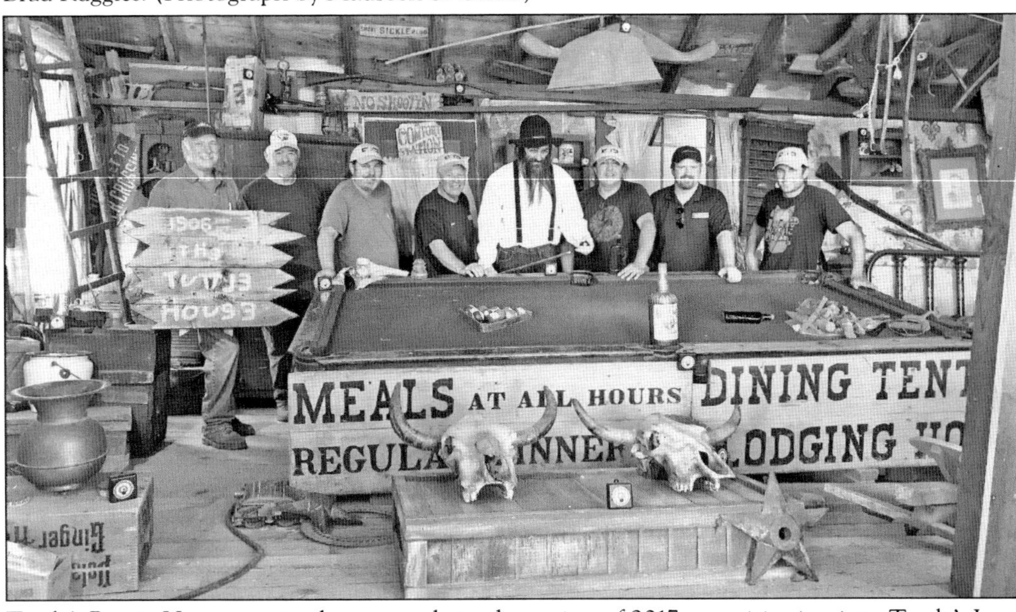

Tuttle's Rustic House received an upgrade in the spring of 2017, transitioning into Tuttle's Laser Shooting Gallery. This interactive attraction retains all the rustic charm of the Tuttle family as guests have a chance to try their skill aiming at 60 laser-activated targets. From left to right are Dave Merrill, Brad Ruggles, Tom Boyd, Fred Englert, Simon Tuttle, Mark Knutsinger, Iain Grant, and Nolan Roddick. (Tom, Mark, and Nolan of Daniels Wood Land assembled and programmed the targets. No last names are available for them.)

During this end-of-year staff party, Clark family members perform a routine to the song, "Let Us Entertain You." From left to right are (first row) Fred Englert, and Katie Mack; (second row) Carol Govoni, Nola Grant, and Anne Englert. (Photograph by Maureen S. Clark.)

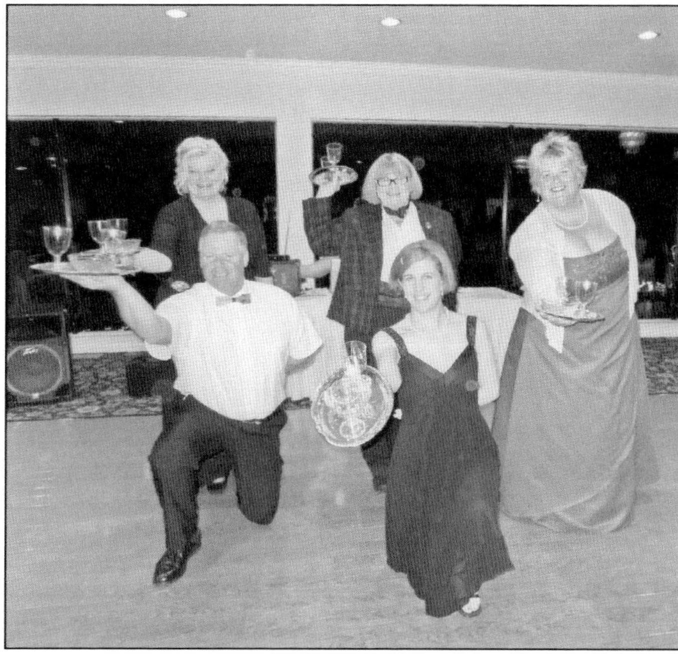

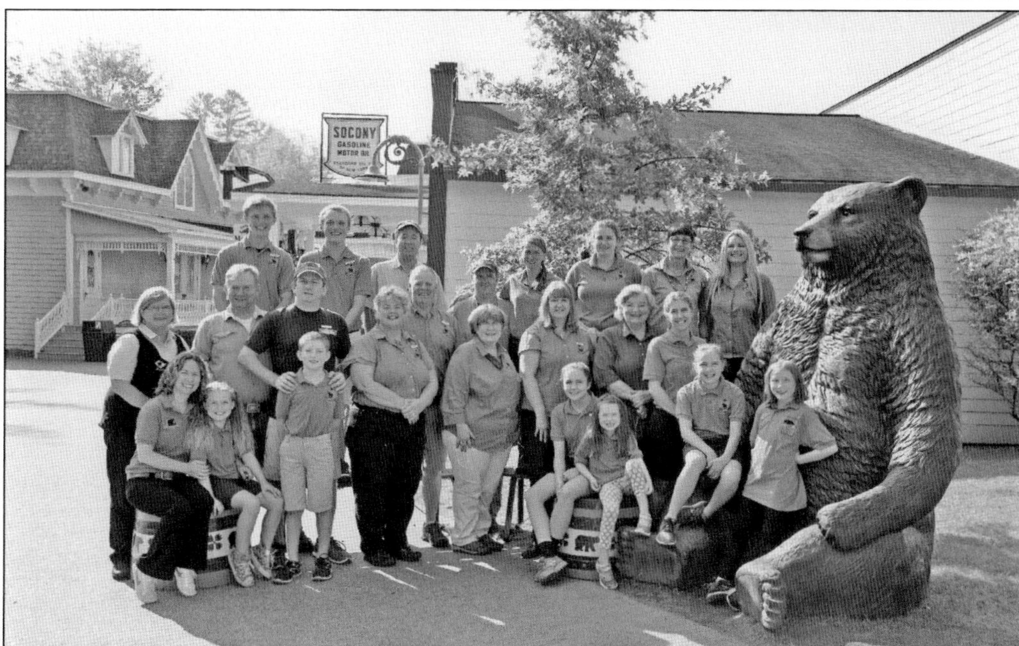

Florence and Edward would be delighted to see how many family members are carrying forward their dream. From left to right are (first row, seated on bear barrels) Sylvia Clark, Willa Clark, Sienna Mack, and Briar Clark; (second row, standing) Maureen Clark, Murray Clark, Andrew Clark with his hands on the shoulders of Mason Clark, Anne Englert, Fred Englert (slightly behind Anne), Nola Grant, Diane Clark, Carol Govoni, Katie Mack, Mackenna Mack, and Emma Clark (seated on the bear); (third row) Liam Clark, Grant Clark, Bob Henderson, Iain Grant, Jodi Grant, Jodie Clark, Elise Clark, and Ashley Clark. (Photograph by Samantha Young.)